BOOKS BY LEE VALLEY

Gardening.

Vegetables From a Country Garden
by Anstace & Larry Esmonde-White

A Gardener's Journal:
A Ten Year Chronicle of Your Garden

Woodworking.

Lettering for Woodworkers

The Woodworker's Logbook

The Craft of Log Building
by Hermann Phleps

The Victorian Design Book

How to Make Wooden Planes
by Leonard Lee

Building Birdhouses for North American Birds
by John Plewes

❧ THE GARDENERS KALENDAR ☙

© 1997 Lee Valley Tools Ltd.

Lee Valley Tools Ltd.
1080 Morrison Drive
Ottawa, Ontario
Canada K2H 8K7

Distributed in the United States by:
Veritas Tools Inc.
12 East River Street
Ogdensburg, New York 13669

Distributed in Canada by:
Lee Valley Tools Ltd.
1080 Morrison Drive
Ottawa, Ontario K2H 8K7

Canadian Cataloguing in Publication Data

Main entry under title:
The gardeners kalendar : the works of each month
in the English garden

2nd ed.
Includes index.
Originally published London, 1766. This text is a
        revision, with illustrations, in part, of the ed.
        published London, 1777 under the title: The
        complete farmer; or, A general dictionary of
        husbandry in all its branches.
ISBN 0-921335-07-5 (bound)

        1. Gardening – Early works to 1800.
2. Gardening – Great Britain. I. Lee Valley Tools.
II. Title: Complete farmer. III. Title: Gardeners calendar.

SB97.G37 1997   635   C97-900611-2

Printed in Canada

ഌ THE ൠ GARDENERS KALENDAR

THE WORKS OF EACH MONTH IN THE ENGLISH GARDEN.

1777

CONTENTS

PUBLISHER'S NOTE

Although nominally a reprint of a gardener's calendar from the *Encyclopedia of Farming* published in London in 1777, this book has been modified in several ways to make it more readable. First, when you read a phrase like "*...requfite to enfure succefs...*" you quickly realize that the British long "s" of the 18th century is an acquired taste. We took out the long "s" root and branch, so to speak. Also, because the calendar had contributions from several experts of the day and because spelling tended to be much more individualistic then than it is now, we regularized the spelling somewhat, choosing the form closest to current usage. In instances where there was consistency in the original text (such as "chuse" for "choose") we used the spelling of the day. Robert S. Lee of Calgary did yeoman work in cleaning up punctuation, sorting out the spelling, and preparing a glossary. Along the way, he sent numerous interesting notes for which we could find no home. Two of them are included here:

> "Numerous references are made to Michaelmas as a time of year for certain tasks to be done. We Anglicans, of course, know that they refer to the feast of St. Michael and all Angels on September 29th, but it may be well to define it for those outside the faith."

> "The *Kalendar* was written for the south of England so instructions are given for such things as handling frost so as to allow planting of radishes in December. Many North American readers will have far colder weather to contend with and will equally find it difficult to obtain the vast quantities of horse dung needed for frost control."

Pity that more could not be included.

Three other people merit special mention. Shawn Allaire, a librarian with Old Fort William, first brought the book to our attention, wondering if it could be used in any way to generate revenue for the Fort. Because of her alertness and love of books, we can offer you this unique text and Old Fort William will collect a handsome royalty from its sale.

Suzanne Graham of Ottawa, designer of A Gardener's Journal, also designed this book. Since the original text was incredibly dense, Suzanne lightened it appreciably by adding relevant 18th century illustrations as well as just leaving more white space that is so necessary for a book to be a relaxing read. Her touch is everywhere in the book.

Lastly, Peter Calamai, longtime friend and avid gardener wrote the foreword, putting all in context by sketching a scene of 18th century England where all this took place.

Leonard G. Lee
Ottawa
July, 1997

FOREWORD

Hoping to be read long after they die, some authors write with one eye on the present and the other on posterity. All too often the resulting work is true to neither. For the authors of practical manuals like this 1777 *Gardeners Kalendar* there is no such temptation; they set out to write for the here-and-now, resigned to their inexorable eclipse by the advances of science and practice. Yet, as a result, their creations sometimes can evoke an era as powerfully as the very best novelists or historians.

All of which is a roundabout way of saying: Hang on tightly, you are about to be plunged without warning into an alien world where plants will be the most familiar items. Imagine a society of six million souls where a few thousand landowners control the bulk of the wealth and almost all the political power — yet a society also on the verge of an Industrial Revolution that will launch the middle-class world we know today. Imagine as well a society where the gardening chores described in this book will actually be done by labourers whose cash wages were no more than seven shillings a week, less than the price of a book, but who seldom had to worry about food or lodging. Finally, imagine a society where at least four out of five adults weren't literate enough to read even the simple, practical advice reprinted here.

Yet all of that — the land-owning oligarchy, the non-cash economy, the widespread ignorance — is seen by the author as the natural order. His* concern is directed instead at problems such as unsightly worm castings on gravel paths which, he reminds us every month, must be daily swept and rolled twice a week. It is this single-minded focus that makes the Kalendar so alive; reading it is like joining a conversation already in progress, with the usual consequences of such precipitate action. You are unsure about some of the references, mystified by the ground rules, fumbling with the assumptions. Allow me to be of help.

---

* There may indeed have been several contributors to the Kalendar, but they were almost certainly all men. Only three English gardening books were even written to appeal to women gardeners between the early 17th and 19th centuries and only the last of these, published after 1800, is known to be written by a woman.

The Settings.

The main scene for our drama is a kitchen garden of unspecified size, but likely between one and three acres. The garden forms part of a country estate, or seat, and is usually situated out of direct sight of the manor house, although close enough for a gentle stroll. (Just as the manor is readily accessible to the garden staff delivering produce, although by a back walk so the gentry aren't distressed by encountering common labourers.) Brick walls enclose the garden, highest on the north side (perhaps 12 feet tall), lowest on the south. Wide walks of spotlessly clean gravel cross the enclosed square, dividing it into quadrants of roughly equal size. In the middle there may well be a fountain with surrounding pond where the wheeled water carts are filled, although there will also be water basins elsewhere.

The walks are often triple bordered. First comes a wooden timber laid on the ground, or possibly a low hedge of neatly clipped box. Behind that lies a wide bed of herbs and salad makings (small salleting) behind which stands a low screen of fruit trees, either espaliered or standards. This defense shields the real working part of the garden — vegetables in raised beds or long rows — from the eyes of the gentry. To avoid offending the noses of the gentry, and make maximum use of space, some vital functions are exiled outside the walls. For example, the dung heaps, composting piles and mushroom bed are all found in the slip, the space between the outside face of a wall and the concealed trench (called a ha-ha) which ensures that sheep and other animals remain bucolically on display in the adjacent pasture. The melon patch on which our author lavishes so much attention is also often found in the slip.

The *Kalendar* author assumes the presence of forcing frames, low wooden rectangles topped by a series of what look to modern eyes like wooden storm windows. Known as "lights," these were no larger than could comfortably be handled by two labourers. A frame itself could range in size from three lights long to thirty or more, sheltering thousands of plants. But the frames were not the only way to extend the season and combat frost; that was another duty of the walls.

When scientists finally got around to measuring such things, they discovered the cleverness of those Georgian gardeners (and the Romans long before them). It turns out that a sunny, south-facing brick wall reflects enough heat seven inches out from the surface to equal temperatures in a garden 7° farther south in latitude. Put simply, a fig growing on a wall in southern England is warmed as if in southern France. This helps explains the author's fixation with the pruning and renailing of tender fruit and vines.

Secondary settings include a nursery for starting plants (of at least an acre), an orchard (bigger is better, we're told) and the pleasure or flower garden, which is introduced almost grudgingly by the author but expands in both space and effort as the *Kalendar* progresses.

The Characters.

Despite the author's mention of husbandmen, it is a safe assumption that *The Gardeners Kalendar* was intended to be read chiefly by the owners of very large farms and of country seats, for the simple reason that they were the only potential audience left by the third quarter of the 18th century. By that time, a few thousand unbelievably wealthy landowners controlled three-quarters of the cultivated land in England, leasing it to tenant farmers in the tens of thousands who, in turn, employed hundreds of thousands of servants and labourers. The small freeholders still common in Belgium, France and Italy had been largely driven from their land in England by the economic and political power of the nobility and the squirearchy.

All these landowners had a country seat, where they spent the bulk of the year when not shooting and fishing in Scotland or participating in the London season. And they had lots of servants. On average, in Georgian and Victorian times, a modest kitchen garden of an acre-and-a-half required a minimum staff of three; add any sort of greenhouses and the total might easily become six. Despite the author's exhortation that the master of the house should "personally . . . direct and superintend the management" of the kitchen garden, this responsibility mostly rested with a head gardener, who was expected to have an encyclopedic knowledge of plants (including the Linnaean classification), be able to read and write, keep financial accounts and planting records, arrange flowers, direct the staff and not leave muddy footprints in the manor. For that he might be paid anywhere between £25 and £75 a year (an innkeeper at the time averaged £100 annual earnings, as did a lawyer). While the head gardener and any journeymen were always male, women were often employed for finicky gardening jobs such as weeding and gathering fruit; garden historian Susan Campbell notes, however, that women were never paid more than half as much as a man for the same work "no matter how experienced they were."

There would also be garden labourers ("very sparing of their work, especially when it is toilsome," warns the author) and a boy of 14 or 15, an apprentice who could — and sometimes did — rise to head gardener. The boy and any unmarried men lived in a garden lodging called a bothy, often little better than a rustic cabin and sometimes closer to a stable.

The Action.

It's little wonder that the author of the *Kalendar* praises the kitchen garden as "the most useful and profitable spot of ground." One acre of intensively cropped kitchen garden could, it has been calculated, supply vegetables and fruit for a family of twelve, so long as cabbages, potatoes and roots were grown elsewhere on the farm. And gardens could be much larger, like that of banker Henry Drummond in Hampshire. Here's an inventory of what was in Drummond's storerooms or on the ground in October, 1795:

> 1200 Savoy cabbages, 700 late cabbages, 2000 early cabbages, 700 purple-sprouting broccoli, 700 cauliflowers, 2200 celery, 600 Brussels sprouts, 1800 lettuces, 2600 endives, 22 poles of spinach, 150 bushels of potatoes, 16 bushels of onions, 30 bushels of carrots, 8 beds of asparagus, 8 rows of artichokes, 10 poles of horseradish and 10 perches* of strawberries.

Even the modest garden of these pages contained between 300 and 400 asparagus roots under glass. So it is no surprise to discover that the work is unrelenting. "Remember to employ every minute that can be spared in digging and trenching the vacant spots of ground," is December's advice. What may surprise is what is missing from the Kalendar. There is, for example, no mention of any chemical pesticides, since they hadn't yet been invented. Tobacco dust, soft soap and an "infusion" of bitter walnuts were about all there was in the Georgian gardener's arsenal. Nor was there any real understanding of plant nutrition, especially the crucial role of trace elements, or the vital importance of the lowly worm. (Even though, at

---

* A perch was a length roughly equal to a rod, i.e. 16 ½ feet. This measurement refers to a square area that is a perch on each side.

precisely the same time, Gilbert Read was writing* that "worms seem to be the great promoters of vegetation," a view Charles Darwin would support scientifically in 1881 in *The Formation of Vegetable Mould through the Action of Worms*.)

Supporting Characters — Plants.

Much of what grows in the *Kalendar* will be easily recognizable to today's home gardener, since the latter half of the 18th century saw British ships and amateur botanists bringing back flowers, fruit and vegetables from around the globe (despite raging maritime wars). China asters, phloxes, chrysanthemums and dahlias — all color for the autumn — arrived in English gardens during this period. So too did the kalmias, catalpa, magnolias and hydrangeas. In the kitchen garden, most varieties of the common vegetables were well established by this time, although the Mazagan broad bean recommended in the *Kalendar* had been only newly introduced from a Portuguese settlement on the coast of Morocco. Surprising to today's gardener may be the fleeting mention of the tomato. Initially grown in 16th century England as an ornamental fruit, the tomato was not embraced by the general public as a food until late in the 19th century. Surprising also — to contemporary readers — must have been the omission of the pineapple, which was a horticultural craze among the nobility and gentry from 1730 well into the 19th century; they were grown in low sloping greenhouses over beds of decaying tanner's bark, with additional heat from coal-fired stoves.

Because domestic production couldn't meet demand, pineapple crowns and suckers had to be imported from the West Indies. For most other plants and seeds, however, the country manor was well served by a network of nurseries and seedsmen who advertised in newspapers and specialized weekly magazines. As early as 1727, the nurseryman Robert Furber had produced a printed catalogue of seeds, bulbs, trees and shrubs — but without prices, uncommon until the 1770s and then often inked in. In 1806, Sutton and Sons became the first to print prices in its catalogues. Of course, experienced gardeners, then as now, also prided themselves on collecting and germinating their own seeds.

---

* Letter XXXV. May 20, 1777 in *The Natural History of Selborne*.

Supporting Characters — Human.

Considering how often he is cited as the authority for some statement, Philip Miller might easily be listed as a co-author of the *Kalendar.* He was the most influential gardener of the 18th century, an influence traceable to three factors: first, his long reign (1722 to 1770) as curator of the Chelsea Physic Garden, where seeds and plants gathered from around the world were grown — and are still today; second, his willingness to experiment; third, his forceful writing in the comprehensive *Gardener's Dictionary* which ran through nine editions.

Never mentioned in the *Kalendar* but important to the future of horticulture nonetheless was Henry Frederick, Prince of Wales, a great garden-lover who died in 1751 from, according to his doctor, "contracting a cold by standing in the wet to see some trees planted, which brought on a pleurisy." To memorialize her husband, the Princess founded Kew as a botanical garden, which led directly to an ambitious plant collection program. Unfortunately, the Prince's early death also cleared the way to the Throne for his unstable son, George III, eventually precipitating the American War of Independence which had already raged for a year when *The Gardeners Kalendar* was published.

Denouement.

It was a time of revolutions, both political and scientific, and *Kalendar* is in that world but not of it. It celebrates the gifted amateur, the gentleman scientist, just as his death sentence was being pronounced by the new Linnaean taxonomy, which would change forever the way man looked at nature. What had once been a great chain of being was now described, analyzed and compartmentalized into species and genuses and families.

One of the greatest of those gifted amateurs was Peter Collison, a Quaker, friend to the powerful in England, correspondent with intellectuals in America and enthusiastic plant collector. His suburban London garden became famous for plants acquired in America and more than 170 new species were either introduced to England by him or first cultivated in his garden. A haberdasher and mercer by trade, Collison was made a member of the Royal Societies of London, Sweden and Berlin. In 1754, the year after publication of Species Plantarum, he wrote congratulating Carl Linnaeus for his "very useful and laborious work." The letter continued:

But, my dear friend, we that admire you are much con-
cerned that you should perplex the delightful science of
Botany with changing names that have been well
received, and adding new names quite unknown to us.
Thus Botany, which was a pleasant study and attain-
able by most men, is now become by alterations and
new names, the study of a man's life, and none but real
professors can pretend to attain it.

It was no use, of course. The Gardeners Kalendar might stubbornly
eschew the Linnaean classification but, as the captions on the drawings
added in this reprint demonstrate, the tide of Latin names could not be
resisted. Botany became something to be studied in books, rather than
observed in nature. Or better still, while gardening.

Peter Calamai
May 1997
Ottawa

FURTHER READING

Fortuitously, what will likely prove the definitive book on kitchen gardens was published only last year, after 15 years of research, by Susan Campbell. Her *Charleston Kedding: A History of Kitchen Gardening* is a joy to own and a pleasure to read. (Ebury Press, 1996)

Equally pleasurable to look at, although with much denser prose, is *The Planters of the English Landscape Garden*, by Douglas Chambers, a University of Toronto professor. The book helps situate the kitchen garden both physically and conceptually. (Yale University Press, 1993)

A classic of the genre is Gilbert White's *The Natural History of Selborne*, first published in 1788 and in print ever since. White, a country parson, focused a discerning naturalist's eye on a single parish. The edition by Richard Mabey can be highly recommended as both affordable and handsome. (Hutchinson, 1988)

Among the many available survey books of garden history, Eleanour Sinclair Rodhe's *The Story of the Garden* is all-encompassing in scope, if not always trustworthy on details, especially dates. (Medici Society, 1932)

GLOSSARY

Many of the following definitions are based on those in the complete *Oxford English Dictionary*, since it records senses of words as used in former times. Where various meanings exist, we have attempted to capture the meaning closest to that in use in 1777, the year of the original publication of *The Gardeners Kalendar*. Some definitions are restricted to only those used in the *Kalendar.*

Back-front: the back of the house, which fronts on the garden.

Bass: the inner bark of the linden (basswood) tree; more loosely, in Falconer's *An Universal Dictionary of the Marine*, a sort of long straw or rushes.

Bell-glass: a bell-shaped glass cover for protection of plants; a century later it was usually called a cloche.

Blanch: to cause the stalks of plants such as celery or endive to become white, by banking the stems with earth to exclude light and prevent the development of chlorophyll.

Blight: a word that entered the language from the lips of gardeners in the 15th century; any harmful influence, such as disease, prevention of blossom setting, cessation of growth, presumed to be carried by the atmosphere; when the cause was unknown, it was called blight and attributed to bad air.

Boscage: a thicket or grove of growing trees or shrubs.

Cabbage: *v.* to form a head, as cabbage or lettuce.

Cardoon: a composite plant *(Cynara cardunculus)*, closely allied to the artichoke. John Parkinson mentioned it in 1629 under the name of *Carduus esculentus* (Edible Thistle), and Darwin said that "Botanists are now generally agreed that the cardoon and the artichoke are varieties of one plant".

Caterpillar: in addition to the current meaning of a moth or butterfly larva, the name was applied in 18th-century England to a leguminous plant of the genus *Scorpiurus* (forget-me-not or scorpion grass) from the shape of its pods.

Coulter: a blade or rotating disc, fixed in front of a plough share to cut the turf so that it turns over without tearing.

Curious: a word having multiple meanings in the 18th century, most now obsolete; with reference to persons, careful, skillful, observant, cautious; with reference to plants, delicate or tender, requiring special treatment, exquisite in beauty or flavour.

Drill: a small furrow made for planting seeds.

Esculent: edible, suitable for food.

Espalier: used both as the trellis on which the growth of trees was directed and the trees themselves. Where we most often see such trees against a wall, the 18th-century English gardener considered the espalier a means of confining the growth of a tree to a plane, making for easy access to all branches for pruning and harvesting.

Farina: pollen.

Foreright: straight ahead, directly to the front; used in *The Gardeners Kalendar* to indicate branches from a walled tree or espalier that grow in a direction perpendicular to the plane in which the tree is being trained to grow.

Glass: used interchangeably with the term 'light' in referring to the transparent cover for cold frames or hot beds.

Gum: *v.* to exude gum as a morbid secretion.

Ha-ha: a boundary or obstacle of such a kind as not to obscure the view, usually a ditch with a wall on the inner side and a sloping face on the outer side. (Readers will find an excellent description of the occurrence of the term in North American place-names in the Jan/Feb 1992 issue of *Canadian Geographic*.)

Haulm: the remains of various cultivated plants after harvest.

Inarching: a method of grafting wherein the scion is attached to the new site, but is not cut from the source stock until after it has become well united with the destination stock.

Layer: a shoot or twig of a tree or shrub, fastened down and covered with earth, so that it might take root and be severed from the parent stock.

Long dung: specifically, stable cleanup with long, undecayed straw; in general, relatively fresh dung straight from the stable rather than from the dungheap.

Michaelmas: the feast of St. Michael and All Angels, celebrated on September 29.

Mould: in general, soil with decayed vegetable matter, rather than a fungal growth (e.g. leaf mould).

Mow: to cut with the scythe (see 'reap').

Nailed: attached to a (brick) wall or espalier by means of a nail to which was fixed a strip of lead for gripping the branch.

Neat: a bovine animal, an ox, bullock, cow (from which neatsfoot oil is derived).

Olitory: belonging to the kitchen garden.

Pale: a pointed stake, or a fence formed of vertical bars or strips, usually pointed.

Poachy: spongy, swampy, retentive of moisture; liable to muddiness.

Point: as applied to directions, e.g., "one point to the eastward of south", the change of direction equal to going fom one point of the compass to the next. As the compass rose had 32 points, this was 11.25°.

Reap: to cut with the sickle (see 'mow').

Riddle: *v.* sift.

Salleting: herbs and vegetables grown as ingredients for salads.

Sea-coal: mined coal, so-called because it came by sea, as opposed to charcoal, which was produced locally and was called simply coal.

Skirret: a species of water parsnip, cultivated for its edible tubers.

Snail: gardeners in 18th-century England used the term to mean both a gastropod and a dwarf annual flower having snail-shaped seed pods.

Tan: ground-up tan bark (usually oak), a waste product of the tannery.

Terras: mortar

Withe: (withy) a tough, flexible twig or branch, used for binding or plaiting.

BEFORE WE PROCEED TO ENUMERATE THE WORK NECESSARY TO BE done in the kitchen, fruit, and flower-gardens, as well as in the nursery, it will be proper to give some directions for laying out these inclosures, consider the nature of the soil best adapted to bring their respective products to perfection; and lay down a few cautions requisite to ensure success.

Neither the husbandman, nor the country gentleman of moderate fortune, who prefers utility to ostentatious show, can set about an easier or more profitable branch of culture, than that of the kitchen and fruit garden, which may very properly be intermixed, and occupy one and the same spot of ground, since they both require a good deep soil, and nearly the same exposure. The walls which inclose the kitchen garden, in order to secure its product, will be extremely serviceable for fruit: and, if elegance should be studied, this united garden may still be placed out of view from the dwelling-house.

The chief things to be considered in the choice of a spot of ground for a kitchen and fruit garden, are, the situation, the soil, the conveniency of water, the extent most proper to be inclosed, and the manner of inclosing it, and laying it out.

If the husbandman can chuse his soil and situation for a garden, the former should be rich, rather stiff than light, and considerably deep. Nor is a moderate degree of moisture here by any means an objection. The situation should be nearly level: because heavy rains would wash away the richest part of the mould, if the declivity were considerable. If he has not a level spot near his house, the ground intended for the garden may be made into flats with terraces supported by strong walls, which will become useful for fruit trees. A gentle inclination may be preserved to answer Mr. Miller's idea of having one part of dry ground for early crops, and the lower part for late crops, in order that the kitchen may be the better supplied throughout the season with the various sorts of herbs, roots, &c.

He should not be discouraged at some seeming disadvantages to which his soil and situation may expose him; for no difficulty is so great, but that it may be overcome by care, industry, and perseverance. Of this we have a striking instance in the following part of a paper which D.J. Beal read to the Royal Society, some years ago, with a view to the improvement of gardening in Scotland.

"I had", says he, "several conferences with Sir Robert Murray (who was an honour to his country, and a blessing to the place where he abode) concerning esculent and olitory gardens, and (under one) nurseries of fruit trees, and other useful vegetable in Scotland. I represented, that, almost within my memory, they are become the chief relief of England; that austere fruit has been found to yield the strong and sprightly liquor which resembles the wine of the grape; that the return of gain from gardens is great and speedy; and that nurseries are neither a chargeable nor a burthensome addition, but a motive of encouragement to persevere in the noblest kind of agriculture. Sir Robert granted all I said: and I am sure he executed all that he could for the benefit of his own country, and of this. But, said he, there are so many rocks, and such bleak winds, in Scotland, that it can hardly draw in the same yoke with England, for gardens and orchards. I replied, that in Devonshire and Cornwall, they fence their gardens and orchards with Flanders furze and tall holly, from the sea winds; that they have lofty firs and goodly pines in Scotland; and that New England, where the winds are as keen, and the snow and frost as deep, and as long lasting as in many parts of Scotland, is nevertheless full of fruitful orchards. And if Scotland be farther in the north, yet Norway is rich in boscage; and the seeds of the hemlock, fir, spruce, and cedar, from New England, Newfoundland, and Virginia, may perhaps rejoice in the exchange of Northern America for the north of this island.

"This, I told Sir Robert, I durst undertake; that when Edinburgh and their chief towns and universities shall plant kitchen gardens, as we do now in England, they shall receive their grateful reward the first year, and bear the charges of their nurseries abundantly, and so hold on, and within seven years secure their posterity of the benefit, and delight themselves with the fruit of their pleasing labour.

"Now for fertilizing rocks, I made bold to repeat it often, that, within a day's journey of the heart of England, I could shew three gardens, the best that I have seen for flowery beauties, English evergreens, and sallads all the winter long; all these on a hard rock, in most places but one foot deep under earth, in some two, and in very few three, with very lofty hills close to the south side, the declivity of the gardens due north, and the rock perfectly bare next to the walls on the north side. I likewise saw rich hop yards in the same case, but in deeper ground, next to the walls on the south side: and these northern hop yards escaped many blasts, which seized on the hop yards on the south side of the hill. On the steep ascent on the north side of one of these rocky hills, where no plough could come, I saw a gentleman ploughing up the shallow turf with a hand-plough, for flax; and I saw good flax grow there, to the largeness of a village-field. His hand-plough had a stem of ash, or sally, about seven feet long, and a plate at one side near the end, to turn the turf; a coulter to be let out shorter or longer, to cut the turf

A kitchen-garden bordered by espaliered fruit trees. Plants are cultivated in deeply dug beds and on raised hotbeds of fermenting dung. Glass cloches protect tender produce.

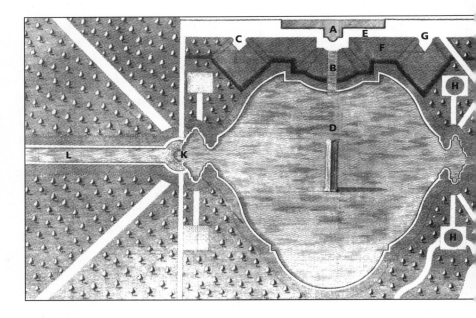

four, five, or more inches deep, as the land permitted, and a small iron wheel. This hand-plough the master and the man, by turns, drove before them, with a walking speed; having leathern aprons before them, to save their clothes. For the causes of this hardy fertility let philosophers account. I am sure the of the truth of what I write.

"It is no hard task to shovel down the shallow and mossy turf, from the deepest declivities of rocks, into places where it may have a receptacle or stay, and there, with the spade to mix and impregnate it with compost for gardens or vineyards. There too the tenth part of an acre in gardening may yield more profit, than ten acres of ordinary tillage in a corn field." *Philosophical Transactions*, numb. 116.

On the other hand we have many proofs that wet, and even very marshy grounds, have been converted into excellent kitchen gardens, after they have been drained. Such was, formerly, all that large part of Paris which still retains the name of *le marais* (the marsh); and such were, evidently, several of our most profitable gardens around London. The marquis of Turbilly has given us farther instances of this truth in several of his noble improvements; and the Memoirs of the truly patriotic Society of Berne remark very justly, that all legumes and pot herbs thrive perfectly well in

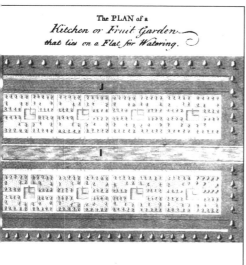

The PLAN of a
Kitchen or Fruit Garden
that lies on a Flat for Watering.

Plan for a kitchen or fruit garden.
Stephen Switzer, 'Seedsman of
Westminster-Hall'.

A. Is the place for a grotto under the house.
B. A cascade of about 50 foot fall.
C. A bastion projecting over the basin.
D. A large basin.
E. A terrace walk looking down upon
   the basin.
F. The horizon of the slope.
G. A bastion projecting over the basin.
H. Cabinets in quarters for greens and
   flowering shrubs.
I. Is a canal.
J. A terrace walk under the wall.
K. A circular cascade or fall of water.
L. A canal and menagerie.

the black, rich, moist, and somewhat rising grounds, which most commonly skirt the borders of marshes.

As warmth is essentially necessary to a garden, it is advisable that the exposure of the ground intended for this purpose be to the south-east or south; and that it be protected from the north and north-east either by high grounds, or plantations of lofty trees at a small distance. Fruit trees require to be likewise protected from the south-west and west, which are apt, in the autumn, to shake the fruit.

The husbandman should here spare no trouble or expense to render his soil of a proper quality and depth: and if it be not naturally so, he must have recourse to one or other of the methods practised for the improvement of soils, according to the nature of his ground.

Whatever the soil be, the mould in which the plants are to live and thrive, should be deep enough to afford their roots full room to extend themselves. It appears by several experiments, that the roots of many plants, not excepting even annuals, pierce to the depth of eighteen inches and more. To allow therefore a sufficiency of room, though perhaps more than may be really wanted, a depth of three feet of good mould should be allotted them here: and if the soil underneath is clay, or retentive of water, which would be apt to chill the roots of plants, it will be right to exceed even this depth.

Trenching is the most effectual way to obtain a considerable depth of well loosened mould. The common method of doing this, when the soil underneath is clay, is to begin with digging a trench four or five feet wide, either along or across the whole ground, then to lay in the bottom of it, about half a foot thick, long dung, fern, leaves of trees, rotten sticks, weeds, or any other such like trash, to rot and keep the soil from binding; then to fill this up with the earth dug out of the next adjoining trench, laying uppermost the spits that were lowest, and so to continue till the work is finished, without ever going deeper than just to the clay, though the surface be never so shallow. But if the clay be dug into, and part of it be turned up and mixed with the other earth, its bad qualities will soon be corrected by the influences of the air, rain, and one winter's frosts; it will become good and fertile mould, and the depth of the staple will be increased thereby, especially with the addition of a little drift sand, coal, or other ashes. The best time for trenching of land, that it may receive the benefit of being well mellowed; is the beginning of winter; when also, being moist, it is easy to dig.

Above A simple sieve for sifting soil.

Right Application of animal manure to garden beds.

When the mould on the surface is but shallow, and lies on a bed of sand, gravel, or loose earth, it will be advisable to lay a layer of stiff earth, inclining to clay, at the bottom of the trench. This will be more especially necessary for the growth of trees, or plants whose roots naturally pierce deep; for by means of this earth, those roots will spread horizontally in the mould, instead of striking down, as they would otherwise do, into barren earth, which would immediately make the trees decay and become stinted. And another advantage attending this method will be, that as water cannot so easily descend through this stiffer soil, the earth will be thereby preserved in a so much moister state; yet even here the clay should not be such as is impervious to water; for this, unless it lie very deep, would be attended with as bad consequences as the other extreme.

The general practice of gardeners is regularly to trench their ground, and lay it rough in the winter, without sufficiently considering the quality of the soil, or the nature of the earth which lies underneath. But a little reflection would convince them of their error. Let us, in this light, see what is the effect of trenching various soils. If the ground is naturally light, and lies on a bed of sand, or gravel, it is to be feared that every substance brought to improve the soil, together with its finest and richest particles, will be car-

ried down into that sand or gravel. Does not too frequent trenching contribute to this loss? As does likewise laying the surface rough in the winter: For the rains wash the finer mould into the hollow places, from whence the depth of the soil being least there, it is most readily carried down into the loose earth underneath. If the soil underneath is stiff, frequent trenching is proper in order to bring back to the surface the rich mould that has been washed down and if it be naturally strong, the laying of it rough in the winter is an advantage, because the winter's frosts will moulder its tough strong particles.

This method of preparing the ground is, undoubtedly, expensive: but its fertility afterwards will yield an ample reward.

Plenty of water is absolutely necessary in this garden, and therefore great care should be taken to provide it, in such manner that it may be come at as easily as possible. If a sufficient supply of it can be obtained from the neighbouring grounds, two or three basins should be made in different parts of the garden, if it be a large one; for when the water is to be carried to a considerable distance, the expense attending this necessary business will be great, and there will be danger of the plants suffering for want of it; labourers being very sparing of their work, especially when it is toilsome, unless they are well looked after. The size of these basins should be proportioned to the quantity of water that will be wanted, or with which they can be supplied: but their depth should not exceed four feet, for fear of accidents, if people should chance to fall into them: besides which, deep water is not so well warmed and tempered with the sun and air, as when it is shallow.

The methods used for collecting and preserving of water in ponds, or reservoirs in the field, are equally applicable to the making and replenishing of these basins in the garden. But it will be proper here to add the following more particular cautions and instructions of Mr. Miller, who, after observing that the best time of the year for lining these basins with clay, particularly in loose or sandy land, and for afterwards covering that clay with a thick layer of coarse gravel, is in autumn, when the sun is declining, and the weather temperate, advises, "as a farther means of securing this clay from being cracked by the heat of the sun, or by frost, to lay upon the rim or top of it, around the sides of the basin, a stratum of sand, then a stratum of good earth, and upon this a layer of thick turf. The grass thus laid will root in the mould underneath, and bind the whole firmly together: and it should be laid as far down the inside of the basin, as the water is apt to shrink to, that no part of the clay may be wholly exposed to the weather.

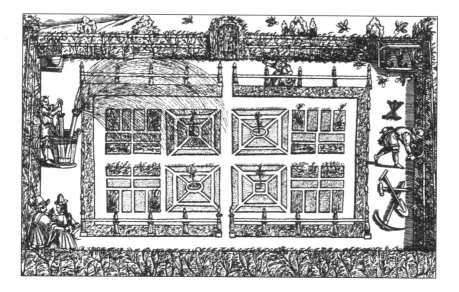

Mechanical watering devices.

Top Water pumped into the garden flows through troughs between the beds.

Bottom A lever-action pump set in a watering tub delivers a fine spray to the garden.

"No trees or shrubs should be suffered to grow near these basins, lest their roots should penetrate into them, and thereby occasion holes through which the water would find an easy passage. Neither should these reservoirs be made near to tall trees, because the shaking of them, by violent winds, would be apt to loosen and crack the clay.

"In countries where clay proper for this purpose cannot be easily had, these basins are frequently lined with chalk beaten into fine powder, and made into a sort of mortar, which is rammed down and worked very hard and firm all over their inside. This cement holds water very well, if the pond be not suffered to remain too long dry: for when this happens, the sun and wind are apt to crack the chalk, and these cracks generally extend through its whole thickness, so as to let out the water.

"Some line these ponds with bricks laid in terras, which is a good method where the ground is very loose and sandy, because when these walls are well built, the surrounding earth may be rammed down close to them. But, as heat is apt to crack the terras, no part of this lining should be left long dry and exposed.

"Others again use for this purpose a cement of powdered tile and lime, two thirds of the former to one third of the latter, beaten well together, and worked up with but little water: for the stiffer it is, and the more it has been beaten, the better it will be. With this cement they cover the surface of the walls of basins, about two inches thick, laying it very smooth, and taking great care that no sticks, straws, or stones be mixed with it. This is generally done in dry weather; and as soon as the whole inside of the basin has been plastered in this manner, it is rubbed over with oil or bullock's blood, and the water is let in immediately after. This cement has the property of hardening under water, so as to be equal to stone; and it will continue as long sound."

Where a supply of water for basins and ponds cannot be obtained, wells must be dug; and it is generally advised, that the water taken out of them be exposed to the sun and air for some time, before it is used, because, says Mr. Miller, the rawness of this water, when fresh drawn, is not agreeable to the growth of vegetables.

The size of this garden should be in proportion to the wants of the family; but with a much larger allowance of ground than is usually allotted, in order that the plants may be benefited by stirring the earth between them whilst they grow. The great and manifest advantages of this practice, especially in the culture of pulse and garden plant, have been so evidently shewn by numbers of experiments, that we cannot but recommend it here as an object of high importance.

It should be inclosed with a wall, either of brick or stone; but brick is best, for the greater conveniency of nailing up the fruit trees which are to be planted against it. The thickness of these walls should be proportioned to their height, which some run up to twelve or fourteen feet, or more; but nine or ten will be enough for almost any kind of fruit; and in this case thirteen inches, that is to say, a brick and a half, will be a sufficient thickness; though two bricks will be better, for duration. Their inside should be built as smooth as possible, and to strengthen them against high winds, piers should be run up with them, at the distance of about twelve or fourteen feet from each other, according to the usual extent of the fruit trees for which they are intended. As to pears, which spread very wide, and frequently grow much above the height here mentioned, they do not require the assistance of a wall; unless it be some of the latest winter sorts, and these the curious, who will be at the expense, may plant against walls built on purpose for them. These piers may project six or eight inches on the outside of the wall, for the sake of greater solidity; they should advance about four inches on the inside, for the convenience of fixing to them trellises, by building the wall on arches; and planting the trees at those arched places, as Mr. Hitt advises, the trees will be thereby enabled to extend their roots underneath the wall; which will prove very advantageous to their growth.

If the quantity of walling which surrounds the kitchen garden be too little to furnish the desired supply of fruit, a cross wall may be built through the middle of this ground; or, where the size of the garden will admit of it, there may be two cross walls; but these walls must not, by any means, be less than eighty or a hundred feet asunder. More will be yet better.

Mr. Miller is clearly of opinion that the best aspect for walls in England, is to have one point to the eastward of the south, because these will enjoy the benefit of the morning sun, and be less exposed to the west and south-west winds (which are very injurious to fruits in this country) than those which are built due south. "I know, says he, that many persons object to the turning of walls the least point to the east, on account of the blights which they think come from that quarter of the spring; but from many years experience and observation, I can affirm, that blights as often attack those walls which are open to the south-west, as those which are built to any other aspect; and I believe those who will be at the trouble of observing for seven years, which aspected walls suffer most from blights, will find those which are built with a point to the eastward of the south, as seldom blighted as those which are turned to any other aspect; therefore in the contrivance of a kitchen garden, there should be as great a length of these walls built as the situation of the ground will admit.

"The next best aspect is due south; and the next to the south east, which is preferable to the south west, for the reasons before assigned: but as there will, for the most part, be south-west and west walls in every garden, these may be planted with fruits which do not require so much heat to ripen them as those designed for the best walls; but wherever there are north walls, those will only be proper for baking-pears, plums, and morello cherries for preserving, or some duke cherries may be planted against these walls, to supply the table till peaches, nectarines, and plums are ripe."

In whatever manner the walls are made, this garden should be well sheltered from the north and north-east, by a distant plantation of high timber trees, if nature has not otherwise provided a sufficient defence from those quarters.

In distribution of this garden, particular care should be taken to lay the walks out so as to obtain the greatest convenience that can be for supplying each part of it with manure and water, and as easy access as possible to its different quarters, which may be surrounded by a border planted with espaliers. The manner of forming espaliers will be directed when we come to speak of the training of fruit trees.

These walks should be firm enough to bear at least the weight of a loaded wheel-barrow, and wide enough for the convenient carriage of whatever there may be occasion to bring into this garden, or to carry out of it. Mr. Miller is against making them of gravel; because, as it will very often be necessary to wheel manure, water, &c. upon them, they would soon be torn up and rendered unsightly; unless care can be taken that the wheel be broad; or rather that it be a roller as wide as the distance between the sides of the wheel-barrow.

For the same reason he rightly condemns turf-walks here, and advises, as the best for a kitchen garden, those which are laid with a binding sand. In effect, these are the easiest kept of any: for when either weeds or moss begin to grow, scuffing of them over with a Dutch hoe in dry weather, and raking them over a day or two after, will render them as clean as when they were first laid: or if they are covered with dust taken from great roads, this will bind and become very firm.

If the soil is stiff and apt to retain water, narrow underground drains should be made by the sides of the walks, to carry off that wet: and where the ground is naturally moist, lime rubbish, flints, chalk, or any other such material as can be procured with the least expense, should be laid at the bottom of these walks; or if neither of these can be had, the sand should be laid thick upon a bed of heath or furze, and the water will drain through this, so that the walks will be firm and good in all seasons.

The same means will also help greatly to drain away the superfluous moisture of the whole ground, if the soil should be naturally too wet; for if they are not sufficient, more under-ground drains may be made across different parts of the garden, according to its declivity: for most kitchen plants are hurt by too much moisture in winter; and trees never produce good fruit when their roots lie in water.

If each quarter of the kitchen garden is to be encompassed by espaliers, the walks which divide those quarters should be wide enough to afford admittance to the warmth of the sun, and to a free current of air. In this case they may be, as Mr. Miller directs, six feet wide in some gardens, and

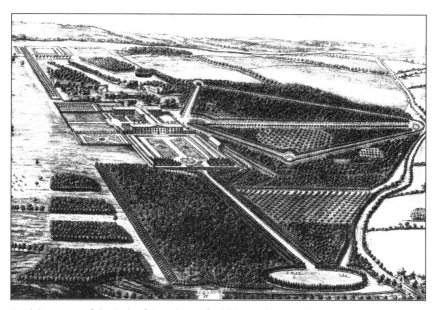

Cassiobury, seat of the Earle of Essex in Hartfordshire. In this grand landscaping scheme, the gardens extend from the traditional enclosed parterre near the house through the countryside by means of a series of radiating 'wood walks'.

ten or twelve in extensive ground. On each side of these walks, the espalier should be planted in a border four or five feet wide; by which means the two espaliers will be far enough asunder for their roots never to injure one another. These borders may be sown with small salleting, or any other herbs that do not continue long or root deep; so that no ground need be lost, and the continual stirring and manuring of it for these productions will be of great service to the roots of the trees.

The borders along the south and other walls that have a good exposure should, in the opinion of this experienced gardener, be at least eight or ten feet wide, in order to allow the roots of the fruit trees that are planted against them full room to extend themselves. Such of these as face the south may be sown for early crops of plants which do not root deep, and those that are exposed to the north will do for late crops: but no deep rooting plant, especially peas and beans, should ever be placed too near the trees; though most gardeners are apt to transgress greatly in this respect, as well to preserve their crops in winter, as to bring them forward in the spring: both which ends might be answered equally well, and without prejudice to their fruit trees, by making reed hedges in some of the warmest quarters, and sowing close to them their early peas, beans, &c. if such fences are found to answer the purpose of forwarding their growth.

It is a general opinion, that plants which are sheltered by walls, so as to be defended from nipping winds, and to have the additional warmth of the reflected heat of the wall, are least liable to be destroyed by the winter's frosts; for which reason it is that early crops are most commonly in borders so situated. The sun will undoubtedly give greater motion to the sap of plants there, and they may, for this reason, seem to be the stronger. But if we consider, that the walls yield no protection against the severity of the night's frost, and that the effect of this frost must be most severely felt by plants whose sap is in the greatest motion, we may rather fear that this situation, instead of being beneficial, may, in fact, counter-act the very end proposed. To be satisfied of this fact, a gentleman sowed some early peas in a border at the foot of a south wall, and at the same time some others, of the same sort, in an open field adjacent to the garden; and he found, that the latter were by much the least damaged by the winter's frosts; nor did he perceive any great difference in the season of their blooming.

A square or an oblong form will be most agreeable to the eye: but it matters not, in other respects, what shape this garden is of; especially as all gross irregularities may be easily hid in the laying of it out. Thus, when

Arboured walls shelter the plantings, grotto and summer house of this pleasant garden.

this is done, any of the slips cut off by the garden wall, may, if large enough, and well exposed to sun, be set apart for a place to make hot beds for early cucumbers, melons, &c. One would wish this spot to be as near as possible to the stables, for the convenience of supplying it with dung; and to have it without the wall is certainly most eligible, because that will save a great deal of filth and litter in the garden, and remove from the nose and eye an object which is not of the most pleasing kind. If this slip is long enough to admit of an annual succession of new beds during two or three years, they will be much better than when they are continued more than one year on the same spot; and as it will be absolutely necessary to fence this melon ground, as it is called, round with a reed hedge, this may be so contrived as to be moved away in panels, in such manner that there will be no occasion to shift anything more than one of the cross partitions, or fences, each year.

The importance of the precept particularly here, will justify our mentioning, that the dunghill, set apart for this, or for any other purpose of gardening or agriculture, should be carefully kept clear from weeds, for if weeds are suffered to scatter their seeds upon the dung, they will be brought into the garden or other cultivated ground, shoot up, damage every crop of useful plants, and occasion a perpetual labour to extirpate them.

Another caution given by Mr. Miller, as absolutely necessary to be observed, is, to carry off all the refuse leaves and stumps of cabbages, the stalks of beans, and haulm of peas, as soon as they have done bearing; for the ill scent which most people complain of in kitchen gardens, is wholly occasioned by those things being suffered to rot upon the ground. The leaves of cabbages may be given to hogs or other animals, while they are fresh, and the rest of the trash may be thrown upon the dunghill, which it will help to enrich; or such as will keep may be preserved, to be thrown in the bottom of trenches, in that part of the garden which is to be trenched the following autumn.

And here we cannot help pointing out a neglect too common among gardeners, we mean, the letting their plants remain on the ground till they have ripened their seeds, and wither: not considering that whilst a plant is in full sap, it preserves the earth in a loose state, probably by means of the moisture perspired from its roots; but if permitted to stand till its seed is ripe, or the plant withers, it leaves the impoverished earth dry and hard, being itself become entirely void of sap.

The most important points of general culture here consists in good digging, keeping the ground clean, manuring the soil, and allowing proper distances between the plants, according to their several kinds and growth.

The kitchen garden, if it be rightly managed, is the most useful and profitable spot of ground that either the country gentleman or farmer can cultivate. It is indispensibly necessary to every family in the country, where the nearest market-town is generally at too great a distance, and, at the same time, too poorly furnished with plants and roots, to afford a proper supply.

We shall conclude our observations on the kitchen garden, with laying down two rules necessary to be observed. 1. Never let the ground be crowded with more plants than it is able to nourish properly. 2. Never let any part of it remain unoccupied, for want of a due succession of crops. By this means the master, whom we would advise to be always his own grdener, at least so far as personally to direct and superintend the whole management, may have his table constantly supplied with such vegetables as he likes best; no part of his ground will lie useless, and each of its productions will be brought to perfection.

We have already observed, that the kitchen and fruit-gardens may very properly be intermixed, and occupy the same spot of ground. But notwithstanding this, their various productions will require a very different treatment, though in the same inclosure: we shall therefore now proceed to consider the latter, more particularly with regard to the method that should be observed.

Making Borders for Peaches,
℅ Nectarines, Plums, Pears, Cherries, &c. ℛ

If the land be a strong clay, take sea sand, if it may be easily had, if not any other sand that is nearest, and about one sixth of the quantity of coal ashes, that has been kept very dry, riddle them, but not too fine, for if some of the larger parts be left, they will disunite the tough body of clay, make it more open and tender and the finer parts that are more burnt, will increase its salts.

But if ashes cannot be had, let one twelfth part of the lime be added to the sand. About one third part of the depth of the border ought to consist of these ingredients; and in trenching the borders, there must be a layer of these, and a layer of the natural soil from the bottom to the surface, in the above proportion, well mixed together.

If the soil of the borders be mixed with large pebbles, they must be picked out, and laid in the drains, where they will be useful. And as this kind of soil is generally of a loose sandy nature, it must be mixed with something more strong and binding, namely with clay, the toughest that can be got near the place. If it be taken from ditches whose soil is naturally a clay, or from ditches where there is sometimes a current of water from arable fields of the same kind of soil, and there leaves its sediment, it will answer the purpose very well.

At the bottom of the borders lay this clay six inches thick throughout, which will prevent the moisture running out too fast in the summer, as it is too apt to do in sandy ground, especially where there are proper drains made. When you have laid down the clay, and by that means formed a sound bottom, let a sufficient quantity of the clay be procured, and to each cart-load of the clay let there be added an equal quantity of the natural soil, three pecks of lime, or rather pigeons dung, and five of soot, and the whole well mixed together: if coal or wood-ashes be used instead of soot, they must be made very fine, otherwise they will open this kind of soil too much; besides, the finer they are made by burning, the more they will enrich the ground by salts.

If the borders are to be planted with trees where others have grown before, the depth and quality of the soil must be examined; and if it be deep enough, and composed of a mixture of sand and clay, it will require to be trenched only, to draw off the too great quantity of moisture, and a proper addition of lime or soot to be mixed with the soil.

But if the borders are designed for vines and figs, the natural soil should be mixed with rubbish, as lime scraps, small pieces of bricks, &c. for a foot deep at the bottom or more; for both the vine and fig tree prosper best, and yield the finest fruit, in a dry soil, with a rock near the surface. If the land be sandy, the lime scraps, &c. may be omitted, and only the soot, &c. added, as before directed.

It will be necessary to observe in trenching all borders, to pick out all the roots of bindweed, common thistle, and all other seeds whose roots strike deep into the earth; but the roots of couch-grass, &c. which run near the surface, may be buried at the bottom of the trenches, which will effectually destroy them without any further trouble.

When these, or, indeed, any borders are first made, they should be raised three or four inches above the height they are designed to continue; for they will settle so much, at least, in a year's time. Those which are ten feet broad, let them have a descent of six inches from the wall, and others in proportion to their breadth: four feet broad will be sufficient for borders made for vines only.

Laying out knot beds using pegs and line.

Foftail Lily
Eremurus elwesii

Ha-ha bounds garden,
but allows uninter-
rupted view beyond.

THE FLOWER OR PLEASURE-GARDEN

The flower-garden being intended solely for ornament and pleasure, a short account only of it will be given here, as the principal design of this work is utility.

The flower-garden should be made near the back-front of the house, from whence a descent of six or seven steps will finely embellish the whole. Proper room should be allowed for a lawn of sufficient extent, which, if it be the first object that strikes the sight, will have a very pleasing effect.

Mr. Miller very justly observes, that the great art of laying out gardens for pleasure, consists in adapting their several parts to the natural position of the ground, so as to have as little earth as possible to remove, which is often one of the greatest expenses that attends the making of gardens.

The boundaries of these gardens, whatever they are fenced with, should be carefully concealed with plantations of flowering shrubs, intermixed with laurels and other evergreens to cover the fences, which have a disagreeable appearance, when they are left naked and exposed. Nor should all the boundaries be seen from any point of view; and if the country around affords a variety of pleasing prospects, it will be right to bound the pleasure-garden with an ha ha ditch and wall, to lay these views open to sight.

THE NURSERY

It is not our intention here to speak of those large and extensive nurseries, where all kinds of plants, trees, and shrubs, are raised for sale; but a nursery that is absolutely necessary for such country gentlemen as are desirous of raising plants, trees, &c. for themselves. Two or three acres of land employed this way may well be sufficient for the most extensive designs; and one acre will be full enough for those of moderate extent. And such a spot of ground may be always employed for sowing the seeds of foreign trees and plants; and also for raising many sorts of biennial and perennial flowers, to transplant into the borders of the pleasure garden; and for raising many kinds of bulbous-rooted flowers from seeds, whereby a variety of new sorts may be obtained annually, which will sufficiently compensate for the trouble and expense; and, at the same time, afford a very agreeable entertainment to gentlemen who are fond of these innocent amusements.

Such a nursery as this should be conveniently situated for water; for where that is wanting, a necessary expense will be incurred by the carriage of it in dry weather. It should also be as near the house as can conveniently be admitted, in order to render it easy to visit at all times of the year; because it is absolutely necessary that it should be under the inspection of the master, who must delight in it, or there will be very little hopes of success. The soil of this nursery should also be good, and not heavy and stiff; for such land will be very improper for sowing most sorts of seed; because, as this will retain the moisture in the spring and winter, so the seed of most tender things, especially those of flowers, will, if sown early, rot in the ground. Therefore, where persons are confined to such land, a good quantity of sand, ashes, and other light manures, should be buried, in order to separate the parts, and pulverise the ground; and if it be thrown up in ridges to receive the frost in winter, it will be of great service to it; as will also the frequent forking or stirring of the ground, both before and after it is planted.

Let the ground be always kept free from weeds, for if these are permitted to grow, they will rob the young trees of their nourishment. Another principal caution is to dig the ground between the young plants at least once a year, to loosen it, and give room for the young fibres of the roots to strike out. But if the ground be stiff, it will be the better if the digging be repeated twice a year, viz. in October and March; which will at once promote the growth of the plants, and prepare the roots for transplanting.

The part intended for the flower-nursery should be well situated to the sun, and defended from strong winds by plantations of trees, or buildings: at the same time the soil should be light and dry, which must always be observed, especially for bulbous-rooted flowers.

In this nursery the off-sets of all bulbous rooted flowers, seedling auriculas, polianthuses, anemonies, carnations, &c. should be planted, and continue there, till they become blowing roots, when they should be removed into the pleasure-garden.

You may also, in this ground, raise the several sorts of bulbous-rooted flowers from seeds, by which means new varieties may be obtained; but most people are discouraged from setting about this work, from the length of the time before the seedlings will come to flower: but it should be remembered, that after a person has once begun, and constantly continued sowing every year, after the parcel first sown has flowered, the regular succession of them coming annually to flower, will not render this method so tedious as it at first appears.

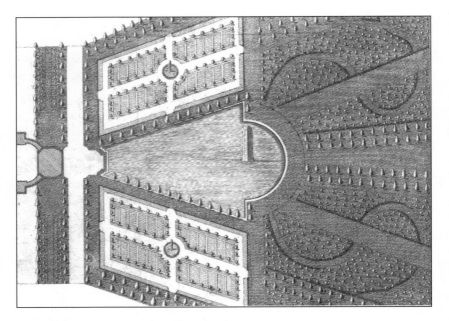

Plan for a fruit garden where the walls are bevel.

ORCHARD

It is a rule among gardeners, that those orchards thrive best which lie open to the south, south-west, and south-east, being screened from the north, and have the soil dry and deep.

In planting of an orchard, great care should be had to the nature of the soil, that such trees as are adapted to grow upon the ground intended to be planted may be chosen, otherwise there can be little hopes of their succeeding; and it is for want of rightly observing this method, that we see, in many countries, orchards planted which never arrive to any tolerable degree of perfection, their trees starving, and their bodies either covered with moss, or the bark cracks and divides; both which are evident signs of the weakness of the trees; whereas, if instead of apples, the orchard had been planted with pears, cherries, or any other sort of fruit to which the soil had been adapted, the trees might have grown very well, and produced great quantities of fruit.

As to the position of the orchard, if you are at full liberty to chuse, a rising ground, open to the south-east, is to be preferred; but we would by no means advise to plant upon the side of a hill, where the declivity is very great; for in such places the great rains commonly wash down the better part of the ground, whereby the trees would be deprived of proper nourishment; but where the rise is gentle, it is of great advantage to the trees, by admitting the sun and air between them, better than it can upon an entire level; which is an exceeding benefit to the fruit, by dissipating fogs, and drying up the damps, which, when detained among the trees, mix with the air, and render it rancid: if it be defended from the west, north, and east winds, it will also render this situation still more advantageous; for it is chiefly from these quarters that fruit trees receive the greatest injury: therefore, if the place be not naturally defended from these by rising hills, which is always to be preferred, then you should plant large growing timber trees at some distance from the orchard, to answer this purpose.

You should also have a great regard to the distance of planting the trees, which is what few people have rightly considered: for if you plant them too close, they will be liable to blights; and the air, being thereby pent in amongst them, will cause the fruit to be ill-tasted, having a great quantity of damp vapours from the perspiration of the trees, and the exhalations from the earth mixt with it, which will be imbibed by the fruit, and render their juices crude and unwholesome.

Wherefore we cannot but recommend the method which has been lately practised by some particular gentlemen with very great success; and that is, to plant the trees fourscore feet asunder, but not in regular rows. The ground between the trees they plough and sow with wheat and other crops, in the same manner as if it were clear from the trees; and they observe their crops to be full as good as those quite exposed, except just under each tree, when they are grown large, and afford a great shade; and, by thus ploughing and tilling the ground, the trees are rendered more vigorous and healthy, scarcely ever having any moss, or other marks of poverty, and will abide much longer, and produce better fruit.

If the ground in which you intend to plant an orchard has been pasture for some years, then you should plough in the green sward the spring before you plant the trees: and, if you will permit it to lie a summer fallow, it will greatly mend it, provided you stir it two or three times, to rot the sward of grass, and prevent seeds growing thereon.

At Michaelmas you should plough it pretty deep, in order to make it loose for the roots of the trees, which should be planted thereon in October,

Grafting techniques. Illustration for 'The Works of Virgil', John Ogilby.

provided the soil be dry; but if it be moist, the beginning of March will be a better season.

When you have finished planting the trees, you should provide some stakes to support them, otherwise the wind will blow them out of the ground; which will do them much injury, especially if they have been plant-ed some time; for the ground at that season being warm, and for the most part moist, the trees will very soon push out a great number of young fibres; which if broken off by their being displaced, will greatly retard the growth of them.

In the spring following, if the season should prove dry, you should cut a quantity of green turf, which must be laid upon the surface of the ground about their roots, turning the grass downward; which will prevent the sun and wind from drying the ground, whereby a great expense of watering will be saved: and, after the first year, they will be out of danger, provided they have taken well.

Whenever you plough the ground between these trees, you must be care-ful not to go too deep among their roots, lest you should cut them off, which would greatly damage the trees; but if you do it cautiously, the stir-ring of the surface of the ground will be of great benefit to them: though you should observe never to sow too near the trees, nor suffer any great rooting weeds to grow about them, which would exhaust the goodness of the soil, and starve them.

If, after the turf which was laid round the trees be rooted, you dig it in gently about the roots, it will greatly encourage them. There are some per-sons who plant many sorts of fruits together in the same orchard, mixing the trees alternately; but this is a method which should always be avoided; for thereby there will be a very great difference in the growth of the trees, which will not only render them unsightly but also the fruit upon the lower trees ill tasted, by the tall ones overshadowing them; so that, if you are determined to plant several sorts of fruits on the same spot, you should observe to place the largest growing trees backwards, and so proceed to those of less growth, continuing the same method quite through the whole plantation; whereby it will appear at a distance in a regular slope, and the sun and air will more equally pass through the whole orchard, that every tree may have an equal benefit therefrom.

The soil of your orchard ought to be mended once in two or three years with dung, or other manure, which will be absolutely necessary for the crops sown between; so that where persons are not inclinable to help their orchard, where the expense of manure is pretty great; yet, as there is a crop expected from the ground besides the fruit, they will the more readily be at the charge upon that account.

In making choice of trees for an orchard, you should always observe to procure them from a soil nearly a-kin to that where they are to be planted, or rather poorer; for, if you have them from a very rich soil, and that where-in you plant them is but indifferent, they will not thrive well, especially for four or five years after planting; so that it is a very wrong practice to make the nursery, where young trees are raised, very rich, when the trees are designed for a middling or poor soil. The trees should also be young and thriving; for, whatever some persons may advise to the contrary, yet it has always been observed, that though large trees may grow, and produce fruit, after being removed, they never make so good trees, nor are so long-lived, as those which are planted while young.

These trees, after they are planted out, will require no other pruning but only to cut out dead branches, or such as cross each other, so as to render their heads confused and unsightly: the too often pruning them, or short-ening their branches, is very injurious; especially to cherries and stone-fruit, which will gum prodigiously, and decay in such places where they are cut: and the apples and pears, which are not of so nice a nature, will produce a greater quantity of lateral branches, which will fill the heads of the trees with weak shoots, whenever their branches are thus shortened: and many times the fruit is thereby cut off, which, on many sorts of fruit trees, is first produced at the extremity of their shoots.

It may, perhaps, seem strange to some persons, that we should recom-mend the allowing of much distance to the trees in an orchard, because a small piece of ground will admit of very few trees, when planted in this method; but they will please to observe, that, when the trees are grown up, they will produce a great deal more fruit than twice the number when planted close and will be vastly better tasted; the trees, when placed at a large distance, being never so much in danger of blighting as in close plan-tations, as hath been observed in Herefordshire, the great country for orchards, where they find that when orchards are so planted or situated, that the air is pent up amongst the trees, the vapours which arise from the damp of the ground, and the perspiration of the trees, collect the heat of the sun, and reflect it in steams so as to cause what they call a fire-blast, which is the most hurtful to their fruits and this is most frequent where the orchards are open to the south sun.

But, as orchards should never be planted, unless where large quantities of fruit are desired, so it will be the same thing to allow twice or three times the quantity of ground; since there may be a crop of grain of any sort upon the same place, as was before said, so that there is no loss of ground; and for a family only, it is hardly worth while to plant an orchard; since a kitchen-garden, well planted with espaliers will afford more fruit than can be eaten while good, especially if the kitchen garden be proportioned to the largeness of the family: and if cyder be required, there may be a large avenue of apple trees extended cross a neighbouring field, which will render it pleasant, and produce a great quantity of fruit; or there may be some single rows of trees planted to surround the fields, &c. which will fully answer the same purpose, and be less liable to the fire-blasts before-mentioned.

JANUARY

1. Horse Radish. *Raphanus rusticanus.*
2. Dittander. *Lepidium sine Piperitis.*
3. Round Onions. *Cepae rotundae.*
4. Long Onions. *Cepae longae.*
5. Leeks. *Porrum.*
6. Garlick. *Allium.*
7. Rampions. *Rapunculus.*
8. Goats Beard. *Tragopogon.*

Melons in this winter garden are planted on raised hotbeds and protected by numerous cloches. The beds are well protected by fruit trees trained to the garden walls.

The Works of this Month in the
KITCHEN GARDEN

January being generally severely cold, there is less work to be done in the garden than in some of the succeeding months, when the weather is more kind and indulgent to all sorts of vegetables.

The gardener is not, however, wholly idle during this inhospitable month, especially with regard to raising early cucumbers and melons, for which preparations, if not made before, must be deferred no longer.

ꙮ Cucumbers and Melons. ꙮ

Let about a load of fresh horse dung, not too full of straw, be provided. Add a small quantity of sea-coal ashes to it, mix the whole well together, and throw it over a second time, laying it up again in a heap: if there be a considerable quantity of straw in it, there will be a necessity for turning it over a third time after having lain a few days; this will rot the straw, and mix it thoroughly with the dung, so that there will be the less danger of burning when the bed is made.

When the dung is thus prepared, mark out the foundation of your bed, in proportion to your light frame, which may very easily be done, by setting it on the place where you intend to make your bed; then mark the place where the corners touched the ground, remove the frame, and drive down a stake in each of the four marks, making an allowance for the bed to be two inches wider each way than the frame.

You should remember that the place where the hotbed is made, must be well sheltered with seed hedges, and the ground very dry. A trench should also be made in the ground of a proper length and breadth, and about a foot deep, into which let the dung be wheeled, and carefully stirred up and mixed; so that no part of it be left unseparated; for where there is not this care taken, the bed will settle unequally. Care should also be taken to beat the dung down close with the back of your fork, in every part of the bed. Some tread the bed; but it will work much more kindly, if suffered to settle gradually of itself.

Green citron melon
Citrullus lanatus citroides

When the bed is finished, the frame and glasses should be put upon it to keep out the rain; but no earth should be laid on the dung till two or three days after, that the steam of the dung may have time to evaporate. Let the glasses be kept close till the heat rises to the top, and then raise them properly, that the steam of the dung may pass away. If there should be any danger of the bed's burning, it will be proper to lay some old dung, or what is still better, cows dung, over the top of the hot dung, which will effectually keep down the heat, and prevent the earth from being burnt.

When the bed has been made four days, take off the frame and glass, and make it perfectly level and the surface smooth. Then put on the frame, and throw upon the dung as much dry earth as will cover it about two inches and a half thick. At the same time fill four or five small pots with rich dry earth, place them on the bed, put on the glasses, and keep the whole close till the earth in the pots is warm. As soon as this is effected, sow a few cucumbers or melon seeds in each pot, covering the seeds about half an inch thick with the same earth as that in the pots. The seeds should be at least three or four years old. Place the pots in the middle of the bed, and draw some of the earth of the bed round each pot. Cover the glasses every night with a single mat only for the three or four first nights after the seed is sown; but the covering must be augmented, as the heat decreases.

As the bed is yet very warm, it will be necessary to examine it every day, that the pots have not too much heat, which you may easily prevent by raising the pots farther from the dung. And this is indeed the true reason why the seeds are sown in pots, because they can be conveniently raised, without giving the least disturbance to either the seeds or plants, and the injury arising from too much heat, easily prevented.

If proper care be taken, the plants will appear in three or four days after the seeds are sown, when it will be proper to give them air, by raising the glasses a little every day; and if the earth in the pots appear dry, refresh

Persian melon
Cucumis melo reticulatus

it moderately with a little water that has stood all night in the bed; but great caution must here be used; for though the cold must be taken off, yet if it be too warm it will destroy the plants. They must also be guarded from the moisture that frequently drops from the glasses, for it will greatly injure them.

If you find that the heat of the bed is strong, let the glass be raised a little with a prop, when you cover it in the evening; and if a mat be nailed to the frame, so as to hang down over the end of the glass that is raised, the plants will be sufficiently guarded from the cold, and at the same time enjoy the advantage of the fresh air. But when the heat becomes more moderate, the glass may be shut close every night, observing to give the plants air in the day-time, and to hang a mat before the place, as already directed.

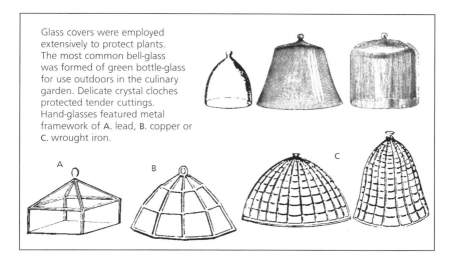

Glass covers were employed extensively to protect plants. The most common bell-glass was formed of green bottle-glass for use outdoors in the culinary garden. Delicate crystal cloches protected tender cuttings. Hand-glasses featured metal framework of **A**. lead, **B**. copper or **C**. wrought iron.

As these plants are very liable to suffer from various causes at this season of the year, it will be very prudent to sow a little more of the same seed in the same bed, and in the same manner as above directed. Nor would it be wrong to sow a little seed at three different times in the same bed, that if one sowing should miscarry, another may succeed.

When the plants have been up three or four days, they should be planted into small pots, and placed in the same bed; but you must remember to fill the pots the day before you intend to remove the plants, with rich dry earth, and set them within the frame till the next day, that the earth in the pots may acquire a proper degree of warmth. This being done, let about an inch deep of the earth be taken out of the pot; forming a small hollow, like that which might be made by pressing on it the head of a small watering pot, in the earth remaining in the pot, and lay the plants on the side of it, with their roots towards the centre, and cover their shanks near an inch thick, with some of the earth that was taken out of the pots. Three or four cucumber plants may be thus placed on each pot; but two melon plants will be sufficient for each pot.

Winter Melon
Cucumis melo inodorus

When all the plants are thus set, let the pots be plunged into the earth in the bed, close to one another, and all the spaces between them carefully filled up with earth. At the same time let the whole surface of the bed within the frame be covered with so much dry earth as will prevent the rising of the steam from the dung, which would destroy the plants. There should always be a magazine of good earth laid under cover to keep it dry in order to earth these beds; for if it be taken up wet it will not only chill the bed, but also occasion great damps in it: it is therefore necessary to have a sufficient quantity of earth prepared long before it is used.

Citron melon
Citrullus lanatus citroides

As soon as the plants are fairly rooted, which will be in two or three days after planting, let them be refreshed with a little water in the warmest time of the day; if the sun shines, it will be the better for the plants; but the water must have stood a sufficient time within the frame before it is used: and as these waterings should be repeated moderately, as often as the earth in the pots grows dry, it will be prudent to keep a quart bottle or two full of water within the frame, that it may be always of a proper warmth to be given to the plants whenever they require it.

As it is necessary to preserve the heat of the bed, you should lay some straw, hay, or fern, round it, and as high as the earth within the frame. By this means neither rain nor snow will chill the bed, which would cause a sudden decay of the heat, and consequently, greatly check the growth of the plants.

When you find the heat of the bed begins to decline, remove the straw, hay, or fern, from the front and back of the bed, and apply a lining of fresh horse dung to both, raising it a little higher than the dung of the bed, and covering the top two inches thick with earth. This covering is absolutely necessary to prevent the rank steam of the dung from entering the frame among the plants, where it would prove destructive.

Common cucumber
Cucumis sativus

This lining will soon revive the heat of the bed, and continue it near a fortnight longer. But you should not wait till that heat subsides: about ten days after the first lining is finished, take the straw, hay, or fern, from the other sides of the bed, and lay there a lining of fresh dung, as before directed: this will again revive the heat; and the dry litter that was laid round the bed, may be now laid round the lining, which will at once protect it from the cold, and prevent, in a great measure, the heat from evaporating. By these precautions the heat of the bed may be preserved for near a fortnight longer.

Cucumber
Cucumis sativus

By proceeding in this manner with making new linings, the plants may be kept in a free growing state in the same bed wherein the seed was sown, till they are fit to be transplanted into the bed where they are to produce their fruit.

You should observe to procure the hottest dung for linings, and to shake it up in a heap eight days before you use it; if in that time it be turned once over, it will be the fitter for the intended purpose.

ᔥ Asparagus. ᔥ

In order to raise asparagus on hot beds, a piece of ground that has been made rich with dung, and well dug and mellowed, must be made choice of. Upon this ground strike out lines seven or eight inches asunder, and plant the asparagus roots in them at four inches distance, when they are a year old: in this nursery they are to remain two years, and be kept clean from weeds, before they are fit for the intended purpose. The hotbed must be made pretty strong, and covered immediately with earth six inches deep, encompassed about with bands of straw. In this bed plant your asparagus roots from the nursery, as close as they can be placed together without trimming them. This being done, cover the buds of the plants two inches thick with earth, and let them remain five or six days, without putting the frames and glasses over them; then lay three inches thick of earth over the whole, and put on the frames and glasses. In about ten days after planting, the buds will appear: and then give them what air the season will permit; for the more air they have, the greener, and better tasted they will be. The bed will last about a month, producing fresh buds daily, if the weather be not too severe. When the heat of the bed begins to decline, warm horse-litter laid upon the glasses every night will contribute as much to facilitate the shoot of the buds, as if new dung were applied to the roots.

ᔕ Radishes. ᘓ

Radishes are sown on a hot-bed having a sufficient thickness of good rich light mould, that they may have depth to root in before they reach the dung. And to have large and clean radishes, make holes as deep as your finger, about three inches distance: drop into each hole a sound seed or two, and cover the seeds a little, leaving the rest of the hole open; by which means they will grow to the height of the hole before they dilate their leaves, and leave a long and transparent root.

Long white
Naples radish
*Raphanus
sativus*

There are several varieties of radishes; as the small-topped, the deep-red, the pale-red, or salmon, and the long-topped striped radish. The small-topped is most commonly preferred by the gardeners near London, because they require much less room than those which have large tops.

If the weather be open at the beginning of this month, you should sow some small-topped and salmon-radishes on a warm border, fully exposed to the sun, and defended from the north winds by a wall or other close fence.

You must however be very careful not to mix the seeds: each sort should be sown by itself; for the small-topped will be fit to draw a full week at least before the other, though both are sown at the same time, and on the same bed. There is also another reason, viz. the latter runs more to leaves than the former. They should therefore have more room to spread, for otherwise their roots will be very small.

Both sorts should be sown pretty thick at this season; because the birds will pick up all they can find, and, if not prevented, destroy the whole. The weather also will destroy some; so that unless great care be taken, and a considerable quantity of seed sown at first, very few plants will come to perfection. Means should therefore be used to keep off the birds; and if the weather should prove frosty after the plants are up, a little straw or dry fern, shook lightly over the bed, would be of great service to the tender plants; nor will they be bruised by this covering, provided care be taken in laying it on, and taking it off the bed.

Rose China winter radish *Raphanus sativus*

You will do well to sow a little of the same seed at least twice in the month, in the beginning and towards the latter end; by which means you will have a continual supply of radishes, till the natural crop comes in.

Some sow their seed on a warm spot in the common ground, covering it with a frame and glasses; by which means they procure a crop at a very acceptable season, and have often the pleasure of seeing this bed produce a better return than that sown on a hot-bed.

℘ Lettuce. ℞

You may also raise lettuce-plants under a frame with glasses, at this season of the year; but you must be careful to let them enjoy the benefit of the open air as often as possible; not by lifting up one of the ends of the glasses, but by taking them entirely off the frame, when the weather is dry and mild; but when it is wet, the glasses must be kept upon the frames, though raised to a very considerable height, that the air may have free admission to the plants. When the weather is severe, they must be kept close night and day; and the glasses covered every night, and even in the day-time if no sun appears, and the wind be very sharp, with mats, or straw.

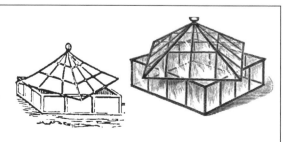

Advantageous in winter months when the base of a conventional glass may be frozen to the ground, the lid of a two-part hand-glass can be reset on the diagonal for ample ventilation.

You must be careful to pick off all the dead leaves as they appear upon the plants; and stir the surface of the ground between them often, taking away all the weeds, or other litter, which would otherwise greatly injure their growth.

You may sow some Coss, cabbage, or brown Dutch lettuce, about the middle of this month, on a warm border, under a wall or pales; observing, when you dig the border, to lay it a little sloping to the sun. If the weather should prove severe soon after the seed is sown, it will be advisable to sow a little more about the latter end of the month, in order to secure a forward crop of lettuce, lest the seed sown first should be destroyed.

৯০ Small Salleting. ০ৎ

As the weather is generally too severe this month for sowing cresses, mustard, rape, &c. in the open air, a slight hot bed should be made, on which the seeds are to be sown. Eighteen or twenty inches deep of dung will be sufficient for the purpose: and if you are in want of frames and glasses, hoops fixed across and covered with mats will answer the intention. The bed must be covered five or six inches thick with light dry mould. In this mould let shallow drills be drawn from the back to the front of the bed, and the seed of each sort sown pretty thick in these drills, covering it about a quarter of an inch deep with mould. But be sure to give the plants air as soon as they appear, by raising the glasses or mats; for otherwise they will mould and spoil, as fast as they come up; so very necessary is the fresh air to the growth of these tender plants.

Cole rape
Rapocaulis

You may make a bed to raise a sallet in a few hours by the help of powdered lime and hot dung. A layer of the lime must be laid first, then one of dung, and over that another of lime: the last must be covered with fine rich mould, and the seed sown upon it, in the usual manner, covering it very slightly.

But if you cannot conveniently make a hot-bed of any kind, you may, if the weather be favourable, sow the seed on a warm border under or near a south wall; observing to lay the border sloping towards the sun, raising it about a foot higher on the north than on the south side. Sow the seeds on this bed, and put on the frame and glasses. The success will be certain, unless the weather prove very severe, when a hot bed will be absolutely necessary to supply the warmth requisite to the vegetation of these plants.

℘ Cauliflowers. ℘

Pick off all the leaves that are either withered or damaged from your cauliflower plants, and suffer no weeds to grow among them. It will also be of great use if you can conveniently stir the surface of the ground about the plants. But however that be, let them have plenty of air every day, by either raising the glasses, or taking them entirely off the frame, when the weather is mild and dry; but do not open them at all in frosty weather.

You should also in severe weather remember to cover the glasses every night, and sometimes even in the day time, with mats, straw, or fern. A little litter laid on the outside of the frame will likewise be of use, especially if the joints of it be not very close, as this method will prevent the frost from affecting the plants.

If your plants are covered with hand or bell-glasses, they must have air given them every day by raising the glasses on the side next the sun; but in sharp weather the glasses must be kept close; and in severe weather long litter should be laid round each glass, which will greatly protect the plants from the injuries of the season. Every mild dry day the glasses may be taken off the plants for four or five hours; but they must be kept close every night; a little earth should also be drawn up round the stem of the plants.

℘ Cabbage. ℘

Let a convenient spot of ground be prepared, when the weather is open, for cabbage plants. The manner of preparing it is this: Lay a sufficient quantity of rotten dung upon the ground, and dig it a spade deep, burying the dung at the bottom of the trench. Into this spot the plants may be removed about the latter end of this month, planting them about a foot and a half asunder. Any of the larger sorts of cabbages may be planted at this season; but the sugar-loaf and early Yorkshire cabbage are the most proper.

In the other beds, where any of the plants have been destroyed either by vermin or the severity of the weather, let their places be new supplied with others.

If you should have neglected to transplant cabbages for seed in the months of November and December, that work may still be done, provided the weather be dry and open. The manner of doing it is this:

Close cabbage
Brassica capitata

Make choice of some of your best cabbages, pull them up, and carry them to some shed, or covered place, and there hang them up by their stalks, for four or five days, that all the water may drain away from between their leaves, then plant them in some border under a hedge or pale, quite down to the middle of the cabbage, leaving only the upper part of it above the ground, observing to raise the earth about it, so that it may stand a little above the level of the ground; especially if the soil be wet, for then it will be necessary to raise them considerably above the surface.

Open cabbage
Brassica patula

If the weather should prove very severe, you must lay a little straw, peas-haulm, or fern, lightly over them, to secure them from the frost, taking off whenever the weather proves mild, lest by keeping them too close they should rot. These cabbages will, by this management, shoot out strongly in the spring, and divide into a number of small branches.

℘ Mint. ℞

A small hot-bed should be made this month for mint, that will be fit for use early in the spring. About nine inches deep of dung will be sufficient for the purpose. This should be covered with earth five or six inches thick, upon which the roots of mint are to be placed, and covered with earth about an inch and a half deep. Let the bed be covered with a frame and glasses, or in want thereof with mats supported by hoops fixed across the bed.

℘ Parsley. ℞

Sweet Parsley
Selinum dulce

If the weather be open, some parsley seed may be sown about the middle or latter end of the month, in a warm part of the garden. The drills should be shallow, the seed sown in them tolerably thick, and covered with earth about an inch and a quarter deep.

Most gardeners sow parsley in a single drill along the edges of the borders near the paths, where it will flourish without taking up too much room.

ᔕᓄ Beans. ᘓ

A great variety of garden-beans are now cultivated in the kitchen-gardens of England, differing both in size and shape; some of them producing their pods much earlier in the year than others, for which they are greatly esteemed.

The Mazagan bean is the first and best sort of early beans at present known: these are brought from a Portuguese settlement, of the same name, on the coast of Africa, just without the Straits of Gibraltar; the seeds of this sort are much smaller than those of the horse bean; and as the Portuguese are but slovenly gardeners, there are commonly a great number of bad seeds among them.

Beans
*Phaseolus
peregrims*

The next sort is the early Portugal bean, which appears to be the Mazagan sort saved in Portugal; for it is extremely like those saved the first year in England. This is the sort generally used by gardeners for their first crop; but these are not near so well tasted as the Mazagan: when therefore the latter can be procured, no person of skill would plant the former.

The small Spanish bean comes next: this will ripen soon after the Portugal sort; and being a sweeter bean, should be preferred to it.

Soon after the Spanish comes the Sandwich bean; this is almost as large as the Windsor bean, but being hardier is commonly sown a month sooner; it is also a very plentiful bearer.

The Toker Bean, as it is generally called, comes about the same time with the Sandwich and being a great bearer, often planted

Both the white and the black blossom beans are also by some persons much esteemed: the beans of the former are, when boiled, almost as green as peas; and this property added to their being very sweet, renders them valuable; but both these sorts are very apt to degenerate, if their seeds are not saved with great care.

The Windsor bean is allowed to be the best of all the sorts for the table; when these are planted on a good soil, and allowed sufficient room, their pods will be very large, and in great plenty. They are also, when gathered young, the sweetest and best tasted of all the sorts: but great care should be used in saving the seed, by pulling up such of the plants as are not perfectly right, and afterwards by separating all the good beans from the bad, when they are taken out of the pods.

If the weather be mild at the beginning of this month, let a proper spot of ground be prepared for a principal crop of Sandwich beans. They may, if the weather permits, be planted the first week in this month. The rows should be six feet distance from one another, and the beans set five or six inches asunder in the row.

Dwarf or French Bean
Phaseolus vulgaris

A few Windsor beans may also be planted about the same time; but it will be more advisable to defer the main crop till near the latter end of the month, for they are less hardy than the Sandwich bean. The rows should be a yard asunder, and the beans planted full six inches apart. The distance between the beans and the rows, is, by some gardeners, thought too great; but Mr. Miller assures us, he has found for many years experience, that the same space of ground will produce a greater quantity of beans, when planted at the above distance, than if double the quantity of seeds were set in it.

Pods and seed of
broad bean
Phaseolus vulgaris

The same ingenious gentleman also observes, that a very bad custom too often prevails in gentlemen's kitchen-gardens, namely, that of planting beans for an early crop close to the garden-walls, on the best aspects, immediately before the fruit trees; which is certainly of greater prejudice to the trees, than the value of the beans, or, indeed, of any other early crop: this practice therefore should be every-where discouraged; for it is much better to run some reed hedges across the quarters of the kitchen-garden, where early beans and peas may be planted, where they may more conveniently be covered from the frost, and to which they may be more easily fastened as they advance in their growth, than to walls, covered with good fruit trees, which must be greatly prejudiced by such practice.

℠ Peas. ∓

There are a great variety of garden-peas now cultivated in England, and which have different titles given them by the gardeners and seedsmen; but as great part of these have been seminal variations, so if they are not very carefully managed, by taking away all those plants which have a tendency to alter, before the seeds are formed, they will again degenerate into their original state. Those persons therefore who are desirous of preserving any variety of peas, should look carefully over those plants they design for seed, at the time they begin to flower, and draw up all the plants they dislike. This is what the gardeners call rogueing their peas, signifying thereby, the separating all the bad plants from the good, that the farina of the former may not impregnate the latter; to prevent which they always do it before the flowers open: by this judicious practice, and by preserving those for seed which flower soonest, they have, of late years, greatly improved their peas, and are constantly endeavouring to procure still forwarder varieties; so that it would be of very little use, should one attempt to give an account of all the varieties now cultivated; it will therefore be sufficient to mention only the titles by which they are generally known, placing them according to the time of their being fit for the table.

ℰℂℛ

The golden hotspur.	Nonpareil.
The Charlton.	Sugar-dwarf.
The Reading hotspur.	Sickle pea.
Masters's hotspur.	Marrowfat.
Essex hotspur.	Rose, or crown pea.
The dwarf-pea.	Rouncival pea.
The sugar-pea.	Gray pea.
Spanish Morotto.	Pig pea.

Pea
Pisum

Some golden hotspurs may be sown the beginning of this month, for a full crop, on a warm piece of ground: let them be sown in rows a yard distance. This crop will succeed that sown in December.

You may also sow at the same time, the first crop of marrowfat peas; and they will succeed the hotspurs; for they will begin bearing as the others give over. This pea is greatly admired in most families; but the dwarf marrowfat is the most proper to be sown at this season.

If you intend to set sticks in the ground for these peas to run, the rows must be at least four feet from one another; but if no sticks are intended, three feet and a half will be fully sufficient.

Those beans and peas, if any, already up, should when the ground is dry, and the weather mild, have some earth drawn up to their stems; for this will at once strengthen the plants, and be of great service in protecting them from the frost.

❧ Celery. ❧

Earth up the celery that requires it, on a dry day, when the weather is open. Take care that the earth be well broken, and laid lightly to the plants, that they may neither be crushed down, nor their hearts buried.

Let the earth be raised very near the top of the plants; for should severe frost set in, all the plants of the celery above the ground will be destroyed; and if any considerable part of the plants should be destroyed, it would even occasion a decay in those parts which are under the surface.

Boston market celery
Apium graveolens dulce

In some families these plants are required every day; some of the rows should therefore be covered with light dry litter, on the approach of hard weather, otherwise it will be impossible to take them up. This method will at once prevent the ground from being frozen, and protect the plants from the piercing coldness of the weather.

❧ Endive. ❧

At this season some of the endive planted about September or October should, when the weather is mild and dry, be taken up, and laid in a ridge

of dry earth to blanch. But be sure to hang the best and largest plants a day or two in a dry place, before they are laid in the earth, that the moisture lodged between their leaves may drain off, otherwise the heart of the plants will be rotten before the blanching is completed.

Let the ridge intended for the reception of these plants be prepared in the driest part of the garden, and where the ground is light and fine. The trench should be about two feet and a half wide, and sideways to the mid-day

Curled-leaved endive
Cichorium endivia

sun. Let it be a good spade deep, and the earth be laid on the north side of the trench, close to the edge, forming a high ridge. Make the sunny side or that next the trench, as upright as possible, in order to drain off the heavy rains; for if water lies about the plants, it will destroy them.

When your ridge is thus prepared, gather the leaves of each plant regularly and close in your hand, make an opening on the sunny side of the ridge, and put the plant sideways into the earth, almost to the tops of the leaves. The plants may be laid pretty near to each other, so that a short trench will be sufficient for a considerable number.

But there is still a surer method of blanching endive at this season; namely by laying some dry earth, or old tan, in a frame, sloping to the sun; and burying your endive plants therein almost to the tops of the leaves. When the weather is either wet or frosty, the glasses and other covering, if you think it necessary, may be put on: and by this method there will be no danger of obtaining excellent endive in the severest season; provided care be taken to lay down a quantity at the beginning of a hard frost. A single frame will hold a very considerable number of plants, as they may be laid almost close to each other.

℘ Carrots. ℘

At any time of the month, when the weather will permit, a warm spot of ground should be prepared for a few early carrots. Let the earth be dug a full spade deep, and the mould broken very fine as you proceed. A small spot will be sufficient for the purpose, as it is only intended to raise a few that may be fit for the table before the general crop. Let the seed be sown when the weather is mild, and raked in as soon as sown.

It you make use of a hot-bed for raising carrots early, the earth should be at least six inches thick, If you have no frame at liberty, let the bed be arched over with hoops, and covered occasionally with mats.

℘ Spinach. ℘

If you are desirous of having spinach early in the spring, a little seed may be sown in a warm spot, about the beginning of the month, and a little more towards the latter end, in order to obtain a regular succession. The smooth-seeded, or round leaved spinach is the best to sow at this season.

℘ Mushroom. ℘

Your mushroom beds will require considerable attendance this month. The plants must have a covering sufficient to defend them from the frost, rain, or snow; and if, by accident, the rain should have penetrated quite through the covering, it must be renewed immediately, or your spawn will be in danger of perishing. Let it therefore be replaced with a good covering of wheat or other straw; and if the wet weather be likely to continue, it will not be amiss to lay some mats, or other covering over the straw; for this will greatly tend to preserve the beds from injury.

Chantarelle
mushroom
*Cantharellus
cibarius*

THE FRUIT-GARDEN AND ORCHARD

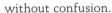

ଔ Vines. ଔ

In pruning vines, which may be done any time this month, observe to take away the lesser and weaker shoots, which bear any fruit, and to leave a sufficient number of the other branches to furnish every part of the wall, without confusion.

The shoots should be shortened to four or five eyes in length; let the branches be cut off about half an inch above an eye, and in a direct sloping from it; and the branches nailed as soon as they are pruned, at about 12 or 13 inches from one another.

You should observe to leave every year some shoots near the bottom of the wall, that you may have a constant succession of young wood coming up in a regular order, in order to supply the place of some of the old and most unserviceable part of the wood, which should be cut away, when it has advanced near the top of the wall, as it will be then in a manner useless. This useless part should be cut away near the bottom, or some convenient young branch growing from it, leaving the latter to supply the place of the former.

All sorts of vines are propagated either from layers, or cuttings, the former of which is generally practised in England; but the latter, recommended by Mr. Miller, is much preferable to the other. He very justly observes, that the roots of vines do not, like most other sorts of trees, grow strong and woody, but long, slender and pliable, and for this reason, when they are once taken out of the ground, they seldom strike out any fibres from the weak roots, which generally shrivel and dry; so that they rather retard than help the plants in their growth, by preventing the new fibres from pushing out: it will be therefore better to set a good cutting, provided it be well chosen, than a rooted plant, as there is very little danger of its growing.

But as there are few persons who make use of proper cuttings, or at least that rightly form their cuttings in England, a few directions for that purpose will be necessary. You should always make choice of such shoots as are strong and well ripened, of the last year's growth; these should be cut from the old vine, just above the place where they were produced, taking a knot or piece, of the two years wood, to each, which should be pruned smooth; you should then cut off the upper part of the shoots, so as to leave the cutting about sixteen inches long. When the piece, or knot, of old wood is cut at both ends, near the young shoot, the cutting will resemble a little mallet; whence Columella calls it Malleolus. In making the cuttings after this manner, there can be only one taken from each shoot; whereas most persons cut them into lengths of about a foot, and plant them all; but this is very wrong: for the upper part of the shoots are never so well ripened as the lower, which was produced early in the spring and had the whole summer to harden; so that if they take root, they never make so good plants; for the wood of those cuttings being spongy and soft, admits the moisture too freely, whereby the plant will be luxuriant in growth, but never so fruitful as that whose wood is close and more compact.

Black Corinth grapes
Vitis vinifera

When the cuttings are thus prepared, they should be planted immediately, or placed with their lower parts in the ground of a dry soil, laying some litter on their upper parts to prevent them from drying: in this situation they may remain till the beginning of April, when they should be taken out of the ground, and washed from the filth they have contracted; and if you find them very dry, let them stand with their lower parts in water six or eight hours, which will dispose them for taking root. The ground being properly prepared, open the holes at about six feet distance from each other, and put one good strong cutting in each hole, laying them a little sloping, that their tops may incline to the wall; but they must be put in so deep that the uppermost eye may be just level with the surface of the ground; for when any part of the cutting is left above ground, as is the common method used by the English gardeners, most of the buds attempt to shoot; so that the strength of the cutting is divided to nourish so many shoots, which must consequently be weaker than if only one of them grew; whereas, on the contrary, by burying the whole cutting in the ground, the sap is all employed on one single shoot, which must, consequently, be much stronger: besides, the sun and air are apt to dry that part of the cutting which remains above ground, and by that means often prevents its buds from shooting.

❧ Apples, Pears, &c. ❧

If any of your wall or espalier trees still remain unpruned, let the work be forwarded now as much as possible. When old pear trees are vigorous, and the space of the wall assigned for each is not sufficient to contain their branches, when properly extended, take away every second or third tree, according as room is wanted, before you prune them. And if the old branches are placed horizontally, lay the new ones left in the middle of the tree in that position between them; but if the old horizontals are too near one another, and the tree not vigorous, part of them may be cut away to make room for the new ones; together with such branches as would shade the young horizontals. There should be nothing left in these places but what will blossom that year; nor should there be too many buds left for that purpose.

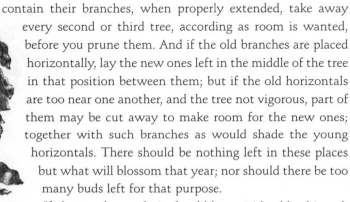

If the tree be weak, it should be considerably thinned, by taking out part of the bearers. You may easily know what buds will produce blossoms by their shapes; they are

Winter Banana
Apple
Malus

more globular than others; these only should be left on those parts of the old horizontals which are nearest the stem, where the young horizontals are interlaid; but let all the collaterals that are not too long for bearers, and near the extremities of the tree, remain.

Every branch, &c. taken from a tree, must be cut off close to the part from whence it proceeded; for when stumps are left, they are apt to produce a number of useless branches.

The hardier sort of apples require much the same management in pruning. Some kinds of apples, especially the nonpareil, will sometimes bear a small number of fruit upon young wood, or shoots of the last year's production; but they generally bear most upon studs, or spurs, proceeding from branches of two, three, or four years old.

When any of the horizontals are cankered, take off the rind as far as the quick, and let all the moss be clean scraped off, both from them and the stem; which may best be done in wet weather; but if the weather be dry, moisten the trees well with brine, and when the moss is taken off, wash them again with the same liquor, which will prevent moss from growing upon them for the future; by this means the eggs of caterpillars concealed in the cavities of the old bark, will be, in a great measure, destroyed.

With regard to the pruning orchard trees, nothing more should be done than to cut out all those branches that cross each other, which if left would rub and tear off its own bark, together with that of the branches it crosses: all decayed branches that are broken by the wind, they should be cut off, either down to the division of the branch, or close to the stem from whence it was produced. But the work should never be done in frosty weather.

Pear 'Winter Grey'
Pyrus

ᔕᗝ Plums and Cherries. ᗒᗩ

Though these trees are somewhat tenderer than the apple and pear trees, yet if the weather be not severe, they may be safely pruned and nailed, either against walls or espaliers.

Cherries of different kinds require different ways of pruning and nailing, because they bear their fruit on wood of different ages; the morello and baremdam bear most of their

Napoleon Cherry
Prunus cerasus

fruit upon the extremities of the last year's shoots, and should therefore be cut and nailed every year, so as to procure a succession of them. With regard to the other sorts of cherries, let it be observed, that all such young shoots of the last year's growth, as are now intended to furnish the wall or espalier with bearing wood, must not be shortened, but every such shoot or branch must be left at its full length; and this should at all times be practised, which is the only way to render the branches fruitful; for the shoots thus treated, will, in two years time, send out many shoots, or fruit-spurs, about half an inch or an inch in length, and from these spurs the fruit is always produced. These spurs generally appear first near the extreme part of the branches; so that by shortening them, that part where the blossom-buds would otherwise have made their appearance, would consequently be cut away.

In nailing these, or indeed any other kind of stone fruit, take care that the rind be neither galled nor bruised by either hammer or nail; for this will cause gum to issue from the wounded part, which will either kill or weaken the part it proceeds from.

Plum trees are observed to produce the best fruit upon the youngest bearers, unless too great a number of them be suffered to remain; these should therefore be carefully preserved; by which means a large quantity of the best fruit will be procured.

We have already observed, that the top or young shoots left for bearing wood, should not be shortened in either apples, pears, or cherries; and shall now add, that the same should be observed with regard to plums. But in some instances this useful rule must be dispensed with; particularly when the trees are about six years old from the budding or grafting, and newly planted against walls or espaliers. For it is necessary that all the shoots produced the two first years after budding or grafting, should be shortened; which should be done in the spring, cutting them to four or five eyes; by which means they will put out lateral branches near the ground, and furnish regularly the wall or espalier with branches from the bottom. After this the branches are to be trained along at their full length, except if should be found necessary to shorten one or two of the middlemost shoots, in order that each may throw out two or three lateral branches, to furnish that part of the tree. Let these lateral shoots also be trained at their full length, unless there are still more branches wanting, when one or two of the most convenient of the last shoots may be likewise shortened, to promote their producing more lateral branches, to cover the wall: for the great art consists in encouraging your fruit trees to produce shoots in proper places, so as to cover the wall or espalier regularly with branches, from the bottom to the top.

Greengage plum
Prunus

But when the trees have acquired branches sufficient to cover the wall or espalier in regular order, you are then to shorten no more of the branches, except in cases where wood is wanting.

ᜈ Peaches, Apricots, and Nectarines. ᜈ

If the weather proves mild, peaches, apricots, and nectarines, may be pruned and nailed any time this month. For though they are rather more tender than any of the sorts above mentioned; yet extreme hard frost only can affect the parts that are newly cut; and in such severe weather no pruning should be attempted.

There is very little difference in the method necessary to be observed in pruning either of these trees; the fruit of them all being produced from the shoots of the last year; a proper supply therefore of the best of the last year's shoots must now be left in a regular manner in every part of the tree; and these shoots must be shortened, in order to encourage them to produce a succession of bearing wood during the succeeding summer; for the wood then produced will bear fruit the summer after.

It will be proper, before you begin pruning, to un-nail the greater part of the tree, that room may not be wanting to use your knife properly: and when you have finished the pruning of one tree, let that be nailed up again, before you proceed to another.

But be careful to remember, in the pruning of these trees, to select the most promising and best situated shoots, which are to be preserved at proper distances in every part of the tree, and room made for them by cutting away the decayed shoots, and old useless wood.

Apricot
Prunus armeniaca

Another circumstance necessary to be remembered is that the shoots should always be shortened in proportion to their own strength and that of the tree. If the latter be weak, the shoots should be left about six or seven inches from one another, and shortened according to their strength: some may be left six, others eight, ten or twelve inches long; varying the length of the shoot in proportion to its strength.

If the tree be neither very vigorous, nor very weak, the shoots should be laid in about five or six inches asunder, and shortened to about eight, ten, twelve, or fifteen in proportion to their strength.

But where the tree is very vigorous, the shoots should be very little shortened; some to the length of ten, twelve or fifteen inches, whilst the strongest may be laid in eighteen inches, or two feet long, and some of them even at full length.

Care should be taken, in shortening the shoots of these trees, to cut them off, if possible, at an eye likely to produce a leading shoot; such eyes are known by their having two blossom-buds; between which there will issue a wood necessary to the welfare of the fruit; for where such shoot is produced at the extremity of a bearing branch, it draws nourishment to the fruit, and renders it much finer than the fruit of those shoots destitute of leaders.

℘ Gooseberry and Currant Trees. ℘

It is a common practice in pruning gooseberry-shrubs, to make use of garden shears, observing only to cut the head round, as is practised for evergreens, &c. whereby the branches become so much crowded, that what fruit is produced, never grows to half the size it would do, were the branches thinned and pruned according to art; which should always be done with a pruning-knife, shortening the strong shoots to about ten inches, and cutting out all those which grow irregular, thinning the fruit-bearing branches where they are too close, observing always to cut behind a leaf bud. With this management the fruit will be near twice as large as those produced upon such bushes as are not thus pruned, and the shrubs will continue much longer in vigour.

The currant tree produces its fruit from the former year's wood, and also upon small snags which come out of the old wood; so that in pruning this shrub, the snags should be preserved, and the young shoots shortened in proportion to their strength. The only care necessary in pruning them is not to leave these shoots too close, and never to prune their snags in order to make them smooth. This, with a small degree of attention in observing the manner of their growth, will be sufficient to instruct any person how to manage the plant, so as to produce great quantities of fruit.

You may during this month, provided the weather be mild, plant both gooseberries and currants; and if the trees are to be set round the quarters of the kitchen-garden, prune them up to one stem, twelve or fifteen inches before you form the head of the tree; for when these trees are suffered to branch away immediately from their roots, they injure all the small crops that grow near them, and render it very troublesome to dig round them.

ભ Raspberries. ભ

The method to be observed in pruning these plants, is to cut away the dead wood close to the ground, clearing away all the small shoots in general, and leaving only three or four of the strongest shoots of the last summer's growth to bear fruit next year, upon each root. All the rest should be cut off close to the surface of the ground.

At the same time those shoots left for bearing, should each of them be shortened, about one third, or at least one fourth, of the length of each shoot.

The spaces between the rows should be well dug to encourage their roots; and if you bury a little rotten dung therein, it will make them shoot vigorously the following summer, and their fruit will be much larger and better.

You may now make plantations of raspberries, leaving at least four feet between the rows, and setting the plants a yard distant in the rows. These plantations are generally made with suckers; but Mr. Miller prefers such plants as are raised by layers, because they will better rooted, and at the same time less liable than the others to send out suckers: and where these are not carefully taken off or thinned, the fruit will be small and in little quantity, especially when the plants are placed near each other, which is too often the case, few persons being willing to allow these plants sufficient room.

THE PLEASURE
OR FLOWER-GARDEN

Unless the utmost care be taken to protect your choicest flowers from inclemency of the season, they will suffer greatly; attention is therefore necessary for them all, though they in general require a different management.

฿ Carnations, Hyacinths, &c. ଔ

Let your carnations that are in pots be well secured from frost, heavy rains, and snow, which would greatly injure, if not entirely destroy them.

The best method is to plunge the pots at the beginning of winter into a bed of dry compost, arched over with hoops, which, when the weather is very wet or frosty, should be carefully covered with mats. But when the weather is mild, let the covering be removed, that the plants may enjoy the free air, so necessary to their health.

You should also in frosty weather cover the beds where you have deposited the choicest kinds of hyacinths, tulips, or any other curious roots. Fern or long litter will do very well for this purpose: but you must remember to remove it, as soon as the severe weather is over.

As soon as any of the above plants begin to appear above ground, let the bed be arched over with hoops; and when the weather is either very wet or frosty, let them be covered with mats, fastened down at the sides to prevent the wind from blowing them off. But be sure to take away the mats as soon as the weather is dry and open.

℘ Auriculas. ℭ

As heavy rains, snow, or sharp frosts, will greatly injure these delicate plants, they should always be removed about the end of October into frames, or on a bed arched over with hoops, and situated in a warm place, where they may be constantly covered when the weather is unfavourable: but remember to take off the covering, whenever the weather is mild and dry.

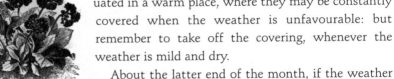

Auricula
Primula auricula

About the latter end of the month, if the weather be mild, take away the upper part of the earth in the pots, as low as you can without disturbing the roots, and fill up the pots with fresh rich earth, which will greatly strengthen their bloom. The best compost for this purpose is good fresh light sandy mould, mixed with very rotten neats dung, or any rotten dung from the bottom of an old hot-bed. At the same time clear the plants from all dead leaves. As soon as this is done, and the pots filled up with fresh mould, let them be returned to the place intended for sheltering them from the weather.

℘ Anemonies, Ranunculuses, &c. ℭ

You may now plant those roots of anemonies and ranunculuses, &c. you reserved, in order to succeed those planted in October and November. But you must chuse a mild day for this work, and take care that the ground be not very wet, which will rot the roots. Let the beds be laid arching, that the rain may run off: they should not be more than four feet wide. In these the roots should be planted in rows nine inches distant, and about six inches between each root. They should be set about two inches and a half deep in the earth.

Crowfoot
Ranunculus Asiaticus
grumosa radice

℘ Tulips. ℭ

A few tulips may now be planted to succeed those set in autumn. They should not be deferred any longer, and therefore the first mild day should be chosen for this purpose; for if they are not planted this month, they will blow but very poorly.

If they are to be planted in beds, let them be made rounding, that the wet may not remain on the surface, and about four feet wide. The roots should

be planted in rows about nine inches distant, and the same distance should be allowed between the roots, which should be set
about four or five inches deep in the soil. If you plant some of
the inferior roots in the borders, they may be set in a row about
a foot from the edge, and the roots about the same distance
from each other.

Tulip
*Tulipa praecox
rubra*

But if you plant them in little clumps, they will make a
more beautiful appearance. For instance, if you plant four or
five roots in a circle about eleven inches in diameter, with
another in the center; and about ten or twelve feet further
such another clump. and so on to the end of the border; the effect, when the
plants are in flower, will be very agreeable.

❦ Crocuses. ❧

These should be planted in borders by the sides of the
walks, within six inches of the edge of the border; but
not in one continued row; for they appear to much
greater advantage when placed in clumps, as was before
observed of tulips. Observe also, if you have different
kinds of crocuses, to plant each sort separate: that is, let
one of the clumps be of the yellow sort, the next of blue,
and so on to the end of the border.

Crocus
Crocus versicolor

❦ Jonquils, Narcissuses, &c. ❧

If you have any left of these, or any other kind of bulbous
roots, they should be planted as soon as the weather will permit. Mild dry weather must be chosen to plant these, and
indeed all other kinds of flower roots. Nor should the ground
be too wet, for that will rot the roots.

These, or any other species of bulbous roots intended to be
set in the borders, should be planted in clumps or patches, as
we before directed for tulips &c.

Daffodil
Narcissus

❦ Double Sweet-Williams, Double Wall-Flowers &c. ❧

All the species of these flowers preserved in pots, should be carefully
secured from severe frost. If the plants are placed in frames, or beds
arched over with hoops, let the glasses or mats be kept over them whenever the frost is sharp, and also in very wet weather. But the glasses or

Double Sweet William
Dianthus barbatus

covering must be taken away in mild, dry weather; for a free circulation of air is of the utmost importance to their health.

Care should also to be taken to protect all the fibrous-rooted perennial plants in general, that are in pots, from the frost. The pots should be plunged to the rims in a dry warm border, and covered during the bad weather with long litter: at least the pots should be removed into some sheltered place, at the approach of severe frost.

ɛᴏ Seedling-Flowers. ᴄᴙ

Be very careful to lay peas-haulm, or fern, over your boxes of seedling-flowers in frosty weather; let the covering be of a considerable thickness, and pressed close down at the edges.

If your seedling flowers are planted in beds in the garden, they should likewise be covered with peas-haulm, fern, or long litter, during the frost: but be sure to remove it both from the beds and boxes, as soon as the weather is mild and open, that the tender plants may enjoy the benefit of a free circulation of air.

ɛᴏ Flowering Shrubs. ᴄᴙ

All the flowering shrubs planted in clumps in the shrubbery, should now be pruned, and all the suckers cleared away from their roots. Never use the shears, but a knife in pruning your shrubs, and be careful to cut away all the dead wood, and thin the branches, where they crowd upon one another. The straggling branches should also be taken away, and the shrubs kept clear from each other, so that every kind may be seen distinctly.

Those flowering shrubs and ever-greens that are set in pots should be protected from the sharpness of the frost, by plunging the pots up to their rims in the ground in a dry part of the garden.

Litter should also be laid round the stems of new planted flowering-shrubs and evergreens, if the frost becomes severe; let the litter extend as far at least from the stems as the roots of the plants.

Let your new planted trees, &c. be supported with stakes, that they may not be displaced by the wind.

The ground between the flowering-shrubs and evergreens should be dug, observing to shorten the straggling roots as you proceed, taking care not to disturb the plants. This will not only be of service to the shrubs, but also give the shrubbery a neat appearance.

You should be very careful at this season of the grass walks in the garden; they should be frequently poled and rolled. The former should be done with a pliable ash-pole, fifteen or sixteen feet long, at least; with which you must break and spread the wormcasts, whenever they appear upon the grass. When this is done, let it be rolled with a wooden roller, which will take up all the wormcasts, and leave your grass walks extremely neat.

This is also a proper season, if the weather is open, for laying turf where wanted, for making or mending grass-walks. Your turfs should be three feet long, one foot broad, and an inch thick.

Almond
*Amygdalus
communis*

The best turf for gardens is that of heaths or commons, where great numbers of sheep are pastured.

As soon as the turf is laid, it should be well beaten with a heavy wooden beater, and afterwards rolled with a large stone or iron roller.

Such of the gravel walks as are not laid up in ridges should be kept clean from litter, and free from weeds; and if they are rolled as often as the weather will permit, it will be of great service.

THE NURSERY

In open weather, let the ground be dug between the rows of young trees and shrubs. It should be dug one spade deep, and the earth turned fairly off the spade, that the weeds may be perfectly buried.

If the weather be frosty, let dung be laid on such parts of the nursery as require it. But observe that the dung be perfectly rotten, otherwise it will be prejudicial to the plants. If a little be laid between the rows of trees, and dug in, it will do them service.

FEBRUARY

1. Imperial Plum. *Prunum Imperiale.*
2. Turkey Plum. *Prunum Turcicum.*
3. Red Primordian Plum. *Prunum praecox rubrum.*
4. Mussel Plum. *Prunum Mytellinum.*
5. Amber Plum. *Prunum Ambariuum.*
6. Queen Mother Plum. *Prunum Regineum.*
7. Green Oysterly Plum. *Prunum viride.*
8. Orange Plum. *Prunum Arantiacum.*
9. Nutmeg Plum. *Prunum Myristicum.*
10. Peasecod Plum. *Prunum Siliquosum.*
11. Gaunt Plum. *Prunum Gandauense.*
12. Date Plum. *Prunum Dactylites*
13. Early Pear Plum. *Prunum Pyrinum Praecox.*

Tree propagation by cleft graft. A budding scion is wedged into a cleft between the bark and wood of a sturdy stock and sealed with grafting clay or wax.

The Works of this Month in the
KITCHEN GARDEN

This is a busy month for the gardener, provided the weather be fine and open; we shall therefore be careful to let our directions be full and intelligible.

℘ Asparagus. ℘

It is not yet too late to make hot-beds for early asparagus. In order to which let some good dung be procured and shook up into a heap, where it must lie about ten days, when it will be fit for your purpose. Let the bed be about three feet high, and the top made very level and smooth. When this is done, lay on the earth six or seven inches thick in every part, and make the surface smooth.

When your bed is thus prepared, raise a ridge of earth about six inches high from one end of the bed to the other, and place the roots against this ridge, as close together as possible, till the whole bed is filled with them; observing to leave a space two inches wide, at least, on each side, to receive some earth against the outside roots.

This being done, cover the crowns of the roots with light earth about two inches thick; which is all that is required to be done till the buds begin to appear through the surface, when three or four depths of more earth must be laid upon the bed; by which means the tops of the roots will be covered five or six inches.

A quantity of sharp pointed stakes, about two feet long, and also some thick bands or ropes of either straw or hay must be procured. These hay or straw-bands are to be carried entirely round the bed, and fastened down with the stakes at proper distances. Upon this border the frame is to be placed; which being done, the glasses must be put on, and covered every night with mats. Be very careful that the hay or straw-bands be directly level with the surface or the earth in the bed.

In about thirty or forty days, the bed, if properly managed, will produce plenty of buds. But it is necessary to remember, that the roots for this purpose be about three years old, never more than four. A three-light frame, if properly placed, will contain three or four hundred roots.

ᔕ Cucumbers and Melons. ᔕ

Your cucumbers and melon plants that have not suffered by any of the accidents that too often attend them at this season, may now be transplanted into the hotbed, where they are to produce their fruit. In order to this, let

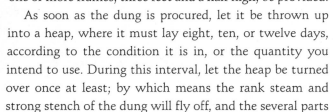

as much horse-dung as will be sufficient for making a hot-bed for one or more frames, three feet and a half high, be provided.

As soon as the dung is procured, let it be thrown up into a heap, where it must lay eight, ten, or twelve days, according to the condition it is in, or the quantity you intend to use. During this interval, let the heap be turned over once at least; by which means the rank steam and strong stench of the dung will fly off, and the several parts

Cucumber
Cucumis

will become mellow, and mix together, when made into a bed; the heat will also be steady and lasting.

In making the bed, observe to shake some of the longest dung into the bottom; after which take it as it comes to hand, shake it equally on every part, and beat it down with the fork from time to time as you proceed. In this manner let the bed be carried up very evenly on each side, to the height of forty inches.

As soon as the bed is finished, put on the frame and lights, which will at once defend it from the rain, and draw up the heat considerably sooner. But it will be necessary to raise the lights a little, when it does not rain, that the steam may pass off. When the bed has been made about a week, look it carefully over; and if it has settled unequally, take off the frame, level the bed, and replace the frame for good.

The bed must now be every day attentively examined: as soon as you find the violent heat is over, the earth may be laid upon the surface.

It is necessary to be remembered, that the earth chosen for this purpose be quite dry, and sufficiently rich. Let about three quarters of a bushel of this earth be laid in a round

Embroidered
market melon
Cucumis melo

hillock about twelve inches high, in the middle of each light; and the spaces between the hillocks, quite to the edge of the frame, be covered with the same sort of earth, two or three inches thick.

As soon as you have put the earth in the above manner upon the bed, put on the glasses; and the next day, if the hillocks of each be warm, level the top of each a little, so that they may be about ten inches high; and then begin to put in the plants.

This being done, take some pots of the strongest plants, lay your hand on the surface of the pot, and take the stems of the plants carefully between your fingers: then turn the mouth of the pot downwards, and strike the edge gently against the frame; by which means the plants, with the ball of earth to their roots, will come out entire. When this is done, make a hole in the middle of each hillock or earth, and place one pot of plants with the ball entire, in each hole, closing the earth well round the ball. Observe to cover the top of each ball about an inch, and to lay the earth close round the stems of the plants.

About eleven or twelve o'clock the next day, give the plants a little water, observing to use such as have stood long enough in the bed to take off the chillness. You should also be careful to let very little, if any, of the water touch either the leaves or stems of the plants at this season.

Common cucumber
*Cucumis longus
vulgaris*

The only difficulty now remaining is to keep up a constant genial heat in the bed, that the plants may be kept in a continual growing state.

But you must remember to raise the glasses a little every day when the weather is favourable, that the plants may enjoy the fresh air; and to open the glass more or less, in proportion to the sharpness or mildness of the weather.

The first week or ten days after the plants are thus ridged out, you must be very careful to prevent the plants from having too much heat; for it sometimes happens that a bed, after the mould and plants are in, will begin afresh to heat, in so violent a manner as to burn the earth at the bottom of the hillocks; and unless some precaution be taken, the burning will soon reach the roots of the plants. It will therefore be necessary, during the first week at least, to examine frequently the bottoms of the hillocks, by drawing away a little of the earth, and, if any burning appears, to remove the burnt earth, replacing it with new. At the same time let part of the earth at the bottoms of the hills be drawn away, leaving them only bases sufficient to support the plants. And in this manner let them continue till the danger of burning is over.

Kolb's Gem
watermelon
Citrullus lanatus

When you give the plants air, you should fasten a mat across the ends of the lights, and let it hang down over the place where the air enters the frame; for this will, in a great measure, destroy the current of wind, so that it will not injure the plants, though there will be a proper proportion of air admitted; and at the same time the steam will have full liberty to evaporate.

Let the glasses be every night covered with mats, and if there be a strong heat and considerable steam in the bed, let the lights be raised a little when you cover up, letting them remain so all night; by which means the steam will fly off through the matting, without the cold air being admitted to the plants.

As soon as the roots of the plants begin to appear through the sides of the hillocks, let some earth be laid round them, and, about three days after that, you may earth the bed all over to the full thickness, so that the whole surface may be level, and equal with the tops of the hillocks.

The heat of the bed will in a little time begin to grow faint: as soon as this happens, let a lining be applied to either the back or front of the bed, or, if the heat be very low, to both.

Common melon
Melo vulgaris

These linings should be composed of dung prepared in the same manner as that for making the bed. They should be about eighteen inches thick, and raised about five or six inches higher than the dung of the bed. Some earth should be laid upon the top of the linings, to prevent the heat from finding a passage that way; for it would otherwise, in all probability, insinuate itself into the frame, and prove detrimental to the plants.

If the plants are not already stopped at the first joint, let it be done now; for this will cause them to send out fruitful runners.

Cucumber and melon seeds should be sown at two or three different times this month, that a fresh supply of plants may be always ready, either for new beds, or for replacing any that may fail.

℘ Cauliflowers. ℘

The glasses should be taken off the frames every mild day, that the cauliflower plants may enjoy a free circulation of the fresh air.

Some of the strongest plants may, about the end of the month, be removed into the place where they are to continue. Let them be planted in a rich spot of ground, and a space of thirty inches, or a yard every way, be allowed between the plants.

Those cauliflower plants also which are under hand or bell-glasses, should be thinned out when there are too many; one plant under each glass will be sufficient, the rest should therefore be taken away. But remember to let the strongest plant under each glass remain; and, at same time, to draw up some earth round their stems. The plants taken up may be planted at the above distance from each other, in another spot of ground.

At the beginning of this month some cauliflower seed should be sown on a slight hot-bed, that plants may not be wanting to succeed the early crop. The bed for this purpose should be about twenty inches thick of dung; and the earth over it five or six inches thick. On the surface of this earth let the seed be sown, and covered with light earth about a quarter of an inch thick. After which let the frame be put upon the bed.

As soon as the plants appear, they must have fresh air given them every day, by raising the glasses a considerable height. In mild weather the lights should be taken entirely away, during the day-time; otherwise they would be drawn up very weak.

If moderate showers of rain do not fall, the plants must be frequently sprinkled with water.

℘ Kidney-Beans. ℘

A hot-bed may be made in the beginning of this month for early kidney-beans.

In order to this some fresh horse dung should be prepared as for other hot-beds; these should be made about two feet and a half high, and long enough for one or

Climbing kidney bean
Phaseolus multiflorus

more frames. Put on the frames, after making the surface of the bed smooth; and when the heat is moderate, cover the bed with rich light earth seven or eight inches thick. Then draw drills an inch deep, and a foot asunder, from the back to the front of the frame. Drop the beans, about three inches asunder, into the drills, and cover them an inch deep with earth.

The yellow, or liver-coloured, kidney-bean is the fittest for this purpose; though the speckled, or dwarf kind will answer very well; for both these will continue bearing longer than the other sorts. As soon as the plants begin to appear, the lights must be raised every day, that the plants may enjoy the benefit of the fresh air, which will strengthen them greatly. Moderate sprinklings of water at proper times will also be necessary when the plants are up.

৪৹ Cabbages and Savoys. ෬

Sugar-loaf and other early cabbage-plants should be removed this month

into the spot where they are to remain. Some rotten dung should have been dug into the ground where these plants are to be set. Let the plants be set in rows two feet and a half asunder, and the same distance between the rows.

A little cabbage seed should be sown about the latter end of the month for autumn use. These will succeed the early plants, for they will be fit to cut in August and September.

Curled Savoy colewort
*Brassica sabaudica
crispa*

About the latter end of the month, Savoy-seed may be sown for the first time. Those plants which are sown now will be fit for the table in September; by October they will be finely cabbaged, and continue good till the end of November.

You may likewise plant this month, if not done before, both cabbages and savoys for seed.

৪৹ Carrots, Parsnips, and Beets. ෬

About the latter end of this month, a sufficient spot of ground should be prepared for carrots, parsnips, and beets.

The farther from trees, and the lighter the ground in which the roots are planted, the larger they will grow; for they thrive best in a light soil and open exposure. The ground should be

Sugar beet
Beta vulgaris

dug one full spade deep at least, and the clods carefully broken.

The seed should be sown in a dry, clear day, with an even hand, not too thick, and the ground equally raked afterwards. Each species of seed should be sown on different pieces.

Those carrots, parsnips, and beets, that are intended for seed, should be planted in rows two feet asunder.

Blood turnip beet
Beta vulgaris

ಎ Beans. ಆ

At the beginning of this month let an open spot be dug for a crop of beans. The Windsor, Sandwich, and other large beans, are the most proper to plant at this season; but they should be planted six inches asunder, in rows a full yard apart.

The Mazagan bean also may now be planted either in the garden, or the field; it is a good bearer, and will, in some soils, answer very well.

ಎ Peas. ಆ

About the beginning of this month a principal crop of peas should be sown in an open piece of ground. If you propose to sow the marrowfats and other large peas, you should draw drills for them, three feet and a half asunder; but if you intend to place sticks for the support of these large kinds of peas, they should be sown in drills four feet asunder.

The hotspur, and other small kinds of peas, should be sown in drills a yard asunder; if you intend to stick them, let the drills be forty inches asunder.

Stratagem
pea
*Pisum
sativum*

All the crops, whether beans or peas, that are up and advanced any considerable height, should now have earth drawn up their stems, which will at once strengthen the plants, and protect them from the frost. It should however be done in a mild day.

ಎ Lettuces. ಆ

If the weather be mild about the beginning of this month, you may sow several sorts of lettuce-seeds on warm borders. The Coss and Silesia are the best kinds for sowing at this season: you may also sow some of the cabbage and imperial lettuces. Let the seeds be sown pretty thick, and raked in as soon as they are sown.

But if the weather should be cold at the beginning of the month, the seed of both the Coss and Silesia should be sown in frames, and covered occasionally to protect it from the severity of the weather. By this means you may procure strong plants in unfavourable seasons, and they may easily be transplanted when of a proper size.

Those plants which have stood the winter in warm borders or frames, should be thinned out, where they stand too close, about the latter end of the month. But you must observe to thin them regularly, leaving them a foot distant each way; for they will require so much room to grow to their full size: the plants which are taken up should be set in an open spot of rich ground, a foot distant every way.

෬ Small Salleting. ෬

Let different sorts of small salleting be sown once a week or ten days, viz. cresses, mustard, radish, rape and lettuce. The seeds should be sown in a frame, the earth light, and its surface laid very smooth.

Shallow drills should be drawn from the back to the front of the

Striped and variegated kales
Brassica oleracea acephala

frame, the seeds sown in the drills, and covered about the fourth part of an inch thick. As soon as this is done, put on the glasses; but be sure to give the plants air as soon as they are above the surface.

If the weather should prove cold and wet, and small salleting be much wanted, a small hot-bed may be made for it. About fifteen inches thick of fresh horse dung will be sufficient for this purpose, and the bed covered with earth four or five inches thick.

Let the seed be sown on the surface, each sort separate, and as much earth sifted over as will just cover it. Put on the frame, with the lights; and when the plants appear, let plenty of fresh air be given them.

If the weather be open and mild, you may, about the middle of the month, begin to sow small salleting on warm borders, in open ground.

෬ Celery. ෬

Prepare a small bed of light rich earth in a warm border, in order for sowing some celery-seeds, about the middle, or towards the latter end of the month. Let the earth be broken fine, the surface raked smooth, and the seed sown not too thick upon it; after which let the seed be covered with light earth about a quarter of an inch thick.

ᔓ Radishes. ᘔ

About the beginning of the month, let some part of a warm border be dug up in order to sow a little radish seed. The small-topped radish seed should be sown at this season, to succeed those of the same sort that were sown in the preceding month.

Red turnip radish
Raphanus sativus

Another piece of ground should be dug at the same time for sowing salmon radish-seed; because these will succeed the small-tops. Some more of the salmon radish seed should be sown about a fortnight or three weeks after the former, that there may be a regular supply of these roots in their proper season.

ᔓ Spinach. ᘔ

If the weather be mild about the beginning of this month, some spinach-seed should be sown in good ground well prepared to receive it. Let the seed be sown thin, regular, and raked in.

Some sow spinach between the rows of cabbages, beans, &c. when ground is scarce. The smooth-seeded kind is the best to sow now; and it will be proper to repeat the sowings every fortnight or three weeks, if a regular supply of this vegetable be desired.

ᔓ Potatoes. ᘔ

About the middle or latter end of this month, provided the weather be open, you may plant potatoes. Let them be set in rows two feet asunder, and a foot or fifteen inches distant from one another in the rows. The roots should be planted about five or six inches deep in the earth.

ᔓ Sorzonera, Salsafy, and Hamburg Parsley. ᘔ

About the latter end of this month, let a spot of light ground, in an open situation, be dug for the above herbs. The seed must be sown thin and even, on separate beds, and raked in equally.

ᔓ Thyme, Marjoram, Savory, and Hyssop. ᘔ

These herbs should be sown upon a dry spot of light, rich ground, in a warm situation, about the latter end of the month. They should be sown thinly on separate beds; and the seeds raked in.

Hyssop
Hyssopus

๑ Parsley, Coriander, and Chervil. ๛

Any time this month, when the weather is open, will be proper for sowing parsley, coriander and chervil. The seed should be sown in
shallow drills, and covered with about a quarter of an inch of mould.

๑ Garlick and Shallots. ๛

The beds intended for planting garlick and shallots
should be about four feet wide, and the roots set in rows
nine inches asunder, and six inches distant from one another
in the rows.

Garlick
Allium sativum

๑ Mushrooms. ๛

You must take particular care to defend your mushroom beds
from heavy rains and frost, as either will destroy the spawn. The
beds should be entirely covered with straw, twelve or fifteen
inches thick at least. And if you should at any time perceive that
the wet has penetrated through any part of the covering, let that
part be removed, and replaced with clean dry straw.

Morel
mushroom
*Morchella
esculenta*

๑ Horse-Radish. ๛

Horse-radish is propagated either by cuttings, or by planting the tops
of the old roots, in the following manner:

Let the trenches in which the cuttings, &c. are to be planted, be dug fifteen inches deep at least. When the trench is ready
procure some knotty roots, and cut them into pieces, about an
inch or two in length, observing that each piece be furnished
with eyes or buds; but it will still be better if you can procure a
quantity sufficient for your purpose, of the tops or crowns.
These may be cut from the tops of small off-sets, which grow
from the main roots, and also from the old roots when they
are taken up for use.

Horseradish
*Amoracia
rusticana*

When you have furnished yourself with a sufficient quantity of cuttings or crowns, place them along the bottom of the trench six
inches from each other. Then let the next trench be dug in the same manner as the first, throwing the earth taken out of the latter into the former
trench, over the plants. In this manner you are to proceed with the rest of
the trenches till the whole quantity intended is planted.

THE FRUIT-GARDEN

⁊ Pruning Fruit Trees. ⁊

As this is the peculiar month for pruning fruit trees, we shall consider this work in general, before we proceed to particular trees.

No part of gardening is perhaps of more general use than that of pruning, and yet it is very rare to see fruit trees skilfully managed. Almost every gardener pretends to be a master of this business, though few rightly understand it. Indeed it requires a strict observation of the different manners of growth of the several sorts of fruit trees; some require to be managed one way, while others must be treated in a quite different manner; and this is to be known only by practice, and carefully observing how each kind is naturally disposed to produce its fruit; some sorts growing on the same year's wood, as vines; others produce their fruit for the most part upon the former year's wood, as peaches, nectarines, &c. and others upon cursons or spurs, which are produced upon wood from three, four, or five, to fifteen or twen-

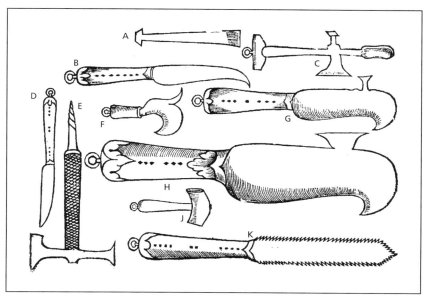

Tools for pruning and grafting of fruit trees. A. Grafting chisel. B. Knife. C. Chisel with wimble bit end for gouging out buds. D. Belt knife for grafting. E. Hammer, file and auger. F. Vine knife. G. Pruning knife. H. Great knife with chisel head. J. Mallet. K. Pruning saw.

ty years old, as pears, plums, cherries, &c. In order therefore to manage fruit trees rightly, provision should always be made to have sufficient quantity of bearing wood, in every part of the trees; and, at the same time, not to have a superfluity of useless branches, which would only tend to exhaust the strength of the trees, and cause them to decay in a few years.

Pruning fruit trees, is founded on the following reasons: first, To preserve trees longer in a vigorous bearing state: secondly, To render the trees more beautiful to the eye: and thirdly, To cause the fruit to be larger and better tasted.

1. It preserves a tree longer in a healthy bearing state; for by cutting off all the superfluous branches, so that no more are left upon the tree than are necessary, or than can be properly nourished, the root is not exhausted in supplying useless branches, which must afterwards be cut out, whereby much of the sap will be uselessly exhausted.

2. By skilful pruning of a tree it is rendered much more pleasing to the eye; but we would not here be understood to recommend a sort of pruning too much practised of late; namely, the drawing of a regular line against the wall, according to the shape and figure they would reduce the tree to, and cutting all the branches, strong or weak, exactly to the chalked line; the absurdity of which will soon appear to every one who will be at the pains of observing the difference of those branches shooting the following spring. All therefore we would be understood to mean by rendering a tree beautiful is, that the branches are all pruned according to their several strengths, and nailed at equal distances in proportion to the different sizes of the leaves and fruit; and that no part of the wall, within the extent of the tree, be left unfurnished with bearing wood. A tree well managed, though it does not represent any regular figure, will still appear very beautiful to the sight, when it is thus dressed, and nailed to the wall.

3. It is of great advantage to the fruit; for the cutting away all useless branches, and shortening all the bearing shoots according to the strength of the tree, will render it more capable of nourishing those which are left remaining, so that the fruit will be much larger, and better tasted. And this is the advantage which those trees against walls or espaliers have over standards, which are permitted to grow as they are naturally inclined; for it is not their being trained to a wall or an espalier, which renders their fruit better than standards, but because the roots have a less quantity of branches and fruit to nourish, and consequently their fruit will be larger and better tasted.

Having thus considered the nature of pruning in general, we shall now proceed to the particular sorts of trees that require pruning at this season of the year.

℘ Prune Standard Fruit Trees. ℭ

Such standard fruit trees, in the orchard and fruit-garden, as require pruning, may be dressed this month. You should be careful to cut from those trees all dead wood and very old branches, and all such as grow in a rambling manner across others. Whenever you free the branches crowded together, let some be cut away, so that the principal branches may stand clear of each other. At the same time be very careful to clear the branches from moss.

Quince Tree
Malus cotonea

℘ Dwarf Apples, Pears, &c. ℭ

If possible, let all your apples, pears, and cherries, planted either against walls or espaliers, be pruned this month.

And in performing this operation, be careful to cut away all the very old branches, and such as are naked, or destitute of bearing wood. At the same time be careful to leave room sufficient for training the young wood and full bearing branches to the wall or espalier, in a regular and handsome manner.

Apple 'Short-hanging fruit'
Malus

Wherever you observe the branches to stand too close together, let the most irregular of them be taken away.

If wood be wanting, leave some of the best situated of the last summer's shoots, in order to fill up the vacant places. But where these shoots are not wanted for the above purpose, let every one of them be cut off close to the part from whence they proceeded, leaving no spurs but what are naturally produced.

It is necessary to observe, that the shoots or branches of these trees must not be shortened, but left at full length, and in that manner trained close and even to the wall, &c. about six inches distant from each other.

℘ Prune Gooseberry and Currant Trees. ℭ

If your gooseberry and currant trees were not pruned last month, it must be done now. In doing this observe to cut away all the irregular branches; that is, all those that grow across, or in a straggling manner from the rest.

Gooseberry
Ribes grossularioides

If you observe the branches in general to stand so close as to interfere with one another, let them be thinned out to proper and equal distances, so that every branch may stand clear of the other; they should be, at least, seven or eight inches apart.

Gooseberry or currant trees may be planted any time this month. But they should never be planted nearer than seven or eight feet from one another.

ଚ Prune Vines. ଜ

If you have any vines that were not pruned last month, let it be done now, but the earlier the better. Observe in pruning vines to cut out the old naked branches, in order to make room for the bearing-wood; which are properly the last year's shoots. Care must therefore be taken to leave a proper supply of the strongest of the last year's shoots in every part of the tree. Care should also be taken to have a succession of young wood coming up regularly from the parts of the vine near the bottom of the wall.

Moore's
early Grape
Vitis vinifera

Let the branches or shoots in general be left at equal distances, and about eight or nine inches from each other.

At the same time you must observe to shorten each shoot in proportion to its strength, some to three, four, or five eyes long, and let the cut be made sloping, about an inch above and behind the eye.

ଚ Raspberries. ଜ

Raspberries, where any remain unpruned, should, if possible, be pruned this month. In pruning raspberries, observe to leave three of the last year's shoots standing on each root, to bear fruit the next summer; but all above that number must be cut away close to the surface of the ground; and all straggling shoots between the rows must also be taken away. All the dead wood must be cleared away.

Black raspberry
Rubus idaeus

All the shoots that are left should be shortened about one third of their original length.

When the pruning is finished, dig the ground between the plants; observing as you dig to clear away all the straggling roots, and leave only those belonging to the shoots which are left to bear.

If the new plantations of raspberries be wanted, they may be made this month. The plants should be set three feet distance from each other in the rows, and the rows four feet asunder.

℘ Strawberries. ℭ

Strawberries should now be cleaned, and have their spring dressing. First pull or cut off all the strings or runners from the plants, and clear the beds from weeds and litter of every kind. When this is done, loosen the ground between and about the plants, adding a little fresh earth between the rows, and close round every plant; this will greatly strengthen the plants, and cause them to produce large fruit.

You may now plant strawberries, but the best time is in August and September. Let a proper piece of ground be prepared for these plants: if the soil be loamy, so much the better; but whatever it be, some rotten dung must be dug in.

Strawberry
Fragari aculeata

Let your ground be now divided into beds four feet wide, with alleys between them at least eighteen inches wide. Let the strawberry plants be set in rows a foot asunder, allowing the same distance between plant and plant in the rows.

℘ Planting Fruit Trees. ℭ

Fruit trees of all sorts may be planted any time this month, when the weather is mild and open.

Peaches, apricots, and nectarines should never be planted closer than fifteen feet from one another; but if you allow eighteen feet, it will still be better.

Apples, pears, plums, and cherries, for walls or espaliers, should be planted eighteen feet asunder; twenty will not be too much. For though these distances seem large at first, when the trees are small, yet in seven years you will be sufficiently convinced of the benefit that will arise from planting them in this manner.

Standard trees should be allowed full thirty feet distance: none should be planted nearer in a garden.

Care should be taken in setting fruit trees that they be not planted too deep; for that is a more material article than most gardeners imagine. And be very careful to open for each tree a hole large enough to

The long sloping windows of this Orangery gain full benefit of the sun's rays.

receive all the roots freely, without pressing them against the sides. When the holes are dug, and the trees ready to be planted, let their roots be pruned, and such as are broken or bruised, taken away. Then set the tree in the hole, carefully observing that all the roots spread freely as they ought to do.

Break the earth well, and throw it in equally about the roots, shaking the tree gently that the earth may fall in close between the roots and their fibres; when the earth is all thrown in, tread the earth gently, to fix the tree in a proper position.

Let all standard trees be supported with stakes, as soon as they are planted, that the wind may not rock them about.

You must also secure dwarf trees against the power of the wind, by fastening them to the wall, or rails of the espalier.

As soon as you have finished your pruning and nailing, let all the fruit tree borders be neatly dug; or, if they have been dug before, let the surface be loosened, where it has been trampled in doing the necessary work about the trees. This will be very serviceable to the trees, and, at the same time, give the borders a clean and neat appearance.

Shield budding technique .

THE NURSERY

You must now finish your digging the ground between the rows of all kinds of young trees and shrubs.

✍ Stocks to Bud and Graft Upon. ✍

You should now make new plantations of stocks to bud and graft the various kinds of choice fruit upon.

These stocks should be planted out as soon in the month as possible, if the weather will permit. Let them be planted in rows two feet and a half asunder, and fifteen inches at least from one another in the rows.

All the stocks that were budded last summer should now be headed down. This should be done with a sharp knife, observing to cut the head off about four inches above the bud.

℘ Grafting. ℭℛ

This curious operation may be performed any time this month, provided the weather be mild.

The most proper sort to begin with are pears, plums, and cherries: and these kinds generally succeed best, when grafted some time in the last fortnight of this month. Apples may either be grafted at the same time, or deferred a fortnight longer.

When grafting is to be performed, you should begin to prepare for it about the beginning of the month.

The first thing necessary to be done is to collect the grafts. In the choice of these the following directions should be carefully observed: First, That they are shoots of the former year. Secondly, That they are taken from healthy fruitful trees. And, thirdly, That you prefer those grafts which are taken from the lateral or horizontal branches, to those taken from the perpendicular shoots. These grafts should be cut off from the trees before the buds begin to swell, which is generally three weeks or a month before the season for grafting; therefore when they are cut off, they should be laid in the ground with the cut downwards, burying them half their length, and covering their tops with dry litter, to prevent their drying: if a final joint of the former year's wood be cut off with the scion, it will preserve it the better: and when it is grafted, this may be cut off; for the grafts never must be cut to a proper length before they are inserted into the stocks; but till then, the shoots should remain their full length, as they were taken from the tree, which will preserve them better from striking. If these grafts are to be carried to a considerable distance, it will be proper to put their cut ends into a lump of clay, and to wrap them up in moss, which will preserve them fresh for a month or longer: but these should be cut off earlier from the trees than those which are to be grafted near the place where the trees are growing.

The reason for grafting is, that as all good fruits have been accidentally obtained from seeds, so these when sown will often degenerate, and produce such fruit as are not worth cultivating; but when the shoots, scion, or grafts, are taken from such trees as yield good fruit, these will never vary from their kind, whatever be the stock or tree on which they are grafted.

The most proper season for grafting is in the spring, just before the rising of the sap, or at least before it rises in any great quantity: but the weather must be neither frosty nor wet; nor should the wind blow very

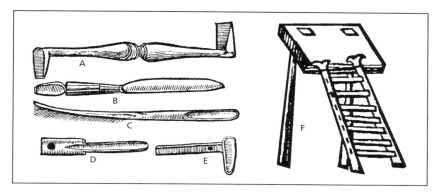

Grafting tools. **A.** Iron grafting chisel with blades of differing sizes. The chisel keeps a cleft open in the stock until the graft is inserted. Chisel blades set at right angles to the handle allow easier removal from the cleft. **B.** Small pen knife. The thin blade makes clean incisions in the stock and is useful for loosening buds before removal. **C.** Pen or quill, halved vertically. This is an ideal tool for the removal of buds. **D.** Ivory tool for bud removal. **E.** Brass shield. The curved shield holds an incision open until a bud is inserted. **F.** Platform ladder. The nurseryman can work comfortably at any height, without damage to the tree.

bleak or strong when this operation is performed: for on these circumstances, and upon the exact joining of the inner bark of the scion with the inner bark of the stock, so that the sap which flows between the bark and the wood may be communicated from the one to the other, the success of grafting chiefly depends.

The implements necessary for grafting are, fine small hand saws to cut off the heads of large stocks; a good strong knife with a thick back to make clefts in the stocks; a sharp pen-knife to cut the grafts; a grafting chisel, and a small mallet to pare away the wood; bass, or woollen yarn, to tie the grafts with; and a quantity of clay, or cement, properly prepared, to lay over the incisions, in order to prevent their bleeding, and keep out the air.

The method of preparing the clay intended for this purpose, is to mix thoroughly together a quantity of strong fat loam, some new stone-horse dung broken into small bits, a little tanners hair, or straw, cut very small, with a little salt, and as much water as will make the whole of the consistence of pretty stiff mortar.

The cement or composition which some have of late used, and which has been found to answer the design of keeping out the air better than the above clay, is made of turpentine, bees-wax, and rosin, melted together. This composition, when of a proper consistency, is laid about a quarter of an inch thick, upon the cut part of the stock round the graft: and has this farther advantage over the clay, that there is no danger of its being hurt by frost; for cold hardens it; and when the heat of summer comes on, by which time it is no longer wanted on the tree, it will melt and fall off without any trouble.

Among the several methods of grafting hitherto known, the following are most approved, and generally practised.

ɷ Cleft-Grafting, Called Also Stock, or Slit Grafting. ɷ

This is used chiefly for middle-sized stocks, from one to two inches in diameter. The season for it is in the months of February and March; and the method, as now practised, is thus:

The head of the stock being sawn, or cut off, with a slope, smooth and clean, a perpendicular cleft is made therein, about two inches deep, with a strong knife, or chisel, from the top of the slope, as near to the pith as may be without touching it. In this cleft, the grafting chisel, or a wedge, is put to keep it open. The graft or scion is prepared by cutting it aslope, in form of a wedge, to suit the cleft, only leaving a small shoulder on each side; and when cut, it is to be placed exactly in the cleft, so as that the inner bark of the scion may aptly, and closely, join to the inner part of the bark, or rind of the stock; in the dextrous performance of which the chief part of the art of grafting consists. That side of the scion which is to be placed outward, at the part where it is cut wedge-wise and inserted into the cleft of the stock, should be much thicker than the other side, the better to facilitate the exact joining of its rind to that of the stock; for if these two do not unite, the graft will not succeed. The rind of the stock chosen for this way of grafting should therefore not be too thick; because it will then be the less manageable. If the cleft pinches too tight, a small wedge may be left in it to bear the stress. As soon as the graft is properly fixed, the cleft should be closely covered with clay, or, which some think better, with moss, or the fresh bark of a tree bound on with ozier.

When this method, which is the most ancient, and most common, manner of grafting, is used to stocks that are not strong, a ligature of bass should be made around the stock, to prevent the opening of its slit; and the whole should then be clayed over, or covered with the cement before described, to hinder the air from penetrating into the slit, so as to destroy the graft, only two eyes of which should here be left above the clay, for shooting.

The straightest and smoothest part of the stock should always be preferred for grafting, in whatever way this operation is performed.

℘ Grafting in the Rind, or Shoulder Grafting. ℘

This is likewise called slicing and packing, to distinguish it from grafting in the bark, which will next be spoken of, and is performed in the following manner, about the latter end of March, or the beginning of April, on more slender stocks than those which are commonly used for cleft-grafting.

The top of the stock is cut off in a smooth, straight place: then the scion, or graft, is prepared by cutting it on one side from the joint, or seam, down slope-wise, making the slope about an inch, or an inch and an half long; and observing it is bent, so that the scion may stand nearly upright when it is fixed to the stock. At the top of the slope, a shoulder is made, whereby it is to rest on the crown of the stock. The whole slope must be plain and smooth, that it may lie even to the side of the stock. The length of the scion used here may be about four inches from the shoulder, for a standard tree; but for a dwarf, or wall tree, it may be six inches. When the scion is prepared, the outside of the sloped end, from the shoulder downward, is applied to the west, or south-west side of the stock, and its length and breadth measured thereon; which done, the bark of the stock, (but not any of its wood) is cut away to those dimensions, that the cut part of the scion may be fitted in as exactly as possible. In doing this, regard must be had to the bigness of the stock, and the thickness of its bark, in order to proportion thereto the length and breadth of the cut part of the scion; otherwise the passages of the sap in the

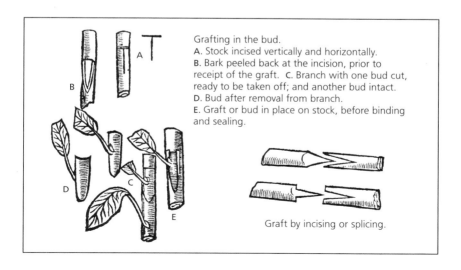

Grafting in the bud.
A. Stock incised vertically and horizontally.
B. Bark peeled back at the incision, prior to receipt of the graft. C. Branch with one bud cut, ready to be taken off; and another bud intact.
D. Bud after removal from branch.
E. Graft or bud in place on stock, before binding and sealing.

Graft by incising or splicing.

stock and scion will not meet, and the scion will then of course perish. When the cut part of the scion is exactly fitted to, and laid on that of the stock, they are bound together with woollen yarn, and covered with clay an inch above, and as far below, the head of the stock; working it round the scion, till it become sharp at top, that the rain may run down it.

This method has several advantages over the former. Among these are, that the wound heals up sooner, and that, in the mean time, it is in less danger from the weather: that it does less injury to the stocks and grafts, by avoiding all severe splittings and pinchings; that the bark is more easily placed in the passage of the sap here, than in the cleft; that the graft thrives and shoots with greater vigour, and bears sooner in this way than in that; and that it is practicable on smaller stocks than the other, which must have a good body, and consistence, before they can bear cleaving.

୨ Grafting in the Bark. ୧୪

This operation is performed thus. Prepare the stock and scion as for grafting in the rind, both as to time and manner; but, instead of cutting out the bark of the stock, slit it down, on the south-west side, from the top, almost as long as the sloped part of the scion, and at the top of the slit loosen the bark with the point of your knife. Then thrust an instrument, made of very hard wood, ivory, silver, or the like, and formed at the end like the slope-end of the scion, but much less, down, between the bark and wood, to make room for the scion; which being put in, the bark is to be so managed, as that

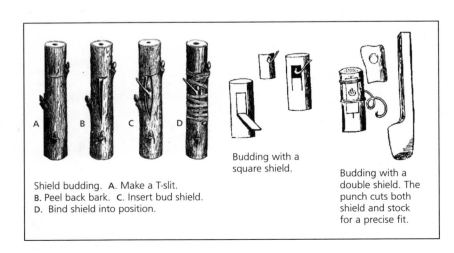

Budding with a
square shield.

Shield budding. A. Make a T-slit.
B. Peel back bark. C. Insert bud shield.
D. Bind shield into position.

Budding with a
double shield. The
punch cuts both
shield and stock
for a precise fit.

it may close exactly to the stock and edges of the scion, and the whole is then to be bound up, and covered as before.

∞ Whip-Grafting, or Tongue-Grafting. ∞

This is proper for small stocks, from an inch diameter to a quarter of an inch, or even less. Mr. Worlidge, Mr. London, Mr. Miller, and others, speak of it as the most effectual way of any, and that which is most in use, because the scion covers the stock much sooner in this method than in any other; for here the scion and the stock must always be of the same thickness. There are three ways of performing it, and all of them may be practised somewhat later than either of the foregoing.

The first is, to slope the scion off a full inch, or more; then to do the same to the stock; and afterwards to tie the one to the other, with bass or yarn, so as to join them closely at every part, but particularly at the rind; and then to cover the joint carefully with well tempered clay. The bass used for this, or for any other binding, should be taken from a found mat, and be soaked in water for some hours, to increase its strength, and render it the more pliable.

The second way is, to make a shoulder in the graft, and, the head of the stock being cut off and smoothed, to join it as in grafting in the rind.

The third method, which is an improvement of the last, is properly named tipping or tonguing. This is done by cutting the stock off slanting, as before, and leaving at its upper side a thin piece, or tongue, as it is called, of the wood, pared away like the lower end of a scion. The scion is then

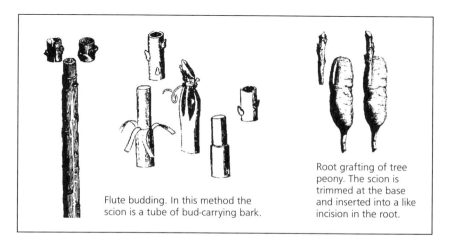

Flute budding. In this method the scion is a tube of bud-carrying bark.

Root grafting of tree peony. The scion is trimmed at the base and inserted into a like incision in the root.

sloped, and tongued, in the same manner as the stock, and a slit is made in each of them, downward in the stock, and upward in the graft, on the side opposite to the tongue, so that each may receive the tongue of the other. The scion is then joined to the stock, as closely as can be, particularly at the bark; a ligature is made round them with bass or woollen yarn, and the engrafted part is well covered with clay or cement.

◌ Side-Grafting ◌

In this, the scion is prepared as in whip-grafting; but the head of the stock is not cut off at the time of performing the operation. Instead of that, so much of the bark as the scion will cover is pared off from the west side of the stock; then both the scion and the stock are slit in the last mentioned manner of whip-grafting, and they are bound together, and closed up with clay. At the year's end, the top of the stock is cut off at the grafted place, slope-wise; and the wound is covered with clay or cement.

◌ Crown-Grafting. ◌

This is only practised in the larger trees, which are capable of receiving a number of grafts, and are too big to be cloven; for these, the head or main branches, being cut off horizontally, four or more grafts are placed round the stock, between the bark and the rind, somewhat in the manner of a crown. The most proper time for performing this is about the latter end of March, or the beginning of April. After the intended number of scions are inserted, which is done exactly in the same manner as that already delivered for grafting in the rind, the whole crown of the stock is well clayed over, and only two eyes of each scion are left uncovered; that being sufficient for their shooting.

This method of grafting was more practised formerly than it is at present; many people having been discouraged by the ill success that has frequently attended their scions, which have been blown out of the stock, by strong winds, after they had made large shoots, and even after they had grown there five or six years. But this accident may be prevented, by tying the scions to stakes fastened to the tree, till they are so firmly fixed, as to have almost covered the stock.

◌ Root-Grafting. ◌

This is a modern invention, the design of which is somewhat different from that of any of the former methods; this being for the propagation, or multiplication, of plants already fitted to produce their fruit.

To perform this, take a graft, or sprig, of a young tree, which you intend to propagate, and a small piece of the root of another tree of the same kind, or of a like genus, and whip-graft them together; observing that the butt-ends of the graft and root be well united, and that the rind of the root joins closely to that of the graft. These may, afterwards, be planted out at plea-sure, and the piece of root will collect the nutritive juices, and feed the graft, as the stock does the other way.

The only objection against this method is, that the young tree grows but slowly at first, which is occasioned by the smallness of the root that feeds the graft; for in all trees the head must follow the increase of the roots, from whence it hath its nourishment.

Grafting by approach, also called inarching, and ablastation.
A branch from one tree is grafted to the stock of another.

ᔈ Reiterated Grafting, or Grafting by a Double or Triple Incision. ᑢ

This is another method mentioned by Agricola, whose work, though chimerical enough in many respects, contains, notwithstanding, several good things. To perform this, first graft a good scion on a stock, and cut it away to one half, or a third part; then fix to that remaining part of the scion another graft, of a better kind; and to that a third; for the oftener the tree is grafted, the finer fruit it produces.

By this method the author above-mentioned assures us, that he produced muscat pears, which were admirable, making at first use of a stock grafted with a pound-pear, on which he grafted a summer bon-chretien; and when the branch of this last had shot, he grafted on it a scion of a bergamot, which he also cut, and grafted on it a scion of a muscat pear.

This is also commended by Agricola, as a very certain and profitable operation; best practised on large, or full-grown, and even old trees.

To do this, half or more of the branches must be lopped off, and grafts of three or four years old be applied to them, taking care to have stakes, or other things, to support them against the wind, &c.

He adds, that by this method you will have, perhaps, the same year, or at least the second or third, such a quantity of fruit, as the youngest and soundest tree would hardly produce.

ᔈ Grafting by Approach, Called Also Inarching, and Ablastation. ᑢ

This is used only when the tree intended to be grafted, and that from which the graft is to be taken, stand so near, or can be brought so near to each other, that they may be joined together. The method of performing it is this: the branch to be inarched is fitted to that part of the stock where it is to be joined; the rind, and part of the wood, of one side of that branch, is then parted away, very smooth and even for the length of three inches; and afterwards the other branch, which is to serve for the stock to which the graft is to be united, is served in the same manner, so that the two may join closely and equally together that the sap vessels may meet. A little tongue is then cut upwards in the graft, and a slit is made in the stock to receive it; so that when they are joined, the tongue prevents their slipping; and the graft is the more closely united to the stock. When they are thus placed exactly together, they must be tied with bass, worsted, or some other soft thing; and the place of junction must be well covered over with grafting clay, to prevent the air from drying the wound, and wet from rotting the stock. A stake must also be fixed in the ground, and both the stock and the graft must be tied thereto, to prevent their being displaced by the wind. When they have remained in this state four months, they will be sufficiently united, and the graft may then be cut off from the mother tree, observing to slope it close to the stock.

It is of great service to the graft then to lay a fresh coat of clay all round the grafted or joined part. This operation should be performed in April or May, that the graft may be perfectly united to the stock, before the ensuing winter. It is chiefly practised upon oranges, myrtles, jasmines, firs, pines, and some other trees, which do not succeed well in the common way of grafting or budding. But though orange trees are here mentioned among the rest, this practice is not to be advised for them, or for any other trees, if they are intended to grow large; for that they hardly ever do in this method; and accordingly it is seldom used but for the curiosity of having a young plant with fruit upon it, in a year or two from its having been raised from the seed. This is, indeed, effected by inarching a bearing branch into a young stock: but the plant so treated seldom lives long.

The walnut, fig, and mulberry, will also take by this method of grafting, though neither of them will succeed in any other way; but still they, like all other trees that are thus managed, will remain weak, and stinted in their growth, besides the shortening of their otherwise usual time of duration.

All grafts, particularly of young scions, are subject to be injured by birds: but that may be prevented by binding some small bushes about the tops of the stocks.

The binding of the grafts, whether it be of bass or yarn, should be loosened at least, if it be not entirely taken off at Midsummer, or thereabout, lest its then too great tightness (as the stock will have increased in bulk, and the binding, perhaps, have been swelled, and consequently shrunk by the weather) should injure the plant.

🙞 Propagating by Layers. ౭

This is the best season for laying down the branches of all kinds of exotics and shrubs.

Layers may also be now made of all such hardy shrubs and trees as are increased by this method, provided it was omitted between Michaelmas and Christmas; and it will succeed with many kinds.

In order to form layers of any kind of trees or shrubs, let the ground be dug round the plant that is to be laid; and as you proceed bring down the shoots or branches regularly, and lay them along in the ground, fastening them securely there with hooked pegs. This being done, let all the young shoots on each branch be neatly layed and covered three or four inches deep with earth, leaving the top of each three or four inches out of the ground.

By next Michaelmas most kinds of layers that are layed now will be tolerably well rooted, and fit to be transplanted.

∽ Transplant Layers. ∝

Let the layers of such trees and shrubs as were layed down last year, and not yet taken off, be now separated; and as soon as taken off, trimmed and planted in rows in an open situation. The rows should be eighteen or twenty inches asunder, and the plants set at about fifteen inches from each other in the rows.

∽ Plant Cuttings of Gooseberries and Currants. ∝

The best method of propagating gooseberries and currants is by cuttings, and this work may now be performed.

Observe to take your cuttings from such of the last year's shoots as are strong. They should be from ten to twelve or fifteen inches in length. Let them be planted in rows twelve inches at least asunder, and set each cutting about half way into the ground.

Experience has sufficiently shewn that gooseberries and currant trees raised from cuttings always produce fruit remarkable large and well tasted; while the fruit produced by trees raised from suckers is generally small and ill tasted.

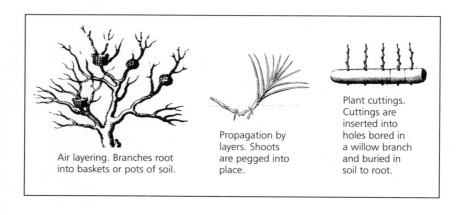

Air layering. Branches root into baskets or pots of soil.

Propagation by layers. Shoots are pegged into place.

Plant cuttings. Cuttings are inserted into holes bored in a willow branch and buried in soil to root.

℘ Plant Cuttings of Honey-Suckles. ℘

This is still a good season for planting the cuttings of honey-suckles and other hardy flowering shrubs and trees.

The cuttings should be shoots of the former year's growth; let the strongest shoots be chosen for this purpose; and let them be from six to twelve inches long. Plant these in a shady situation, in rows twelve inches asunder, and six or eight between each in the rows. They must be set about half way in the earth.

By next October, most of the cuttings planted now, will be sufficiently rooted, and therefore may be removed at that season.

℘ Transplant Flowering Shrubs. ℘

Flowering shrubs of all kinds may be now safely transplanted, provided the weather be mild and open. Observe to let the whole of this work be completed by the latter end of this month, if the weather will permit.

℘ Transplant Hardy Fruit and Forest Trees. ℘

All kinds of hardy fruit and forest trees may be removed this month; but the sooner it is done the better, provided the weather be mild and open.

℘ Pruning. ℘

All flowering-shrubs that want pruning must now undergo the operation; for you must finish your pruning this month.

You should observe to train all your plants with a single stem; and if you find their heads growing irregular, cut out or shorten such shoots as you think necessary, in order to form the head into some handsome form.

Be careful to take away all suckers that rise from the roots of any kind of shrubs. The best of them may be planted out at proper distances, and in two or three years time, they will become good plants.

℘ Sow the Stones of Plums, &c. ℘

The stones of plums, and kernels of other fruits, should now be sown in order to raise a supply of stocks to bud and graft upon.

The sooner they are sown in the month the better, provided the weather be mild and open. Let the spot chosen for this purpose be in a sheltered situation, and the soil perfectly clean and light. The stones should be sown on beds about four feet wide, and covered about an inch deep with earth.

Gladiolus
'Triumph of Paris'
Gladiolus

THE PLEASURE OR
FLOWER-GARDEN

ঙ Sow the Seeds of the Auricula and Polyanthus. ⊂খ

The seeds of the auricula and polyanthus may be sown any time this month, when the weather is mild and open. The plants will rise freely from this sowing, and thrive well. A warm spot of ground should be chosen for the purpose, unless you chuse to sow the seed in pots or boxes filled with rich light earth.

Grey-edged
auricula
Primula auricula

But which ever method be used, the seeds should be sown tolerably thick, and covered about a quarter of an inch deep with rich light earth.

If the seeds are sown in pots or boxes, place them in a situation well defended from the northerly winds, and open to the morning and mid-day sun: in about two months they must be removed into a more shady situation.

ঙ Sow Curious Annual Plants. ⊂খ

The choicest kind of annual plants, such as double balsams, cockscombs and tricolars, globe amaranthos, marvel of Peru, diamond sicoides, or ice plants, egg plants, China asters, &c. require a hot-bed in order to their blowing early in any tolerable degree of perfection.

Let therefore some new horse dung be thrown up in a heap about the middle of this month, and in about eight or ten days it will be in a proper condition for making the bed; which should be about two feet and a half thick of dung. Let the surface be levelled, and the frame and glasses placed upon it.

Hunch-backed
amaranth
Amaranthus

As soon as the burning heat of the bed is over, lay on a quantity of rich, light, and perfectly dry, earth, sufficient to cover the bed five or six inches deep.

Make the surface of the earth level and smooth, and sow the seeds on the surface, each sort separate, covering them about a quarter of an inch deep with light earth, well sifted. Let the glasses be covered over night with mats; and give the plants now and then little sprinklings of water.

Sunflower
Helianthus argophyllus

℘ Sow Ten-Week Stocks. ℝ

A little of the seed of ten-week stocks may be sown at the latter end of the month, in order to raise a few plants for blowing early in the summer.

It will be best sown on a slight hot-bed, as the plants will be much stronger, and flower three weeks or a month earlier than they would otherwise do. But as the plants are tolerably hardy, they may be sown in a warm border.

Let the ground be neatly dug, and the seed sown tolerably thick, in a bed about three feet broad. Arch the bed over with hoops, and cover it every night with mats in bad weather. If you have a spare frame and glass to cover the bed, or hand-glasses for the plants, they will thrive the better.

℘ Sow Hardy Annual Flowers. ℝ

If the weather be mild, dry, and open, about the latter end of the month, many sorts of annual flower-seeds may be sown in warm borders, and other parts of the flower-garden; particularly the lark spur, flos adonis, convolvulus, lupines, sweet scented and Tangier peas, candy tuft, dwarf lychnis, Venus looking-glass, Venus navel-wort, Lobel's catchfly, dwarf poppy, dwarf annual sun-flower, oriental-mallow, lovetera, hawk-weed, &c.

Morning Glory
Convolvulus major

You must observe to sow all the above seeds in the places where the plants are intended to flower; for they will not succeed if transplanted.

The best method therefore of cultivating these annual flowers is this: dig with a trowel, at proper distances, small patches of about eight or nine inches over, breaking the earth very fine, and laying the surface even. When the ground is thus prepared, draw a little of the earth off the top to one side, sow the seeds thin, and cover them with the earth that was drawn off; the seeds should be covered about half an inch deep; but the larger, as the sweet peas, &c. near an inch.

When the plants appear, let them be judiciously thinned, by taking away the weaker and less promising plants, that the remainder may have proper room to grow and flourish.

℘ Transplant Flowering Shrubs. ℜ

Hawthorn
*Cratagus
laevigata*

If the weather be mild and open, you may at any time this month, safely transplant most sorts of flowering shrubs, particularly the gelder-rose, syringas, laburnum, lilacs, honey-suckles, roses, spiræas, althæa-frutex, hypericum-frutex, Persian-lilac, double-blossom cherry, double flowering-peach, almonds, flowering raspberries, double bramble, cornelian cherry, and double hawthorn. Bladdersena, scorpion-sena, privet, Spanish-broom, jasmines, sumach, cytisuses, acacias, and many other sorts of hardy plants, may be now transplanted.

℘ Transplant Hardy Fibrous-Rooted Flowering Plants. ℜ

Most of the fibrous-rooted flowering plants, particularly the polyanthuses, primroses, London pride, violets, double-daisies, double-camomile, thrift, gentianella, hepaticas, saxifrage, &c. may be removed to the proper situations.

You may also now remove rose-campion, rockets, campanula, catchfly, scarlet-lychnis, double-feverfew, bachelors-button, sweet-williams, columbines, Canterbury-bells, monkshead, greed-valerian, tree-primrose, fox-glove, golden-rod, French honey-suckles, and several others of that kind. But you should remember in planting the above, or indeed any other flowering plants, to mix them in such a manner, that, during the flowering season, there may be both a variety of colours, and a regular succession of flowers in the different parts of the garden where they are planted.

Foxglove
Digitalis

℘ Transplant Carnation Plants. ℜ

The choicest carnation plants may, about the latter end of this month, be removed into the pots where they are intended to blow, provided the weather be mild and open.

Let the pots be filled with rich light earth, then take up the plants, with as much earth as will readily hang about their roots. Set a single plant in the middle of each pot, and close the earth well about the body of the plants, giving them immediately a moderate watering, by which the plants will be properly settled in their places.

You must remember to place the pots, as soon as the flowers are planted, in a situation properly defended from the cold winds.

℘ Transplant Evergreens. ℞

Most of the hardy kinds of evergreen-shrubs and trees, particularly phillyreas, yews, evergreen-oaks, junipers, hollies, firs, cypress, cedars, lauristinus, pyracanthas, arbutus, &c. may be transplanted any time this month when the weather is mild.

Care should be taken to dispose the most curious sorts of flowering shrubs and plants in such a manner, that they may be easily seen from the walk or lawn near which they are planted. You should also be careful not to plant them too close together, nor suffer them, as they grow up, to interfere with one another; because great part of the pleasure of seeing these shrubs to advantage, will, if they stand too close together, be destroyed.

℘ Transplant Box. ℞

If box be wanted for edgings, borders, or to supply gaps in edgings formerly made, it may be safely planted, in mild weather, any time this month; it will take root readily, and there is no fear of success.

℘ Dress Auricula Plants. ℞

The choicest sorts of auricula plants in pots must now be treated with more than ordinary care, as their flower-buds will soon begin to appear; the plants must therefore be carefully defended from frost and cold heavy rains, by covering them with canvas, mats, or glasses. But remember to let them be entirely uncovered every mild and dry day.

Primrose
Primula auricula

They must also be carefully dressed; and if some fresh earth were not added last month, let it be done now, and the sooner the better.

℘ Tulips, Hyacinths, &c. ℞

Let the beds of tulips, hyacinths, anemonies, and ranunculuses, be carefully defended from frosts and heavy rains; and those in which the choicest sorts are planted, be now, unless done before, arched over with hoops, and covered with mats or canvas, in frosty and extreme wet weather.

෨ Prune Flowering Shrubs. ⨾

You must now finish your work of pruning flowering shrubs and evergreens.

Observe, in doing this work, to cut all the dead wood, and either to shorten or cut off close all straggling irregular branches, and those which interfere with other shrubs; for every shrub shows itself to the greatest advantage, when it is clear of any other.

When the pruning is finished, and the cuttings cleared away, let the ground be neatly dug between and about the plants, observing to take off all suckers arising from the roots.

Border pinks
Dianthus

෨ Dress the Borders, Beds, &c. ⨾

All flower borders and beds in general, should now be thoroughly cleaned from weeds, and every kind of litter. Let therefore the surface of the beds and borders be carefully loosened with a hoe in a dry day, and neatly raked.

This will give the whole an air of liveliness, which is always very pleasing to the eye.

෨ Mow Grass-Walks and Lawns. ⨾

One necessary requisite in rendering grass-walks and lawns beautiful is neatness. The season for mowing them now begins to approach; let them therefore be poled and rolled once or twice every week. A wooden roller is best to take up the worm casts; but when these are taken away, the walk should be rolled with an iron or stone roller, in order to render the bottom firm, and the surface smooth and even.

෨ Turf. ⨾

You may, any time this month, lay turf, where it is wanted, either to make new, or mend old walks. Observe to beat it well, and roll it with a heavy roller now and then, in order to make it firm and even; and it will grow freely and with very little trouble.

MARCH

1. Common Cucumber. *Cucumis longus vulgaris.*
2. Long Yellow Spanish Cucumber.
Cucumis Hispanicus.
3. Common Melon. *Melo vulgaris.*
4. Pumpkin. *Pompion.*
5. Greatest Musk Melon. *Melo maximus optimus.*
6. Common Strawberries. *Fragari vulgaris.*
7. Great Bohemia Strawberries.
Fragari Bohemica maxima.
8. Prickly Strawberry. *Fragari aculeata.*

Setting out vegetables in the kitchen-garden. Wide gravel walks separate the raised beds of this formal garden.

The Works of this Month in the
KITCHEN GARDEN

☙ Cucumbers and Melons. ୡ

Be very careful to examine frequently the state of your cucumber and melon hot-beds, with regard to the degree of heat; for it must be both lively and moderate, to preserve the plants in a state of free growth. If this be properly regulated, the plants will show plenty of fruit, which will grow to a handsome size.

If you find the heat too faint, let a lining of fresh horse-dung be applied either to the back or front sides of the bed; but if the heat be not much declined, a lining on one side will be sufficient at a time; but let the other be lined about ten or twelve days after.

Let the linings be eighteen or twenty inches thick, and raised about five or six inches up the frame. The tip must be covered with earth about two inches thick, to keep down the steam.

Remember to let the plants have fresh air every day, and to raise the glasses in proportion to the heat of the bed, and the warmness of the weather.

Let a bottle or two of water be kept always in the frame, to be in readiness to refresh the plants now and then. The best time for doing this is from ten to two o'clock in a mild sunny day; but let it always be done moderately.

The glasses should be covered every night with mats, and uncovered in the morning about an hour and a half after the sun.

Figari melon
Cucumis melo

Some seeds of cucumbers and melons should be sown at three different times this month, viz. at the beginning, middle, and latter end, that a continual succession of plants may always be in readiness, either to plant into new beds, or to supply the place of such as may fail in others.

At the beginning of this month you should make hot-beds for planting out the cucumber and melon plants that were sown in January.

It has already been observed, that the success will, in a great measure, depend upon the due preparation of the dung, before it is made into a bed. Let the bed be about three feet high; the dung beaten down well with the fork, when laid on the bed, but not trodden: when the bed is finished, put on the frame and lights, and let it be managed in every respect as before directed in the former month. The same directions will also be sufficient for managing the plants, whether cucumbers or melons.

If dung could not conveniently be procured for making hot-beds for early cucumbers or melons, last month; it is not yet too late, provided the bed be made about the beginning of the month: for the fruit from the seeds sown now will be ready to cut by the middle or latter end of May.

The cucumber and melon plants intended to be reared under hand or bell-glasses, should be sown about the middle of this month.

ၼ Cauliflowers. ငၡ

Let those cauliflower plants as have stood all the winter in frames or hot borders, be now transplanted.

Cauliflower
*Brassica oleracea
botrytis*

The ground for this purpose should be well trenched, and a good quantity of rotten dung buried in the trenches. Then level the ground; and if it be naturally a wet soil, raise it up in beds about two feet and a half, or three feet broad, and four inches above the level of the ground; but if the ground be moderately dry, it need not be raised at all.

Let the most promising plants be set in the beds prepared as above in rows two feet and a half asunder, allowing the same distance between plant and plant in the rows.

Draw up some of the earth to the stems of cauliflower plants, under hand or bell-glasses, taking great care that none of the earth fall into their hearts; this will at once strengthen the plants and promote their growth. But remember to give them air by raising the glasses on props an inch or two in height; and when gentle showers fall, take the glasses entirely away, for this will greatly refresh the plants. Should there be more than one or two plants under each glass, let them be removed the beginning of this month: for never more than two plants at most should be suffered to grow under one glass. And if the glasses are small, one only should remain.

Those cauliflower plants which were raised from seed sown the last month, should now be pricked into a slight hot-bed, which will bring them forward amazingly. Let the bed be eighteen inches high, and either covered with a frame, or arched over with hoops. Cover the bed with rich earth six inches deep, prick the plants therein at two or three inches apart, and refresh them with a little water. Every mild day let the glasses or other covering be taken off, but the bed kept covered every night.

At the beginning of this month cauliflower seed may be sown on a slight hot bed, where the plants will soon come up, and flourish.

You may also sow cauliflower seeds in a natural bed of rich light earth, provided the situation be warm; but the plants, though they will grow freely, will be near a fortnight later than those sown upon a slight hot-bed.

℘ Cabbages. ℘

Cabbage plants of all kinds may be set any time this month, but the sooner it is done the better. They should be planted in good ground, at about two feet and a half distance every way.

It must however be remembered, that this distance is to be understood of such plants as are intended to grow to their full size; for eighteen or twenty inches will be sufficient for those which are intended to be cut up young.

Early York Cabbage
Brassica oleracea capitata

The seeds of cabbages intended for autumn and winter use, may be sown any time about the middle of the month; observing to sow each sort separate, and in an open spot of ground.

About the middle or latter end of the month, a little red cabbage seed may be sown, in order to raise plants for the winter.

Savoy seed, for a principal crop intended to serve the family from about Michaelmas to Christmas, should be sown, in an open situation, about the latter end of the month.

ભ Carrots and Parsnips. ભ

Carrot and parsnip seed, if not sown last month, should be sown at the beginning of this, for a principal crop.

Carrots delight in a deep, warm, light, sandy soil, which should be dug two spades deep, that the roots may run down with greater ease; for if they meet with any obstruction, they are very apt to grow forked, and shoot out lateral roots, especially where the ground is too much dunged the same year the carrots are sown, which will also occasion their being worm-eaten.

When therefore there is a necessity for dunging it the same year the carrots are sown, the dung should be well rotted, and thinly spread over the ground; and in the digging of it into the ground, great care should be taken to disperse it through the different parts, and not to bury it in heaps. When the ground is inclinable to bind, too much care cannot be taken to break and divide the clods; large spits therefore should never be taken in digging for carrots; they should be very thin, and the clods well broken.

Half-long scarlet carentan carrot *Daucus carota*

The ground, when dug, should be laid level and even, otherwise, when the seeds are sown, and the ground is raked over, part of the seeds will be buried too deep, and others in danger of being drawn up into heaps; by which means the plants in some places will come up in bunches, and in others the ground will be naked; both which should be always carefully avoided.

As these seeds have a great quantity of small forked hairs upon the borders, by which they closely adhere, so it is very difficult to sow them even, or prevent their coming up in patches; the seeds should therefore be well rubbed with both hands before they are sown, in order to separate them. A calm day also should be chosen to sow them; for if the wind blows, it will be impossible to sow the seeds equal; because, as they are very light, they will be blown into heaps. When the seeds are sown, the ground should be trodden pretty close, to bury them, and then raked smooth and level.

When the plants are come up, and have got four leaves, the ground should be hoed with a small hoe three inches wide, cutting down all young weeds, and separating the plants to three or four inches distance each way, that they may get strength. When the weeds begin to grow again, the whole should be hoed over a second time, when care should be taken not to leave two carrots close to each other, and also to separate them to a greater distance, cutting down all weeds, and slightly stirring the surface of the ground in every part, which will at once prevent fresh weeds from springing up, and facilitate the growth of the carrots.

∞ Sowing Turnips. ∾

About the middle, or towards the latter end of this month, as the weather is more or less favourable, turnips should be sown in a light soil, and open situation. They may indeed be sown at the beginning of the month, if thought necessary; but it should be remembered, that those which are sown so early are apt to run to seed before they apple, or, at least, before they obtain any considerable size.

Turnip
Brassica rapa

∞ Sow Onions, Leeks, &c. ∾

The seeds of onions and leeks intended for the principal crop, should, if not done in February, be sown the beginning of this month. Let each sort be sown on separate beds of rich mellow earth, and raked in evenly, that the plants may come up equally in every part.

If the earth be very light and rich, the ground should, as soon as the seeds are sown, be trodden all over, and then well raked, in order that the seed may be buried more regularly.

But where the ground is any thing wet and stiff, it will not be so proper to tread the seed in. The ground should therefore be divided into beds of four, five, or six feet wide, with alleys between them; and in these alleys the gardener should stand to sow the seed, and afterwards to rake it into the ground. Some, for the more certainty of burying the seed, throw a little of the earth in the alleys over it, and then lightly rake the whole.

∞ Sow Radishes. ∾

Let some radishes be sown at three different times this month; viz. at the beginning, the middle, and end, that there may not be wanting a fresh succession of young radishes for the table. The spot where the seed is sown at this season should be open, the soil good, and somewhat moist.

The crops of early radishes should now be thinned where the plants stand too close together, by pulling up the worst, and leaving the best plants, at about two or three inches distance. At the same time the bed should be cleared from weeds.

Long scarlet radishes
Raphanus sativus

These early crops should also be frequently watered in dry weather; otherwise they will grow but poorly, and, at the same time, the roots be hot and sticky.

࿇ Sow Spinach. ࿇

About once every fortnight some spinach seed should be sown, that there may be a regular supply for the table; for one sowing will not continue above a fortnight before it will run to seed. The seed should be of the round leaved kind, sown thin in an open spot, and raked in equally.

The plants of the early crop of spring spinach should now be thinned, so that the plants may be five or six inches distance from one another.

Savoy-leaved spinach
Spinacia

The crop of winter spinach should be kept clear from weeds, and the earth between the plants stirred with a hoe.

࿇ Sow Lettuce. ࿇

Lettuce-seed of different kinds should be sown about the beginning, middle, and latter end of the month, that there may be a constant supply for the table.

Let the seeds be sown in an open spot of ground, a rich soil, and the earth well broken. Sow the seeds evenly on the surface, and rake them in lightly, taking care to lay the surface smooth and level.

Thin those lettuce plants which have stood the winter in warm beds or borders, where they stand too close. But remember to do this regularly, drawing out the weaker and letting the strong plants remain, at about ten or twelve inches from one another. At the same time loosen the earth between the plants with a hoe, and clear away all the weeds and litter from the beds and borders.

The plants drawn out should be planted in an open spot of rich earth, at about twelve inches from one another.

࿇ Sow Asparagus. ࿇

Let the seeds of asparagus be sown this month, either to make new plantations the following year, or for raising beds of that vegetable immediately from the seed.

You should be very careful to procure good seeds of asparagus, as the success of the whole plantation will greatly depend upon that particular. In order to this, a sufficient quantity of the fairest buds should be marked early in the spring, and permitted to run up for seed, for those which run up after the season for cutting the asparagus is over, are generally so backward as not to ripen their seeds unless the summer be warm, and the autumn very favourable. In the choice of buds for their seed, great regard should be had to their size and roundness, never leaving any that are inclinable to be flat, or that soon grow open-headed; let therefore the roundest and closest-headed be chosen. But as several of these will produce only male flowers, which are barren, a greater number of buds should be left than might be necessary, if there could be a certainty of their being all fruitful. When the buds are left, it will be proper to thrust a stake down by each, taking care not to injure the crown of the root. These stakes will not only serve as marks to distinguish them from others, when they are all run up, but also to fasten the shoots to when they have advanced in height, and put out lateral branches; this caution will prevent their being broken by the wind, which otherwise frequently happens, before the other shoots are permitted to run up; after which there is indeed little danger, as they will then be sheltered by the other stalks.

Towards the latter end of September the berries will be fully ripe, when the stalks should be cut down, and the berries stripped off into a tub, where they should remain three weeks or a month to sweat, by which means the outer husks will be rotten. Then fill the tub with water, and break all the husks by squeezing them between your hands. The husks will now all swim upon the water, and the seeds sink to the bottom; so that by pouring the water off gently, the husks will be carried away with it; and by pouring in fresh water two or three times, and stirring the whole about with your hands, the seeds will be entirely clean.

Asparagus
Asparagus officinalis

Let the seed be now spread upon a mat or cloth, and exposed to the influence of the sun and air in fine weather, till it is perfectly dry; when it should be put into a bag, and hung up, in a dry place, for use.

The seed being thus procured, a plantation of asparagus may be raised immediately from the seed; and this is a very good method, though the beds will require a year longer, before any buds can be cut, than those which are planted with roots: but as the roots of asparagus always send forth many long fibres, which run deep into the ground, so when the seeds are sown where they are to remain, these roots will not be broken or injured, as those must be which are transplanted; they will therefore strike deeper into the ground, and make much greater progress. At the same time the fibres will push out on every side, which will cause the crown to be in the centre; whereas in transplanting, the roots are rendered flat by the side of the trench.

The ground where you intend to make asparagus beds, should be trenched, and a good quantity of rotten dung turned equally at the bottom of each trench. It will be necessary to dig the trenches so deep, that the dung may be buried fifteen inches below the surface of the dug ground. Then level the whole spot very exactly, taking away all large stones, and divide it into beds four feet wide, with alleys two feet wide between them.

The ground being thus prepared, draw a line across it, and with a dibble make holes at a foot distance, and about half an inch deep. Into each of these holes drop two or three seeds, lest one of them should miscarry, and cover the seed by striking the earth in upon it. Remove the line a foot further for another row, and proceed in this manner till the whole spot is sown. Some time after the plants appear, they must be thinned, leaving only two of the strongest plants in each hole; and afterwards thinned a second time, leaving only one plant in each hole.

If the seed be only intended for raising plants for new plantations, or supplying deficiencies in others, it should be sown on a spot of rich light earth; and when the plants come up they must be kept perfectly free from weeds, by a careful hand-weeding, and now and then refreshed with water in dry weather.

耹 Planting Asparagus. Ѯ

New plantations of asparagus may be made any time this month when the weather is mild and open.

In order to this the ground must be trenched, prepared, and divided into beds, in the manner above directed for raising asparagus from seed.

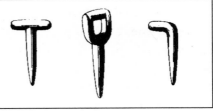

The dibble, which some call dibber in Kent, is a useful device for making holes in the mould for setting seeds, bulbs, young plants and the like,

The beds being finished, strain your line, and open four drills with a spade from one end of the bed to the other, twelve inches asunder; observing that the two outside drills be not nearer the side than six inches; and when you have opened one drill, to plant that before you open another.

Place the plants ten or twelve inches asunder, and nearly upright against the back of the trench or drill, and in such a manner that the crown of the roots may lie between two and three inches below the surface of the ground, and be all placed at an equal depth; spreading their roots in a regular manner, drawing, at the same time, a little earth up against them with the hand, in order to fix the plant in due position. When one drill is thus planted, draw the earth immediately into the drill over the plants with a rake; and then proceed to open another drill, planting and covering it in the same manner; and so on till the plantation is finished. When the whole is planted, let the surface of the beds be raked smooth, and cleared from stones; driving into the corner of every bed a firm stake, as a mark for the alleys.

The gardeners about London generally sow a thin crop of onions the first year on their new asparagus beds; nor will this hurt the asparagus in the least, provided the onions are not suffered to grow too near the plants.

A common error has long prevailed, that the dung used for manuring the beds, communicates a strong rank taste to the asparagus; but this is a great mistake, the sweetest asparagus growing upon the richest ground, while that growing on poor ground has the rank taste so often complained of. Nor is this to be wondered at, when it is remembered that the sweetness of asparagus is owing to the quickness of its growth, which is always proportioned to the goodness of the soil, and the warmth of the season. Mr. Miller tells us, that in order to prove this he planted two beds of asparagus upon ground which had been dunged a foot thick; and the beds were every year after dunged extremely well; and the asparagus produced from these beds were much sweeter than any he could procure, though they were boiled together in the same water.

ᔓ Dress Asparagus Beds. ᘒ

About the middle of the month fork up your asparagus beds; taking particular care that the fork does not reach the crowns of the roots.

Some time after the beds should be raked even; but remember not to defer it longer than the end of the month, or at farthest the first week in April; for by that time the buds will begin to advance near the surface, and consequently, be in danger of being injured by the teeth of the rake.

℘ Planting Artichokes. ℭ

In order to make a new plantation of artichokes, let the surface of the ground you intend for this purpose be spread over with rotten dung, and dug in. When the ground is thus prepared, a sufficient quantity of young shoots slipped from old roots must be procured. Let these shoots, taken from old stocks, be clear, sound, and not woody, having some fibres to their bottom; then with your knife cut off that knobbed woody part which joined them to the stock; and if that cuts crisp and tender it is a sign of their

Artichoke
Cynara scolymus

goodness, but if tough and stringy, throw the shoot away as good for nothing. Cut off also the large outside leaves of the plants intended for planting, pretty low, that the middle or heart leaves may be above them.

Your plants being thus prepared, they should, if the weather be dry, or the shoots any time taken from the stocks, be set upright in a tub of water three or four hours, which will greatly refresh them. This being done draw a line across the ground that the shoots may be set in a row, and with a measure-stick plant them at two feet distance from each other in the rows, and the rows five feet asunder, if designed for a full crop. The plants should be set about four inches deep, and the earth closed very fast to their roots; observing, if the season grows dry, to water them two or three times a week, till they have taken root, after which they will require none. Those artichokes which are planted in a moist rich soil, will always produce the largest and best fruit, which will be fit for the table in August and September; so that where such a spot can be found, it will be proper to make a fresh plantation every spring, to succeed the old stocks, and supply the table in autumn. But the roots will not live through the winter in a very moist soil; so that the stocks intended to remain to supply the table early, and furnish you with plants, should be in a drier situation. You should also remember to plant artichokes in an open spot of ground, not under the drip of trees; for they will there draw up very tall, and produce only small insignificant fruit.

℘ Dress Plantations of Artichokes. ℭ

About the beginning or middle of the month, according to the earliness of the season, or the forwardness of the old artichoke stocks, the plantation must be dressed in the following manner.

Remove with your spade all the earth from about the stock, down below the part where the young shoots are produced, clearing away the earth from between the shoots, so as to be able to judge both of the goodness of each, and their proper position upon the stock. Then make choice of two of the clearest, straightest, and most promising shoots produced from the under part of the stock; for these are far preferable to the strong thick plants which generally grow upon the crown of the roots, these hav-

ing hard woody stems, and never produce good fruit. The market gardeners about London call them rogues, from their having very little bottom, and the scales of their heads being placed irregularly. When you have made choice of two plants, slip off the other shoots with your hands, observing carefully not to injure the plants you intend to remain for a crop. This being done, draw the earth with your spade about the two plants which are left, closing it fast to each of them with your hands, and separating them as far asunder as they can conveniently be

Thistle artichoke
Cynara silvestris

placed without breaking them. At the same time crop off the tops of the leaves that hang down with your hands. Then level the ground between the stocks, and the whole operation will be finished.

The shoots which were stripped off will do to form fresh plantations of artichokes, where wanted, in the manner above described; for there is no other method of increasing artichokes, than by planting the young shoots.

ᔕ Plant Beans. ᘰ

Beans of all kinds may be planted at this season: let some be put into the ground once a fortnight, by which method the table will be constantly supplied with young beans during the season. The white blossom bean, as it is a great bearer, will answer the purpose exceedingly well.

Let the larger sorts of beans be planted in rows a yard asunder; but two feet and a half will be sufficient for the lesser kinds.

Broad bean plant
Faba vulgaris

ᔕ Sow Peas. ᘰ

All kinds of peas may be sown any time this month; so that if you sow a few every fortnight, or thereabouts, a constant supply will be the conse-quence. Let drills be drawn for the different kinds of peas, according to the directions given in the foregoing month; sow them regularly, and cover them with earth about an inch and a half deep.

Let the earth be drawn up to the stems of such peas and beans as are now grown to some height; this will greatly strengthen the plants, and encourage their growth.

℘ Plant Kidney-Beans. ℛ

About the latter end of the month, if the weather be mild and dry, and the ground not too wet, a few kidney-beans may be planted close under some warm wall; but without that precaution they will not succeed.

In such a warm situation let drills be drawn for them, about two feet, or two feet and a half asunder. Plant the beans in the drills about two or three inches apart, and cover them with earth about an inch deep.

Potatoes
Solanum tuberosum

℘ Plant Potatoes. ℛ

You may plant potatoes any time this month, but the sooner you do it the better.

Be careful to procure roots perfectly sound and of a tolerable size for planting. When a sufficient quantity of these is procured, let them be prepared for planting by cutting or quartering them; that is, let each root be cut into two, three, or more pieces, carefully observing that each piece be furnished with one or two eyes.

When you have thus prepared your roots, let them be planted in rows about a foot and a half or two feet asunder, and twelve or fifteen inches apart in the rows. They may be planted as you proceed in digging the ground, placing the roots in the trenches, and it would be of great advantage if a little dung were laid over every row of potatoes, and the earth thrown in upon the dung.

Mr. Miller observes that many of the roots cut in the above manner often rot, especially if the weather should prove wet, soon after they are planted; and therefore recommends the fairest roots to be planted entire in the rows, instead of the separate parts; and to allow them a larger space of ground both between the rows and between the roots. By this method he assures us, that the roots will be in general large the following autumn.

It is the practice of some gardeners to dig holes about two feet and a half over, and eight inches deep, and to throw into each hole as much rotten dung as will half fill it, laying the dung highest in the middle, and then to place the potatoes upon the dung about half a foot asunder, covering them six or seven inches deep with the earth that was thrown out of the holes. The holes must be at least a yard every way asunder. By this method fine crops of very large potatoes are procured.

℘ Plant Jerusalem Artichokes. ℭ

These roots will thrive in almost any soil; but when they have once taken root, it will be difficult to clear the ground of them, for the least bit will grow.

They may be planted any time this month, in rows two feet asunder, and about fifteen inches apart in the rows.

Jerusalem artichoke
Helianthus tuberosus

℘ Plant Mint. ℭ

New plantations of mint may be made this month, with little trouble.

It is propagated either by slips or parting the roots; but the former is generally practised. The method is this:

About the latter end of this month slip off and draw up with all their roots, a proper quantity of the best of the young plants, from such old beds of mint as are well stocked with them. The best manner of doing this is to draw up the young plants gently with the help of your knife, separating them carefully as they rise from the old roots. If this be properly performed, every plant will rise with tolerable good roots.

When a sufficient quantity of these plants are procured, let them be set in rows six inches asunder, and the same distance apart in the rows. As soon as they are planted, let a tolerable watering be given them to settle the earth about their roots.

If you intend to form a plantation of mint by roots, a sufficient quantity of them must be procured, and parted in a proper manner. Then draw drills with a hoe six inches asunder, place the roots about six inches apart in the drills, covering them with about an inch deep of earth, and rake the whole spot of ground. This method will succeed best if done the beginning of this month, or in October or November.

℘ Plant Chives. ℭ

Chives may be planted any time this month, in the following manner: let a sufficient quantity of slips from old roots be procured, and planted in beds about eight inches from one another.

Chives
Allium schoenoprasum

℘ Plant Garlick, Shallots, &c. ℭ

Both garlick and shallots may now be planted in the same manner as directed last month; but the sooner it is done the better.

℘ Plant Onions. ℭ

Such of the dry onions as begin to shoot in the house, may be now plant-ed in a small spot in the garden: they will serve to pull up for scallions.

℘ Plant Rosemary, Rue, Southernwood, &c. ℭ

Any time this month you may plant the slips or cuttings of rosemary, rue, southernwood, or lavender. A shady border should be chosen for this purpose, and the slips or cuttings planted six inches apart. They will take

root freely, if watered in dry weather. When they are well rooted, and have acquired a considerable degree of strength, they may be transplanted into a more open situation.

If the plantation be made with cuttings, let these be taken from shoots produced the last year. They should be from five or six to eight or nine inches long, and each cutting set about two thirds of its length into the earth.

Golden rue
Ruta graveolens

But whenever you can produce slips, or suckers, that rise immediately from the roots of older plants, these should be chosen; because they are often well furnished with roots.

℘ Plant Sage, Hyssop, Thyme, Penny-royal, &c. ℭ

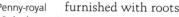

The slips or cuttings of sage, hyssop, thyme, &c. may be planted any time this month.

These cuttings should be taken from the last year's shoots, and about five, six, or seven inches long; but as there are sometimes slips, or suckers, arising from the bottoms of the old plants, these should be chosen, especially if they are

Penny-royal
Pulegium

furnished with roots.

Let these, whether cuttings or suckers, be planted in a shady border, where they will soon take root, and, in three or four months, become good plants, provided they are watered in dry weather. When they are well rooted, they may be taken up, and planted at proper distances in beds of rich earth.

℘ Sow Purslane. ℭ

If purslane be required early, it should be sown on a hot-bed the begin-ning of this month. Eighteen inches deep of dung will be sufficient for this purpose: put the frame on, and cover the bed with earth five or six inches thick. Sow the seed on the surface, and cover it about a quarter of an inch with light earth.

About the end of the month, if the weather be warm, the seed may be sown in a natural bed of rich earth.

ഔ Sow Parsley, Chervil, &c. ଔ

Parsley, chervil, and coriander seeds may be sown any time this month. In order to which, let some shallow drills be drawn eight or nine inches asunder, and in these the seeds sown, each sort separate. Cover the seeds when sown about half an inch deep with earth.

You may sow parsley, in single drills, at the edge of the quarters, or borders of the garden: it will make a useful, and, at the same time, a neat edging, if not suffered to grow too rank.

ഔ Sow Celery. ଔ

If you omitted to sow celery last month, let it be sown the beginning of this, for an early crop; more of the seed may be sown about the middle, or latter end, of the month, for a principal crop. The seed sown at the beginning of the month should have a warm spot of rich earth. Let the seed be sown on the surface, and either covered about a quarter of an inch with light earth, or raked in lightly with an even hand. Remember to sprinkle the bed with water frequently in dry weather.

Fennel
Foeniculum vulgare

ഔ Sow Fennel, Dill, Savory, Hyssop, Thyme, &c. ଔ

The seeds of fennel, dill, burnet, sorrel, marygold, &c. should be sown the beginning of this month, if omitted in February.

With regard to hyssop, thyme, savory, and sweet-marjoram, they will succeed, if sown any time this month.

All these seeds should be sown separately, in spots of light earth, and raked in with an even hand.

Giant Fennel
Ferula tingitana

ഔ Sow Small Salleting. ଔ

All kinds of small salleting, such as cresses, mustard, radish, rape, and turnip, should be sown, once a week, at least, in a warm border. Let the seeds be sown, each sort separate, in shallow drills, three inches asunder, and covered lightly with earth.

ఴ Sow Capsicum. ಞ

Long & round
capsicums
*Capsicum
annum*

The seeds of capsicum should be sown in a hot-bed, about the middle, or towards the latter end of the month; when the plants appear, let them have a large portion of free air, and frequent sprinklings of water. When they are fit to remove, which will be about the latter end of May, they must be transplanted into beds of rich earth, in the common ground.

ఴ Sow Cardoons. ಞ

About the middle of this month you may sow cardoons in a bed of light rich earth, in an open situation. The seed must be sown thin, and the bed watered frequently in dry weather.

ఴ Sow Nasturtiums. ಞ

Nasturtiums require a dry soil, and open situation; in such a spot therefore let drills about an inch deep, and two feet distance, be drawn. Let the seeds be placed in these drills about two or three inches apart, and covered with earth the depth of the drill. When the plants, which are of the climbing kind, rise and begin to run, set sticks, as you do for peas, to support them.

ఴ Sow Hamburgh Parsley. ಞ

Skirrets
Sisarum

The seeds of Hamburgh, or large-rooted parsley may now be sown, if omitted the foregoing month. Let the seed be sown thin, and equally, on beds of rich earth, in an open situation, and raked in with an even hand. When the plants are up, and have acquired a little strength, they must be thinned to six inches distance, that the roots may have room to swell; for the root only of this plant is eaten.

ఴ Sow Scorzonera, Salsafy, and Skirrets. ಞ

The seeds of scorzonera, salsafy, and skirrets, may be sown any time this month. But remember to sow each sort on separate beds, in an open situation, and to rake the seed in lightly.

THE Nursery

ᔥ Sow the Seeds of Hardy Exotics. cx

The seeds of many sorts of hardy exotic trees and shrubs may be sown this month; such as the tulip tree, larch tree, and plane tree; the sassafras, arbor judæ, Virginia dogwood, American cypress, Virginia walnut, acacias, and many others of the like kind.

The method of sowing the seeds of these hardy kinds, many sorts of which will grow freely, and with very little trouble, is this:

Dig a spot for them where the ground is dry, of a loose texture, and in a situation not too much exposed. Let the earth be well broken, and the surface made very level.

Cedar of Libanus
Cedrus libani

When this is done, let the piece be divided into beds three feet and a half wide, and sub-divided into as many parts as you intend to sow different kinds of seed.

Let each seed be sown, or planted, according to the kinds and sizes of the different seeds, in its separate spot.

Cover the seeds with fine light earth, taking care that each sort, according to its size, be covered a proper depth; some half an inch, some an inch, and others an inch and a half, according to the size of the seeds, fruits, or nuts.

The beds must be frequently sprinkled with water, in dry weather; and, when the sun is hot, a little shading with mats will be of service.

Sow the Seeds of the Cedar of Libanus, Pines, Firs, ᔥ and Other Hardy Evergreen Trees and Shrubs. cx

This is the proper season for sowing the seeds of the cedar of Libanus, pines, firs, cypress, juniper, and the like.

Let a small spot of light earth be dug for these seeds, divided into small beds, the seed sown thereon, each sort by itself, and covered with rich earth about half an inch thick.

You should remember to water and shade your plants in hot dry weather, especially while the plants are young, for then both will be of most service.

This is also the season for sowing the seeds of the arbutus, or strawberry tree; but there will be more certainty of success, if it be sown on a hot-bed. The method is this.

Fill some small pots with light fresh earth, sow the seed therein, covering it about half an inch, and plunge the pots up to their rims in a hot-bed.

Sprinkle the surface of the earth in the pots frequently with water; and when the plants appear, give them a large quantity of fresh air.

These seeds will grow, if sown in a bed of natural earth; but the growth of the plants will be much less in the same time, and success more uncertain.

You may now also sow the acorns of evergreen oaks, the seeds of the phillyrea, bay, and other evergreens.

All these seeds should be sown in light earth, the acorns covered about an inch deep, but the other seeds only half an inch.

∾ Propagating Exotic Trees, &c. from Cuttings. ∾

Exotic trees and shrubs may, at this season, be propagated from cuttings. The method is this:

Dig a spot for them where the ground is somewhat moist and not stiff; break the earth well with the spade, and rake it smooth. This being done, divide the spot into as many parts as you have different sorts of plants to propagate.

Let the cuttings be taken with a sharp knife from the trees you intend to increase, and from the shoots of the last summer. They should be from six to ten inches long, and planted in rows, each cutting being planted half way into the ground. Close the earth well about them, water them in dry weather, and keep the whole spot clear from weeds.

Evergreen or Holm oak
Quercus ilex

∾ Transplant Evergreens and Exotic Trees. ∾

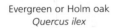

This is a proper season for transplanting most kinds of evergreen trees and shrubs from the seed-beds, or other places where they stand too close together; particularly the evergreen oak, phillyrea, alaturnus, pyracantha, lauristinus, Portugal laurel, arbutus, cytisus, hollies and yews. Also cedars and cypresses, pines, firs, and junipers, may now be transplanted with safety.

Exotic trees or shrubs may also be removed at this season.

California evergreen oak
Quercus agrifolia

℘ Transplant Flowering Shrubs. ଔ

You may now remove most kinds of the hardy flowering shrubs.

But you should remember to perform this operation in calm cloudy weather, when either the more tender kinds or the evergreen plants, are to be removed; for upon this particular, and the expedition with which they are planted after they are taken up, the success of the operation will, in a great measure, depend.

Be careful in planting them to break the earth perfectly fine, and see that it falls in properly between and about their roots.

As soon as they are planted, let them be well watered, and the waterings occasionally repeated in dry weather.

You should also cover the surface of the ground with mulch, or long litter, in order to prevent the sun and wind from drying the earth too much about their roots. Let firm stakes be fixed in the ground, and the stems of those plants which require support, be fastened to them.

℘ Plant Vines. ଔ

This is a proper season for propagating vines from cuttings.

The cuttings should be taken from shoots of the last year's growth, shortened to ten or twelve inches; and, if possible, have an inch or two of the branch from whence the shoot was taken, at the extremity of each cutting.

Let the cuttings be planted in a slanting direction, and so deep that one eye only may be seen above the surface.

By this method most of the cuttings will succeed; they will take root freely, and even produce tolerable shoots the same season.

Grapevine
Vitis vinifera

Water them moderately in dry weather, and keep the ground perfectly free from weeds.

Let these cuttings be planted in the place where they are to remain; for they never succeed so well after transplanting.

℘ Grafting. ଔ

Apples, pears, plums, cherries, &c. may be grafted any time this month.

You may cut off the stocks which are to be grafted for standard trees to what height you please.

The same method is to be pursued in performing the operation of grafting, as mentioned in the work of the nursery last month.

so Dress the Beds of Seedling Trees and Shrubs. ca

Look attentively over the seed-beds of young trees and shrubs; and where any weeds appear, let them be carefully picked out by the hand; for if they are suffered to continue, their roots will mix with those of the young plants, and consequently render it difficult to remove the one without injuring the other.

so Water the Seed-Beds of Young Trees and Shrubs. ca

You must remember to refresh the seed-beds of young trees and shrubs with water now and then in dry weather; a little at a time will be sufficient for the purpose. This will be of the utmost service to them, as you will soon perceive by their growth.

Delicate trees which wintered in the orangery are removed from tubs for summer display.

THE FRUIT-GARDEN

∾ Plant Fruit Trees. ∾

From the beginning to about the twentieth of this month, all kinds of fruit trees may be planted with success. And in moist soils there will be little danger of their growing, if planted at the latter end of the month; but the sooner it is done the better.

Turkey plum
Prunum turcicum

The trees that are now planted will take root in a short time; and, with the assistance of a little water in dry weather, shoot freely.

Observe the directions given in the former month with regard to the distances at which fruit trees either for walls, espaliers, or standards, ought to be planted.

Let a large hole be dug for each tree, and when carried to the depth intended, let the mould at the bottom be well loosened.

When the tree is ready for planting let all the ragged roots, and those which are bruised, be cut off: and the ends of all the rest be trimmed.

As soon as this is done, place the tree in the hole, break the earth well, and throw it in equally about the roots. When all is in tread the surface round the tree.

Remember to secure all new planted fruit trees against the violence of the wind; stakes should be fixed in the ground for the support of standard trees, and those planted against walls or espaliers be fastened thereto.

∾ Plant Fig Trees. ∾

This is a very proper season for planting fig trees; for they will now take root in a very short time.

It is necessary to observe, that fig trees are propagated either from layers, or suckers arising from the roots of old trees.

Fig
Ficus carica

When therefore it is intended to plant those trees, let a sufficient number of good suckers of a moderate growth, and such as are firm or well ripened, be procured at the beginning of this month, and planted where they are to remain.

But fig trees raised from layers made from the branches, are preferable to those from suckers; because the latter are more apt to run to wood than the former. The time for laying down the branches in order to raise young trees, is either in this month or in October or November: but remember to cover them with long litter in hard frosts. In one year's time the layers will be sufficiently rooted, when they should be separated from the old stock, and planted where they are to remain.

Remember to make your layers from branches of fruitful trees, for those which are made from the suckers, or shoots produced from old shoots, have very soft branches, full of sap, and therefore are in danger of suffering from the frost. They will also run greatly into wood, and not be very fruitful. Let the shoots therefore that are laid down be woody, compact, and well ripened; not young shoots full of sap, and whose vessels are consequently large and open.

Fig
Ficus carica

If fig trees are to be planted against walls, or pales, they should not be set nearer to each other than twenty feet.

℘ Pruning Fig Trees. ℞

This is the best season of the year for pruning fig trees; for if they are pruned at the latter end of autumn, as is often practised, many of the young bearing shoots, which are tender, are very liable to be killed by the severe frosts; but if the pruning be omitted till this month, when the frosts are over, there is great reason to hope, that though some of the bearing branches may have perished by the severity of the weather, enough of them will have escaped the frost, to furnish the wall.

Observe in pruning fig trees, to leave a sufficient supply of the last summer's wood, from the bottom to the extremity, every way, and in every part where there is proper room to train the shoots, so that the tree may be equally furnished with them at moderate distances; for these bear the figs the ensuing season.

Remember to train in every year some young shoots at or near the bottom, that there may be a proper supply of young branches, coming out regularly one after another, to supply the places of old naked branches, which will appear every season, in some part or other of the tree. At the same time let all the old branches which are destitute of young wood be cut out; by which means there will be sufficient room to train the bearing branches neatly and at proper distances; for they should neither be left, nor laid in too close.

You must never shorten, or top, the young branches of fig trees; they must be left at full length; for by shortening the branches you will not only cut away the part where the fruit would otherwise have appeared, but also occasion the branches to run greatly to wood, and never produce half a crop of fruit.

Observe to nail every branch strait and close to the wall, and at about seven or eight inches from one another.

❧ Prune Apricot, Peach, and Nectarine Trees. ☙

All the apricot, peach, and nectarine trees that were not pruned last month, must be now pruned and nailed, and the sooner the better; for the whole must be finished before the middle of the month.

The greatest care should now be taken in pruning and especially in the nailing of these trees; because as the buds are now considerably swelled for bloom, the least touch will rub them off.

This same method is to be observed in pruning trees now as in the former months.

Apricot
Prunus armeniaca

❧ Guard the Apricot, Peach, and Nectarine Trees from Frost. ☙

You should be careful to defend the choicest kinds of your apricot, peach, and nectarine trees, when in blossom, from frosts, which often happen at this time of the year.

In order to this, mats, of the larger kind, should be nailed from one end of the wall to the other, letting them hang down over the trees. The lower ends of the mats should also be fastened down, to prevent their being blown to and fro by the wind, which would inevitably beat off many of the blossoms.

But whenever the weather is mild, the mats should be taken away; for the blossoms require this kind of shelter in sharp frosts only.

❧ Prune Cherries, Plums, Apples, Pears, &c. ☙

You must now forward the pruning of cherries, plums, apples, pears, and all other kinds of fruit trees, whether stan-dards or planted against walls or espaliers, which could not be pruned in the foregoing month, with all the dispatch possible: let the whole be finished by the middle of the month at farthest.

Dwarf cherry
Chamacerasus

❧ Pruning and Ordering Young Apricot, Peach and Nectarine Trees. ☙

This is the proper season for heading down young apricot, peach, and nectarine trees, which have been planted since Michaelmas last, with their first shoots from budding at full length.

This operation should be performed just as the trees begin to push; you will therefore do well to watch the proper opportunity, and let their heads be then shortened; for this will prove of the utmost advantage to the young trees.

The head should be cut down to the third or fourth eye from the bottom; and if there are two shoots from the same stock, let both be shortened in the above manner.

Long Carnation peach
Persica Carnea longa

By this method the trees will produce some strong shoots near the ground, which will enable you to furnish equally every part of the wall with branches.

On the contrary, by omitting to head the trees, they would run up with a head like a standard tree, and hardly furnish a single branch within two or three feet of the ground; and, consequently, that part of the wall would be rendered wholly useless.

With regard to those young apricot trees that were headed a year ago, and each produced three or four shoots the last summer, you should now shorten these shoots to such lengths as may encourage each shoot to produce two or three new ones the same season.

Let each shoot be shortened to about one half of its original length; that is, such as are twenty inches long should be about ten or eleven inches; and such as are fifteen inches, or thereabouts, in length, should be shortened to eight or nine; and so in proportion to the different lengths of the shoots.

ɕɔ Prune Young Apple, Pear, Plum, and Cherry Trees. ɕɔ

Let the heads of young dwarf-apple, pear, plum, and cherry trees, lately planted against walls or espaliers, be now pruned down, in order to induce them to put out some good shoots, near the ground, to furnish that part of the wall or espalier.

If the heads of these trees are only of one year's growth from the bud or graft, let them be shortened to three or four eyes, observing what was mentioned before, namely, to do it just when the buds begin to break.

If they are two years from the bud or graft, and the first shoots were, last spring, cut down as above; let the shoots which were produced from them last summer, be now also shortened to six or seven inches.

You must observe the same rule with regard to these trees, as mentioned above for the apricot and peaches; for it is by a judicious shortening the first and second year's shoots from the budding and grafting, that the whole success depends with regard to the forming at once a useful and a beautiful tree.

When a young wall or espalier tree is once well furnished with branches near the ground, these will easily supply you with more in their turn, to cover the wall or espalier upwards.

But in the common course of pruning apple, pear, plum and cherry trees, their shoots or branches should not be shortened; for after the young trees are furnished with a proper supply of branches at the bottom, their shoots must then be trained to the wall at length, shortening only a particular shoot at places where more wood may be required to cover the part.

Pear
Pyrus communis

℘ Prune and Dress Gooseberries and Currants. ∝

If there be any of your gooseberry or currant bushes yet remaining unpruned, let the work be done at the beginning of the month.

Remember to keep the branches thin, and the middle of the tree open and clear of wood, so as to admit the sun and air freely; for by that means the fruit will be larger and much finer tasted.

At the same time let the ground be dug between the gooseberry and currant trees, where it has been omitted in the former months. For the loosening of the ground about these shrubs is of the utmost advantage to them, and at no time more useful than at present, when they are just beginning to shoot.

℘ Prune and Dress Raspberries. ∝

Let all the pruning of raspberries be now finished; observing to cut out all the dead wood; and where the live wood stands too thick, let part of it be taken away, as mentioned in the former month, shortening at the same time the shoots that are left.

Remember also to dig the ground between the rows of raspberries, where it was not done before; for this will at once strengthen the shoots, and give the bed a clean and neat appearance.

You may still make plantations of raspberries, provided the whole be finished by the middle of the month.

The plants will take root soon after they are set, and grow freely, provided they are now and then refreshed with water in dry weather.

Remember in planting raspberries to make use of the young shoots produced from the old roots last year; choosing those whose roots are well furnished with fibres, and ejecting those whose extremities are naked and sticky. The instructions for planting these shoots given in the former month, will be sufficient for the purpose, and therefore need not be repeated.

❧ Dress Fruit Tree Borders. ❧

Let all the fruit tree borders be dug at the beginning of the month, if it was not done the preceding. This will be of great service to the trees, destroy the weeds, and give the borders when raked, a neat and pleasing appearance.

At the same time the borders which were dug the preceding month, should be stirred with a hoe, and then raked very smooth. This will greatly retard the growth of the young weeds, and make the whole appear neat and decent.

❧ Dress Strawberries. ❧

If any of your strawberry beds still remain undressed, let the work be done as fast as possible; for the plants will now begin to push apace.

Clear the beds from weeds, and the plants from strings and other litter;

at the same time let some of the plants be taken away, wherever they are found to stand too thick.

The best method of keeping these plants is in single trenches as it were, separate from one another, so that there will be room to dig round them with a narrow spade or a trowel.

As soon as you have cleared the beds from litter, loosen the earth between the plants; and if you add a little fresh earth to the beds it will strengthen the plants, so that they will flower much stronger, and produce large fruit.

Chili strawberry
Fragaria chilensis

❧ Plant Vines. ❧

Cuttings of vines may be planted any time this month; they will take root freely.

Let the cuttings be planted somewhat slanting, and so deep that one eye only may be above the ground, and that close to the surface. And be sure to plant them where they are to remain.

The cuttings must be shoots of the last year, and shortened to about twelve inches in length; and let each cutting have about an inch of the preceding year's wood at the bottom.

❧ Prune Vines. ❧

If any of your vines still remain unpruned, let it be done as soon as possible at the beginning of the month; for those vines that are pruned too late seldom produce a good crop of grapes.

A formal garden in which the regular beds contain each a single variety of plant. The garden is enriched by plants in pots brought out from the greenhouse for the summer.

THE PLEASURE OR FLOWER-GARDEN

❧ Sow Tender Annual Flowers. ❧

About the beginning of this month a hot-bed should be made for sowing tender annual flowers, provided that work was not done in February. They should be made entirely in the same manner as directed in the foregoing month; and the same kind of seeds should be sown. By good management the plants raised at this season may be brought to flower strongly and beautifully in July.

❧ Transplant Tender Annual Flowers. ❧

Let a hot-bed be made about the middle or latter end of this month, in order to prick the tender annual flowers that were sown in February. Let the bed be about three feet high, and the surface even; then set on the frame; and when the great heat is over, let it be covered with light, rich, and perfectly dry earth, six inches thick.

As soon as you perceive the earth is warm, prick the plants therein at three or four inches each way, and give them a gentle sprinkling of water. Put on the glasses, but remember to raise them a little every day to let the steam escape; and shade the plants from the sun till they have taken root.

When the plants have taken root, and begin to push, let the glasses be raised a considerable height every day, that they may have a sufficient quantity of fresh air; and, at the same time, remember to give them frequently a gentle sprinkling of water.

Sʐ Sow the Hardier Kinds of Annual Flowers. Sʐ

In the beginning of this month, a hot-bed should be made for sowing the seeds of the hardier kinds of annual flowers.

The bed should be two feet high, made in the usual manner, and covered with rich earth four or five inches thick.

On this bed you may sow the seeds of China aster, Indian pink, marvel of Peru, balsam, palma-Christi, capsicum, mignonette, French and African marygolds, ten-week stocks, chrysanthemum, tree and purple amaranthus, persicarias, love-apple, seabiouses, convolvulus major, stramoniums, and several others of the like sorts.

Amaranth
Amaranthus caudatus

Let the seeds be sown each sort separate, in shallow drills, drawn from the back to the front of the frame, two or three inches asunder. Cover the smaller seeds about a quarter, and the larger half an inch. When the plants are come up let them have air by raising the glasses a considerable height every day; and as soon as they have gathered a little strength, they must be gradually hardened to bear the open air, by taking the lights entirely off every mild day. Remember to refresh them often with moderate sprinklings of water. About the middle of next month some of them will be fit to prick out, and the remainder in May.

It sometimes happens that dung cannot be spared at this season for making a hot-bed; when this is the case, the above annual flower seeds may be sown in a warm border, where the earth is rich and light; and if the weather be warm, they will succeed extremely well; particularly China aster, ten-week stock, Indian pink, African and French marygolds, chrysanthemum, purple and tree amaranthus, persicarias, scabiouses, and convolvulus major. Let the seeds be sown thin, each sort separate, the beds arched over with hoops, and covered with mats every night in bad weather.

Dwarf Indian marigold
'Legion of Honor'
Tagetes

By observing this management the plants will grow freely, and, if you refresh them with water in dry weather, they will be fit to plant out in May, or the beginning of June, and flower pretty strongly in autumn.

℘ Sow Hardy Annual Flowers. ℛ

About the middle of the month you may sow in the borders, and other parts of the garden, the seeds of all sorts of hardy annual flowers: particularly the large and dwarf annual sun-flower, oriental mallow, lavatera, larkspur, flos Adonis, sweet sultan, large flesh-coloured blue, and yellow lupines, convolvulus major, sweet-scented and Tangier peas, and nasturtium. Soon after you may sow the seeds of the Spanish nigella, purple and white Candia tuft, Venus looking-glass, Venus navel-wort, dwarf double poppy, Lobel's catchfly, dwarf annual lychnis, convolvulus minor, and some others.

Catchfly
Lychnis sylvestris latifolia

You should remember in sowing the above, or any other kinds of annual flower seeds, to sow each sort separate in patches, in the different borders, in the manner mentioned in February. The plants must remain to flower in the places were they are sown, for they do not succeed well after transplantation; let them therefore be thinned, where they have risen too thick. At the same time remember to water the seeds in dry weather, and also the plants after they are come up.

℘ Dress the Pots of Annual Flowers. ℛ

Clear the plants of the double wall-flowers, double stock july-flowers, double sweet-williams, rockets, rose campions, catchfly, campanulas, scarlet lychnis, &c. that were potted last autumn, from decayed leaves. Then take some of the earth out of the pots, but do not go so deep as to displace the roots of the plants. Fill up the pots again with fresh earth, and give them some water. By this means their roots will be strengthened, the plants will grow freely, and produce large and beautiful flowers.

Wall-flower
Erysimum cheiri

℘ Transplant Chrysanthemums. ℛ

The cuttings of the double chrysanthemums planted in pots or boxes last autumn, should now be removed into single pots, where they are to flower. At the beginning of next month, some of them may be planted out in the borders among other flowers, where they will blow strong, and make a handsome appearance.

ᔕ Nurse Auricula Plants. ଓଃ

You should be very careful to defend your choice auricula plants from too much wet, cold, winds, and frost; for either will greatly injure their flower-buds, which are now in great forwardness. The pots should therefore be continued under the hoop-arches, where the plants may enjoy the benefit of the open air, and when there is occasion, be sufficiently defended by drawing the mats over the hoops.

Primrose
*Primula
cortusoides amoena*

But, at the same time, remember not to debar the plants from a warm and moderate shower of rain now and then, if any should happen, for such showers will be of the greatest service to the plants. Remember also to refresh them often in dry weather with moderate sprinklings of water, just enough to keep the earth about their roots a little moist.

ᔕ Transplant and Dress Carnations. ଓଃ

You must transplant all the carnations which were omitted last month, at the beginning of this.

Remember to take up the plants with a ball of their own earth about their roots, and place each plant in the middle of each pot, unless the pots be large, in which case two plants may be set in each pot; observing to close the earth well about them, and give them a moderate watering to settle the earth well about their roots. Let the pots be set in some proper place where the plants may be defended from cold winds, and let them have moderate waterings frequently in dry weather.

Carnation
*Dianthus
caryophyllus*

At the same time the carnation plants which were removed last autumn into the pots where they are to remain, should now have fresh earth given them, by removing the old earth from the tops of the pots, and filling them up with fresh.

In order to this, let the plants be first cleared from all dead leaves, then take out as much earth as possible out of the pots, without disturbing the roots of the plants, and fill the pots with fresh mould, laying it close round the plants; after which let them be moderately watered to settle the earth. By this means the plants will be so greatly strengthened, that they will shoot strongly, and produce large and beautiful flowers.

☙ Protect Your Tulip, Hyacinth, and Ranunculus Beds. ೞ

The more curious kinds of tulips, hyacinths, ranunculuses, and anemonies, must be protected from the frosts and cold rains, which frequently happen this month, and which will greatly injure your plants, if they are not well guarded; for their flower-buds are now advancing apace. Let therefore the hoop arches be still continued over the beds, and mats drawn over the hoops every night in heavy rains and frosty weather. By this precaution your flowers will blow large and in great perfection.

Tulips
Tulipa

But remember to take away all the mats when the weather is mild, that the plants may enjoy the benefit of the fresh air; nor should they be covered in a moderate shower of rain, for that would be of great service.

It will not be amiss, if your beds were at first covered with low hoops, to remove them, and place taller in their stead, as this will give the plants more air when the mats are drawn over the hoops, and there will be less danger of injuring the beds in drawing the mats over the hoops.

☙ Support Hyacinths. ೞ

You must now be careful to support with sticks the flower-stems of your large double hyacinths, for they now begin to grow apace, and the flowers are too heavy to be supported by the stock alone. Remember to use some soft tying in fastening the flower stalks to the sticks, which must be fixed in the ground very near the plant.

Holland
hyacinth
Hyacinthus

☙ Sow Perennial Flower Seeds. ೞ

Most kinds of perennial flower seeds may be sown this month, particularly carnations, pinks, sweet-williams, wall-flowers, and all the species of stock july-flowers. You may also sow single rose campion, catchfly, scarlet lychnis, columbines, Greek valerian, scabiouses, and Canterbury-bell.

☙ Sow French Honey-suckles, Hollyhocks, &c. ೞ

The seeds of French honey-suckles, hollyhocks, tree primrose, campanulas, fox-gloves, and many other sorts, may be sown this month. A spot of ground in a warm situation, but not too close to the walls or fences, should be dug for the above flower-seeds. Let the spot, when dug, be divided into beds of three feet and a half wide, and subdivided into as many parts as you intend to sow different kinds of seed, for each kind must be sown separate. Let the seeds be sown thin and covered properly with earth, the larger about half an inch, and the smaller about a quarter of an inch deep.

Some gardeners sow all kinds of perennial flower seeds in shallow drills, proportioning the depth of each drill to the particular sort of each seed, so that they may be covered with their proper depth of earth. Others, after raking the surface of the bed smooth, draw off equally, with the back of the rake, about a quarter of an inch deep of earth, into the alleys: when this is done they sow the seed, and with the teeth of the rake cover them with the earth before drawn into the alleys. Either of these methods may

be practised with success; perhaps the drills are more proper for the larger kinds of seed, and the broad cast for the smaller.

But whatever method be used in sowing the seeds, you must remember to sprinkle the beds frequently with water in dry weather. Your plants will be fit to prick out in May or June.

Anemonie
Anemone fulgens

✺ Plant Ranunculuses, Anemonies, &c. ✺

You may now plant some ranunculuses and anemonies: they will blow and make a fine appearance in May and June, when the early sorts are over. But remember to water the plants frequently after they are up, in dry weather, and then they will flower tolerably strong.

✺ Plant Carnations, Pinks, &c. ✺

This is the season for planting in clumps, in the borders, carnations, pinks, sweet-williams, both double and single; bachelors buttons, double feverfew, golden rod, perennial sun-flowers, perennial asters, French-honeysuckles, columbines, Canterbury-bells, monkshood, fox-gloves, tree-primrose, and various other sorts of the same tribe.

Japanese
Chrysanthemum
Chrysanthemum

All the above plants will take root in a very short time, and flower this season, provided they are now and then refreshed with water in dry weather. Plants may also now be planted in the borders at the beginning of this month; such as polyanthuses, auriculas, double camomile, London pride, violets, hepaticas, thrift, primroses, gentianella, and a great variety of others of the same kind. Give them a little water when first planted, and repeat it at times in dry weather: they will grow freely, and make a fine appearance in blossom.

Cut-flowered
Chinese pink
*Dianthus
superbus
cardneri*

℘ Plant Flowering Shrubs. ℛ

In any part of the garden, where flowering shrubs are wanted, they may now be planted; for most sorts will succeed: particularly the althæa-frutex, spireas, syringas, golden-rods, and honey-suckles.

℘ Transplant Exotic Trees. ℛ

The greater part of the hardy exotic flowering trees or shrubs may be transplanted any time this month.

℘ Transplant Evergreens. ℛ

This is a very good season for transplanting evergreens; for they will take root sooner now than at any other time of the year: particularly the arbutus, or strawberry tree, magnolias, bays, pyracanthas, phillyrea, alaturnus, laurel, Portugal laurel, lauristinus, evergreen oak, hollies, yews, and a great variety of others.

You may also transplant pines and firs of all sorts, cedars of Libanus, cypress, junipers, and others of that kind.

Remember in planting evergreens, and indeed shrubs of every kind, to let the work be done as expeditious as possible, after they are taken up. Let a hole be opened for each shrub, large enough to receive the root freely; and when it is deep enough, let the ground be well loosened at the bottom. As soon as the holes are ready, bring the shrubs, and have pruned away the broken or bruised roots, place them upright in the hole, break the earth well, and throw it in equally about their roots, and cover them of a proper depth. Let the surface of the earth round each shrub be made hollow like a basin, to hold the water when given in dry weather; and let some mulch or long litter be laid upon the earth round the tree; this will keep the ground moist about the roots.

Let each shrub be well watered as soon as planted, in order to settle the earth about the roots; and, at the same time, let stakes be fixed in the earth, and such as require support be fastened thereto.

Be careful to plant your shrubs, of whatever kind, at proper distances, that when they grow up, they may not crowd one another: for shrubs always show themselves to most advantage when they are separate. In a word, there must always be room sufficient left to dig, and hoe and clean the ground between them.

❧ Plant Box Edgings. ❧

Box planted at this season, will soon take root and flourish, provided it be properly watered. Where therefore any gaps appear in edgings formerly planted, they should be now filled up; for nothing has a worse appearance than ragged and uneven edgings.

If you like thrift better than box for edgings to borders or flower-beds, it may be planted at the beginning of this month; and it will succeed, if watered at proper intervals in dry weather, till it has taken root.

❧ Dig the Borders. ❧

The borders and other parts of the garden that have not already been dug, must now be done. Let them also be raked smooth, which will at once give them a neat appearance, and put them in a proper condition for receiving the seeds of annual flowers.

❧ Hoe and Rake the Borders. ❧

Those borders which were dug and planted with flowers last autumn, must have their surface loosened with a small hoe, and the earth stirred carefully between the plants, taking care of the tender shoots of bulbous plants, which are now just breaking through the surface. A dry day should be chosen for this work, and, as soon as the earth is loosened with the hoe, let it be neatly raked, clearing away all the rubbish, weeds, and decayed leaves which appear about any of the plants.

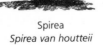

Spirea
Spirea van houtteii

This will greatly promote the growth of the flowers, and at the same time prevent the first growth of seed weeds.

❧ Dig the Clumps in Shrubberies. ❧

Let the ground between the flowering shrubs and evergreens in the clumps and borders, be dug at the beginning of this month, if it was not done the preceding. This will greatly help the plants, and the freshness of the ground will give them an additional beauty.

ℬ Gravel Walks. ℭ

You must now be very careful to keep your gravel walks free from weeds, and all kinds of litter.

If you intend to make any new gravel walks, this is a very proper season for doing it.

In order to this, you should chuse that sort of gravel which consists of smooth even pebbles, mixed with a due quantity of loam; for this will bind exceeding close, and look very beautiful.

But if the only gravel you can procure be loose or sandy, you should take one load of strong loam to two or three of gravel, cast them well together, and turn this mixture over two or three times, that they may be well blended together; if this be mixed in proper proportion it will bind well, and not stick to the feet in wet weather.

There are different opinions with regard to the choice of gravel; some are for having the gravel as white as possible, and in order to make the walks more so, they roll them with stone rollers, which are often hewn by the masons, that they may add a whiteness to the walks. But this renders it very troublesome to the eyes, by reflecting the rays of light too strongly. This should therefore be avoided, and such gravel as will be smooth, and reflect the least, should be preferred.

With regard to the depth of gravel walks, six or eight inches may do well enough; a foot thickness will be sufficient for any; but there should always be a depth of rubbish laid under the gravel, especially if the ground be wet; in which case there cannot be too much care taken to fill the bottom of the walks with large stones, flints, brick rubbish, chalk, or any other materials that can easily be procured, which will drain off the moisture from the gravel, and prevent its being poachy in wet weather. If these materials cannot be procured to lay at the bottom of the walks, let a bed of heath, or furze, be laid under the gravel to keep it dry. If either heath or furze be laid in green, they will continue a long time, as they will be covered from the air. This bed will prevent the gravel from getting down into the clay, and also keep it dry. If these precautions are omitted in the first laying of gravel upon clay, the water detained by the clay will render the gravel poachy, whenever there is much rain.

Gravel walks are apt to be laid too round, which gives them a narrow appearance, and, at the same time, renders them not so well to walk upon. A gravel walk of twelve feet wide should have a rise of about two inches and

a half in the middle; that is, the middle should rise gradually so much higher than the sides.

The same proportion should be allowed to every gravel walk; one of
twenty-four feet wide should not have above five inches rise in the middle,
and one of six feet wide not more than one inch and a quarter; and so in
proportion for any other breadth.

You must also, in making gravel walks, have great regard to the level
of the ground, so as to lay the walks with easy descents towards the low
parts of the ground, that the wet may be drained off easily; for when
this is omitted, the water will lie upon the walks a considerable time
after hard rains, which will render them unfit for use, especially where
the ground is naturally wet or strong: but where the ground is level, and
there are not declivities to carry off the water, it will be proper to have
sink-stones laid by the sides of the walks, at convenient distances, to
carry off the wet; and where the ground is so naturally dry, that the
water will soon soak away, the drains, from the sink-stones, may be contrived so as to convey the water into cesspools, where it will gradually
sink away; but, in wet land, there should be subterraneous drains to convey the water off, either into ponds, ditches, or some other place proper
to receive it; for where this is not well provided for, the walks can never
be either handsome or useful.

In order to destroy worms, that too often spoil the beauty of gravel
walks, some recommend the watering them well with a strong and bitter
infusion of walnut tree leaves, especially those parts of the walks most
annoyed with these reptiles. This bitter infusion will, it is said, as soon as it
reaches them, force them out on the surface, so that they may be easily
gathered up, and taken away. But if, in the first laying of the walks, a good
bed of lime rubbish be placed in the bottom, there will be no need of having recourse to bitter infusions; for no worms will ever harbour near lime.

With regard to old gravel walks, you must now remember to roll them
twice a week, as least, when the weather will permit, by which means they
will be firm, and the surface smooth. They will also appear very beautiful,
and be agreeable to walk upon.

But where the surface is dirty, or over run with weeds or moss, they must
be turned; by which means the moss and weeds will be destroyed, and the
walks will appear fresh as when first made.

Such gravel walks as were broken up, and laid in ridges, at the beginning
of winter, should now be levelled down, and put into their proper form.

But surely this ridging of gravel walks, in winter, is one of the most unnecessary, and, at the same time, the most ill-looking contrivances that was ever introduced into a garden. For the walks are thereby rendered entirely useless, in the winter season; nay, even in some gardens, rendered incommodious both to the proprietor and the gardener himself; and, in all gardens, has a desolate and confused appearance. Nor can any good reason be given for this absurd practice; for it will not prevent the growth of weeds, as pretended, and, at the same time, will at once, both deaden the colour, and destroy the binding quality of the gravel.

However, where this has been practised, let the ridges be levelled down some time this month.

In turning gravel walks, remember to tread, rake, and roll them every twenty feet at least. The method is this:

When you have advanced with the turning about twenty feet from the end, let that be trodden all over equally; then smooth it off with the back of the rake, and roll it directly. In this manner you are to proceed to the end of the walk; for gravel never binds so well as when fresh stirred.

₲ Clean Grass Walks. ℛ

Let your grass walks and lawns be kept perfectly clear of worm-casts, for these spoil the grass, and have an unsightly appearance.

Where ever, therefore, any of them appear, let them be broken, and spread about with a taper and pliable pole, and the grass be immediately rolled with a wooden roller; by which means the earth thrown up by the worms will be taken away, and you may mow the grass close and even.

If the weather be mild, the grass will now begin to grow apace; let therefore your walks, or lawns, be mowed in good time, before the grass is rank, other wise you will not be able to cut it close enough, to procure a fine and even bottom.

At the same time, let all the edges of the walks, or lawns, be neatly cut with a sharp-edged iron; this will give them a very pleasing and neat appearance.

₲ Lay Turf. ℛ

Any time this month you may make new grass walks or lawns, for the turf will now grow freely, provided it be laid down as soon as it is cut.

Remember to beat it well after it is laid, and to roll it sufficiently after rain; for by this means the surface will be rendered firm and smooth.

APRIL

1. Small Black Grape. *Vitis nigrae minores.*
2. Great Blue Grape. *Vitis caerulea majores.*
3. Muscadine Grape.
Vitis Moschatellinae.
4. Burlet Grape. *Vitis Burletenses.*
5. Raisins of the Sun Grape.
Vitis insolatae.
6. Fig Tree. *Ficus.*

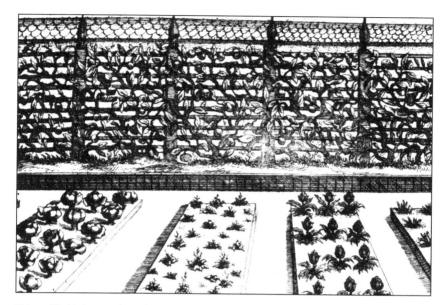

This prolific kitchen-garden is bordered by fruit trees trained to a wooden frame.

The Works of this Month in the
KITCHEN GARDEN

∞ Cucumbers and Melons. ∞

Be careful to examine the heat of your cucumber beds; for if that be deficient, you must not expect either a plentiful crop, or fine fruit.

If therefore you perceive the heat of the beds to be faint, let no time be lost in renewing it, by adding a lining of horse dung to the sides of the bed, as directed in the former month. By this addition the heat will be revived, the plants preserved in a growing state, the fruit will set freely, swell kindly, and grow to a handsome size.

But, at the same time, remember to give the plants air every day, by raising the ends of the lights at the back part of the frame with props, higher or lower, in proportion to the state of the weather.

A little before sun-set; mats be thrown over the glasses, and removed every morning about an hour after the sun is up.

Let moderate quantities of water be given the plants occasionally; the cucumber plants will require it more frequently than the melon; but be sure not to give them too much at one time.

The melons will also require water; but as their fruit will now begin to appear, it must be applied very moderately.

Whenever you perceive any decayed or damaged leaves on any part of the plants, whether cucumbers or melons, let them be taken away together with all the decayed flowers.

When the weather is hot, and the beams of the sun fierce, so that you perceive the leaves of the cucumbers or melons to flag, you should be careful to shade them either with a mat, or loose hay thrown over the glasses, for two or three hours, while the heat continues.

ভ Make Ridges for Cucumbers and Melons. ভ

About the middle or latter end of this month, according to the warmth of the season, you must make ridges for such cucumber and melon plants as are to be planted under hand or bell-glasses. These ridges are made in the following manner:

Dig a trench about three feet wide, and, if the soil be dry, ten inches deep, but if wet, not above three inches, levelling the earth at the bottom of the trench. Then put in your dung, prepared as directed in the preceding months for making hot beds. The dung should be at least two feet thick. If you propose to make more than one ridge, the interval between the ridges should be four feet; and these spaces, or alleys, are, in about a month or five weeks, to be filled with new hot dung, and covered with earth; for this will revive the heat in the ridges, and give fresh vigour to the plants.

Cucumber
Cucumis sativus

When this is done, and the dung in the ridge has a proper degree of heat, cover it with earth about four inches thick round the sides, raising hillocks in the middle of the ridge, three feet and a half asunder. Set the glasses upon the hills, leaving them close down about twenty-four hours, in which time the earth in the hills will be sufficiently warmed.

Stir up the earth of the hillock with your hand, and make it a little hollow in the middle, in the form of a basin, in each of which let three or four cucumber, or two melon plants be set, observing to shade them until they have taken root; after which, you must be careful to give them air, by raising the glasses on the opposite side to the wind, in proportion to the heat of the weather: but remember that this is to be done only about the middle of the day, till they are able to bear the sun without flagging, when they should enjoy both freely.

Remember to cover the glasses every night with mats, till the latter end of May.

If your plants have not been stopped before, remember to do it now. This operation should be performed when they have two, three, or four leaves, by pinching off the top of the plant; by which means each plant will produce two, three, or four shoots, or runners: and when these runners have three joints, it will be proper to stop them also, by pinching off the top of each at the third joint, which will cause each of these runners to put out two, three, or more shoots. By this means, the plants will be furnished with fruitful runners; for it is from these lateral shoots we are to expect the fruit; but if the plants were not to be stopped as above directed, there would not be above one or two runners from each plant, and these perhaps extend a yard in length without shewing a single fruit, especially the cucumber.

When the fruit appears upon the plant, there will also appear many male flowers on different parts: these may at first sight be distinguished; for the female flowers have the young fruit situated under them; whereas the male have none; but have three stamina in their centre, loaded with a golden powder, intended to impregnate the female flowers; and when the plants are exposed to the open air, the soft breezes of wind convey this farina, or male powder, from the male to the female flowers. Under frames the case is different: the breezes of air are wanting to convey

Pumpkin
Cucurbita pepo

the farina from the male to the female flowers; and for want of this, many of the fruit drop off, because the flowers were not impregnated. The curious have often observed, that the bees which have crept into the frames when the glasses have been raised to admit the air, have supplied the want of these gentle breezes of wine, by carrying on their hind legs the farina of the male into the female flowers, and left there a sufficient quantity of it to impregnate them. These industrious insects have taught the gardeners a method of supplying the want of a free circulation of air under the frames, so necessary to the impregnation of the female flowers. The method is this:

They carefully gather the male flowers at a time when this farina is fully formed, and carry it to the female flowers, turning them down over them, and gently striking, with the nail of one of their fingers, the outside of the male flower, so as to cause the farina on the summits of the stamina to fall into the female flowers; by which means they will be sufficiently impregnated. By practising this method, the gardeners have now a much greater degree of certainty than formerly, in procuring an early crop of cucumbers and melons; and by this method the florists also have arrived to greater certainty of procuring new varieties of flowers from seeds, which is done by mixing the farina of different flowers.

ଔ Sow Cucumber and Melon Seeds. ଔ

The beginning of this month, you should remember to sow some cucumber and melon seed, in order to raise plants for ridging out, under hand or bell-glasses, in May.

ଔ Cabbages and Savoys. ଔ

If you did not transplant all the cabbage plants you intended to remove this spring, in March, let it be done at the beginning of this month, that the plants may take root before the dry weather comes on. Remember to water the plants as soon as they are set.

Let the earth be drawn up round the stems of forward cabbage plants; this will at once strengthen them, and increase their growth.

Sow savoy and cabbage seed, to raise plants for a full winter crop. The situation of the spot where the seeds are sown should be open, and the seeds raked in equally.

You should now prick out into beds those cabbage and savoy plants which were sown in February and March; for by this means they will gain strength before they are planted where they are to remain.

Henderson's early summer cabbage
Brassica oleracea capitata

The beds you intend for them, should be prepared of good earth, in an open situation, and about three feet and a half broad. Let the largest plants be drawn out regularly from the seed bed, and planted in the beds prepared for their reception, at four or five inches distance every way. Remember to water them immediately after they are planted, and to repeat it occasionally in dry weather.

At the same time let the plants left in the seed-bed be cleared from weeds, and well watered to settle the earth about their roots, which had been disturbed by drawing the larger.

ଔ Cauliflowers. ଔ

Draw up the earth about the stems of your early cauliflower plants, for this will be of great service in promoting their growth; but be careful that no earth be drawn into their hearts, as that will greatly injure them.

The cauliflower plants raised from seed sown early in the spring should, about the latter end of the month, be planted out for good, in an open situation, on a piece of rich ground, into which some good rotten dung has been dug. They should be planted at about two feet and a half distance every way.

As soon as they are planted, let them be watered, and the operation frequently repeated in dry weather, till the plants have taken root.

Let your bell-glasses be now raised on props, in order to give the plants more air; and whenever any gentle showers fall, remember to take them entirely from the plants, for nothing refreshes them more than gentle showers.

As soon as you find your plants grow so fast as to fill the glasses with their leaves, dig slightly about the plants, and raise the ground about them in a bed, large enough to support the glasses, about four inches high, which will give your plants a great deal of room, by raising the glasses so much higher, when they are set over them again; and by this means you may keep them covered till the middle of this month, which could not otherwise be done without prejudice to the leaves.

℘ Plant Kidney-Beans. ℘

At the beginning of this month you may plant kidney beans of the early kind, on a spot of dry ground, defended from cold winds, and open to the sun.

Let them be dropped three inches apart, into drills an inch deep, and two feet and a half asunder. Let the earth be drawn equally over them, but do not let them be covered above an inch deep.

Remember to chuse a dry season for planting these beans, because much wet will rot them; a rainy season is therefore very improper for this work.

Kidney-beans for a principal crop may be planted about the middle of this month. The speckled dwarf kidney-bean, and the Battersea white, are the proper kinds for planting now.

They should be planted in an open situation, and the rows two feet and a half, or three feet distant from each other.

Mr. Miller recommends the scarlet bean, as preferable to all the other sorts in goodness, and at the same time as much hardier. This sort may now be sown in the same manner, and on the same soil, as those mentioned above; but they will be a fortnight later. This defect will, however, be well supplied by the continuance of the scarlet bean; for it will continue till the frost puts a stop to it in autumn. At the same time the pods of this sort, when old, are seldom stringy, have a much better flavour than the young pods of the other sorts, and will boil greener.

Parsnip
Pastinaca latifolia

⅏ Carrots and Parsnips. ⚬

You may yet sow carrots; but it must be done at the beginning of the month, if you desire to have your roots of a tolerable size.

But if a supply of small young carrots should be desired, you must sow a little seed at two different times this month; at the beginning and towards the latter end; by this means young carrots will be always ready for the table; for when the roots of the first sown become too large, those of the second will supply their place.

You may also, at the beginning of the month, sow parsnip seed, where wanted; but if you delay it any longer, it will not succeed.

⅏ Spinach. ⚬

Spinach seed may be still sown; it will grow, if sown any time this month; and where a constant supply of this plant is wanted, a little of the seed should be sown often, at least once a fortnight.

Let the spinach sown the preceding months be now hoed, and the plants thinned out to four or five inches distant.

⅏ Radish. ⚬

You should sow a little radish seed at three different times this month; for by that means a constant supply of young radishes may be obtained. About eight or nine days between each sowing will be sufficient.

The seed should be sown in dry weather on a rich spot of ground, in an open situation; but you must remember to water it frequently, both before and after the plants are come up.

Indeed all the crops of radishes should be often watered in dry weather; for otherwise the roots will be small, hot, and sticky.

Let all your crops of radishes be thinned, where they have come up too thick; the plants should be at least two or three inches asunder; and the beds carefully weeded.

⅏ Asparagus. ⚬

You may yet plant asparagus as required; the plants will grow freely; but they rarely succeed well, if not planted by the middle of the month. The same method is to be observed in planting asparagus now, as mentioned in the former month.

If any of your asparagus beds remain undressed, let them be forked up by the end of the first week in this month, and raked immediately after; for the buds are now in great forwardness; so that great care is necessary not to injure them.

ᔥ Artichokes. ᙅ

Artichokes may be yet planted if required; they will succeed, provided you plant them early in the month.

The same method is to be observed in planting them, as described in the preceding month.

Globe Artichoke
Cynara scolymus

ᔥ Beans. ᙅ

Beans should be planted at three different times this month, at the beginning, the middle, and the end.

The long podded beans are proper for planting now. This bean is a remarkable good bearer, and a fine eating bean; consequently very proper for a family. This sort may be planted any time this month. Allow a good distance between the rows.

You may also plant the Windsor, the Sandwich, or indeed, any of the larger kinds.

Maule's butter wax beans
Phaseolus vulgaris

The Mazagan and white-blossom bean, which are great favourites with many persons, may also be planted any time this month. Let the rows be two feet and a half asunder.

Both these are plentiful bearers, their stalks being generally loaded with pods from the very bottom to the top; and though small, none exceed them for eating.

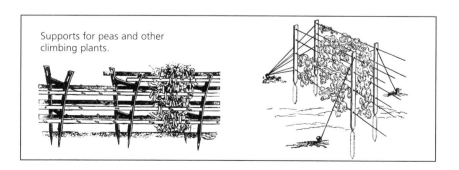

Supports for peas and other climbing plants.

⅏ Peas. ⊘

A quantity of peas should now be sown to succeed those sown in March: and if a constant supply be desired, some should be sown every fortnight at least.

The marrowfats are very proper for sowing at this season of the year; though any other of the larger kinds of peas may be sown any time this month; there is no danger of their succeeding if the weather be kind.

You may even sow hotspurs, or any of the smaller kinds of peas, at this season; for these will succeed if sown early.

Let the earth be drawn up to the stems of peas which are come up, and advanced a little height. This will greatly strengthen the plants, and forward them in their growth.

Potato plant
Solanum tuberosum

When the plants are advanced about six inches in height, the sticks should be placed where you intend them; or the peas will now begin to want support.

⅏ Potatoes. ⊘

If you omitted to plant potatoes in the former month, you may still do it, but the sooner it is done the better; for they rarely succeed well if planted after the middle of the month.

⅏ Turnips. ⊘

Turnips may be sown any time this month; and the plants will appear in a few days after the seed is in the earth.

Let the seed be sown thin and equally in an open spot of ground, and raked in with a light and even hand.

Those turnips which were sown the former months should now be hoed, and the plants thinned out to seven or eight inches distant from one another.

⅏ Lettuces. ⊘

Coss, Silesia, Imperial, or any other sorts of lettuce may be sown any time this month; and as a regular succession of these plants is generally desired, a little seed should be sown about once a fortnight.

The spot of ground intended for this purpose should be in an open situation, and the earth well broken. When the ground is prepared let the seed be sown equally, not too thick, and raked in lightly.

The coss, Silesia, or any other sorts of lettuce sown last month, or in February, should now be transplanted.

In order to this let a spot of ground be chosen, and a little rotten dung spread over it. Dig the ground well, bury the dung properly, and rake the surface very smooth.

The lettuces should be planted about ten or twelve inches distant from one another, every way. When this is done let the plants be watered immediately, and the operation frequently repeated in dry weather, till they have taken root.

∽ Small Salleting. ∝

Cress, mustard, rape, radishes, and other plants of that kind, generally called small salleting, should be sown once a week at least.

In order to this a spot of rich ground should be chosen, and the seed sown, each separately, in shallow drills, and covered lightly with earth.

Curled Colewort
Caulis crispa

As soon as the seeds are sown, water them moderately, if the weather be dry; for this will greatly promote their growth.

∽ Celery. ∝

Let a little celery seed be sown the first or second week in this month, in order to raise plants for succeeding those which were sown in March.

A rich light spot of earth must be chosen for this purpose, and the ground broken fine, and the surface made very smooth and even. The seed is then to be sown equally, not too thick, and either lightly raked in, or covered with fine earth about a quarter of an inch thick.

A few hoops should, at the same time, be fixed across the bed, and a mat drawn over the hoops occasionally, when the sun is hot, to prevent the earth from being too much dried. Water the bed now and then, and the plants, by this method, will rise well, and grow freely.

Half-dwarf celery
Apium graveolens dulce

Prizetaker onion
Allium cepa

⚬ Onions and Leeks. ⚬

You may yet sow the seed of onions and leeks; either of them will succeed, if sown at the beginning of the month; but if deferred any longer, there is great danger of success, especially with regard to the onions.

⚬ Purslane. ⚬

Purslane may now be sown on a bed of light rich earth in the common ground. Water the bed often in dry weather, and shade it from the heat of the sun, till the plants are come up, and have acquired a sufficient degree of strength.

⚬ Scorzonera and Salsafy. ⚬

About the middle of this month the seeds of scorzonera and salsafy should be sown for the principal crop; for that sown any time before the middle of this month will soon run up to seed, and consequently become useless.

⚬ Pot and Physical Herbs. ⚬

Baum, penny-royal, and camomile, should now be planted; but remember to plant them where they are to remain, and at about eight inches from one another.

Mint will also succeed if planted this month, especially if the following method be pursued:

Sage
*Salvia minor
primata*

Draw up from the old beds a proper quantity of the best plants, that is, those which are strongest, and five or six inches high. These plants must be taken up very carefully, with some roots to each.

Plant them in rows, allowing six inches between each row, and set them about six inches apart in each row. Water them as soon as they are planted, and repeat the operation frequently in dry weather, till the plants are well rooted.

Tansey, tarragon, chives, and sorrel, may also be planted at this season; but remember to plant them where they are to remain, and to allow eight inches between every plant.

Slips of sage may likewise now be planted; they will grow freely. Let the slips be about six or seven inches long, and planted in a shady border four or five inches apart from one another. Put the slips into the ground within two inches of their tops, and water them frequently in dry weather.

Tansy
Tanacetum
vulgare

They will become fine plants by September, when they may be transplanted into beds of good light earth, at about eight or nine inches distance every way.

Thyme, hyssop, savory, and marjoram will grow freely from slips or cuttings, planted any time this month. They should be planted in a shady place, and treated in the same manner as before directed for sage.

Rue, rosemary, lavender, southernwood, wormwood, and lavender-cotton, may also now be propagated by slips or cuttings.

These slips or cuttings should be about six or eight inches long, and planted in a shady border six inches from one another. Remember to set the slips or cuttings full half way in the ground; and to water them frequently.

Thyme
Thymus

They may be transplanted, in September, to the place where they are intended to remain, at the distance of a foot from one another.

Nasturtium seed may be sown in a drill about an inch deep. Let the seeds be placed two or three inches apart in the drill, and the earth drawn equally over them. They will grow and flourish freely.

Thyme, marjoram, savory, and hyssop, may now be sown separate on a bed of light earth. Let the seeds be sown, in separate spots, on the surface, and raked in with a light and even hand.

Borage, bugloss, clary, carduus, burnet, sorrel, and marygold, may now be sown in separate spots of good earth, and raked in evenly.

Belleville
sorrel
Rumex

It is not yet too late to sow parsley, chervil, and coriander. Let the seeds be sown equally, not too thick, in shallow drills, and covered with earth about a quarter of an inch thick.

THE NURSERY

ᔭ Grafting. ᑫ

The operation of grafting may still be performed on fruit trees of the latest kind; but it must be done during the first week in the month, or it will not succeed.

Hollies of the variegated kinds may be grafted till the middle of the month; for they are not so forward as the fruit trees.

The common plain holly is the proper stock to graft the variegated kinds upon; but the stocks for this purpose must be four years growth at least; if they are five or six it will be the better.

In order to this let some good cuttings, or grafts of the best variegated kinds be produced; they must be cuttings of the last summer's growth. Let these be carefully grafted, in the manner already described, and there will be little reason to fear the success.

ᔭ Inarching. ᑫ

The operation of inarching may also be now performed on evergreens, or indeed, on whatever kind of trees or shrubs you may be desirous of propagating by that method; which is principally intended for those kinds of trees and shrubs which are not easily raised from seed, or any other general method; for it should be remembered, that most sorts may be propagated by inarching.

With regard to the evergreen kinds, they may be inarched with safety this month; but the other sorts generally succeed best, when inarched at the beginning.

ᔭ New Grafted Trees. ᑫ

Your new grafted trees should be carefully examined; for the clay is too often subject to fall off, or at least crack in such a manner as to admit both air and wet to the grafts. Whenever you find this to be the case, let the old clay be taken entirely away, and some more, which has been previously well wet, and well wrought, placed immediately in its room. Observe to close this perfectly in every part, so that neither air nor wet can penetrate to the graft.

If you find any shoots produced from the stock below the graft, let them be rubbed off close; for these will impoverish the grafts, and perhaps in the end destroy them.

ℵ) New Budded Trees. ℭ

Look over your new budded trees frequently about this time, for those which were budded during the last summer will now be making their first shoots, and therefore require some care and attention.

Insects often attack the tender shoots from the buds and if not prevented will greatly hinder their progress, if not totally destroy them. Attention therefore is necessary; and by attention the injury may be, in a great measure at least, prevented.

In order to this, examine the extremities of the young shoots, and where you find any of the leaves curled up, let them be carefully taken off, for they are full of small insects. By continuing this practice, the vermin will be destroyed, and consequently the injury prevented from spreading any further.

At the same time be very careful to rub off all the shoots besides the bud, that the whole efforts of the stock may go to support the buds; for all the others will have a tendency to injure and starve them.

ℵ) Transplanting. ℭ

At the beginning of this month, you may transplant most sorts of evergreens; particularly cedars, cypresses, firs, phillyreas, alaturnuses and pyracanthas, bays, hollies, ever-green oaks, cistuses, and several other sorts of evergreen.

Remember to chuse a calm cloudy day for this work, and if gentle showers of rain fall, so much the better; for calm showery weather is much the best for removing trees and shrubs at this season.

As soon as they are planted, let them be well watered to settle the earth about their roots. Some mulch or litter should also be laid on the surface of the ground; for this will prevent the sun's drying the earth too much, and preserve a proper degree of moisture to the roots.

ℵ) Destroy Weeds. ℭ

The weeds will not grow very fast between the rows of young trees; let them therefore be destroyed, by hoeing the intervals.

But remember to use a sharp hoe, and chuse a dry day for this purpose. By this means you will easily keep your plantations clean and neat, without much labour; but if they are suffered to grow for any length of time, it will require double labour to extirpate them, besides the injury they will do to the young trees.

৬ Sow Evergreens, Flowering Shrubs, &c. ৪

All the seeds of evergreens, and other seeds intended to be sown this spring, must be put into the ground this month.

The seeds of hardy greens, such as the cedar, cypress, juniper, evergreen oak, acorns, and bays, are the sorts that will yet succeed.

They must be sown in beds of light earth, in the common ground. Some indeed sow them in boxes or pots, in order to remove them to different parts of the garden, according to the season of the year.

Let the beds be about three feet broad, the earth broken very fine, and the surface laid perfectly even.

Each sort of seed must be sown separate, and covered with a proper depth of rich light earth; that is, from half an inch to an inch, according to the size of the seed or kernels.

If you should now sow any of the more choice or tender kinds of trees or shrubs, you would do well to let it be done in pots, and the pots plunged into a hot-bed; for this will greatly forward their growth. Where this convenience, however, is wanting, they may be sown in beds, in the common ground, where very few, especially of the American sorts, will miscarry.

৬ Management of Seed Beds. ৪

Let the seed-beds be watered once every two or three days in dry weather, both before and after the plants begin to appear. Let the waterings be moderate and gentle; for if you at any time apply the water hastily, it would probably wash away the earth from the seed, and also from the young plants when they begin to appear.

You should also be careful to shade, in the middle of hot sunny days, all kinds of seedling trees and shrubs, from the time they appear till they have been up for some time. This will be almost as necessary as water.

It may easily be done by fixing hoops across the bed, and drawing mats over them when necessary.

If your seeds are sown in boxes, pots, or tubs, let them be removed to a shady situation about the middle or latter end of the month.

But wherever they are sown, remember to keep the beds, pots, &c. free from weeds; for if this be neglected the weeds would choke the plants, as they grow much faster. As soon therefore as any weeds appear, let them be taken away; at least before they get any great head. This must be done carefully by hand weeding.

THE FRUIT-GARDEN

❧ Plant Fruit Trees. ☙

You may yet plant apple, pear, plum, and cherry trees, where wanting; they will still succeed; but the sooner it is done the better. It should not be delayed beyond the first week in the month.

White Norman apple
Malus

Be sure you give each tree a good watering as soon as planted; it will be of the utmost service, as it will nourish the tree, and settle the earth close about its roots. The waterings should be repeated once a week, in dry weather.

❧ New Planted Trees. ☙

All new planted trees in general should be watered once a week in dry weather, and remember to water their heads as well as their roots.

At the same time let some mulch be laid on the surface of the ground round their stems; this, with moderate water-ings, will preserve a proper degree of moisture to their roots, and prove very serviceable to their growth.

Gratiola Pear
Pyrum cucumerinum

❧ Vines. ☙

As your vines planted against walls will, by the latter end of the month, have made some shoots, they should then be looked over; and all such as appear to be useless, rubbed off. The old branches generally send forth shoots; but as these rarely produce either grapes or wood proper to bear fruit, they should all be rubbed off close.

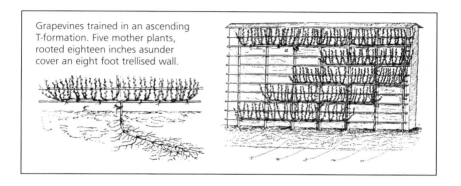

Grapevines trained in an ascending T-formation. Five mother plants, rooted eighteen inches asunder cover an eight foot trellised wall.

The shoots that arise from the last year's wood should not be taken away at present, except where two shoots arise from one eye, the worst of which should be rubbed off; for if both are left they will starve each other, so that the fruit of neither will be good.

Muscadine grape
*Vitis
moschatellinae*

Having thus cleared away all useless shoots, let the others, when of a due length, be trained close to the wall in a regular manner, so that each may equally enjoy the advantage of the sun and air; this will at once promote the growth of the shoot and that of the fruit.

By practising this method the grapes will be fine, the bunches large, and they will ripen early and well.

With regard to vines planted in the vineyard, stakes should now be fixed near them for their support, provided it was not done before. Let these stakes be firmly fixed in the ground, and the vines tied to them at equal distances.

Remember to keep the ground between the rows of vines entirely free from weeds; for the success, with regard to the growth and fineness of the fruit, greatly depends upon keeping the surface clean.

Propagation
of grapevine
by layering.

Whenever, therefore, any weeds make their appearance, let them be destroyed by the hoe the first dry day, before they arrive at any considerable bigness.

☙ Peach, Apricot, and Nectarine Trees. ☙

About the latter end of this month, look over your peach, apricot, and nectarine trees, displacing all such young shoots as are evidently useless. That is, all shoots produced foreright should be rubbed off close: together with those which arise in parts of the tree where they are not wanted, or where they cannot be neatly trained in.

Queens peach
Persica reginea

But all shoots properly situated for training in must be left, and, when of a proper length, trained close and in a regular manner to the wall.

☙ Pruning. ☙

If any pruning still remains to be done, let it be entirely finished the first week in the month; for after that time no tree should be touched with the knife.

℘ Grafting. ℘

Apples, pears, plums, and cherries, may yet be grafted with success, provided the operation be performed at the beginning of the month; but after that time the grafts will not take.

℘ New Grafted Trees. ℘

Look frequently over your new grafted trees, to see if the clay keeps close about them; for it is apt to crack and fall off. Where this happens, let the old clay be taken away, and new placed in its stead; for no wet must be admitted to the graft.

At the same time all the shoots that rise from the stock below the graft, must be rubbed off as soon as produced; for these, if suffered to remain, would rob the graft of its nourishment, and, consequently, prevent its shooting.

℘ New Budded Trees. ℘

Your new budded trees must also now be looked over; we mean those which were budded last summer; for they will now begin to shoot. Examine them carefully with regard to insects, destroying them wherever they are found. If the leaves curl up, insects are the cause of it, and will, if not prevented, spoil the shoot. Let therefore the curling leaves be picked off; this will prevent the mischief from spreading further.

Cherry
Cerasus ilicifolia

Remember that no shoots which come from the stock should be suffered to remain. Let them, therefore, be taken off as soon as they appear, and nothing to be left to draw nourishment from the bud.

℘ Thinning of Fruit. ℘

About the latter end of this month, look over your apricot trees, and where you find the fruit too thick, let some of it be taken away; observing to leave the most promising and best shaped fruit, but not so close together as to touch when grown to their full size.

In order to this begin at one side of the tree, and look over the branches regularly, one by one, singling out on each branch all the fruit you would leave before any are taken away. When the fairest and best situated fruit are thus singled out, let the rest on that branch be cleared away. When you have finished one branch go to the next; and proceed regularly from branch to branch through the whole tree.

℘ Strawberry Beds. ℃

Take care that your strawberry beds be now kept free from weeds. You should also clear away the runners from the plants as they advance; unless

new plantations are wanted, when some of the strongest runners should be suffered to remain.

They will require very frequent waterings in dry weather, especially when they are in bloom; for if they are not well supplied with water at that season, the crop will be thin, and the fruit small and ill tasted.

Manchester
strawberry
Fragaria

℘ Destroy Insects. ℃

Insects are very destructive to fruit trees, so that too much care cannot be taken to destroy them. This is the season when they begin to breed on the leaves of young trees. and also on those of old trees, which are of weaker growth. Proper means should therefore be taken to remove the evil before it spreads too far.

In order to this look over your trees frequently; and where you perceive any of the leaves curled up, you may be sure to find insects there. Let the worst of these leaves be taken off immediately, and the branches well and frequently watered in dry weather.

If you perceive your trees, whether old or young, over-run with insects, pluck off all the curled leaves, and scatter tobacco dust over the branches where the insects are found. This should be done in the morning, and suffered to remain two or three days on the tree.

If tobacco dust cannot easily be had, steep some tobacco in water, about twenty-four hours, and sprinkle the trees where the insects are, with the solution, which will totally destroy them, without injuring either the fruit or the tree.

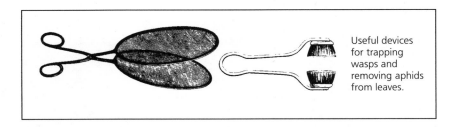

Useful devices
for trapping
wasps and
removing aphids
from leaves.

Large-flowered
painted daisy
Bellis perennis

THE PLEASURE OR FLOWER-GARDEN

❦ Sow Perennial and Biennial Flowers. ❧

You must sow all the perennial and biennial plants intended to be sown this season.

The sorts proper to sow now are sweet-williams, wall-flowers, columbines, stock july-flowers, Canterbury bells, pyramidal campanulas, tree primrose, Greek valerian, hollyhocks, French honey-suckles, single catchfly, rose campion, and scarlet lychnis.

Canterbury bells
Campanula medium

The seed should be sown in beds of light earth three feet wide; and the smaller about a quarter of an inch deep.

Sprinkle the beds frequently with water, in dry weather, both before and after the plants appear above the surface. By this means the plants will grow freely, and soon acquire a sufficient degree of strength.

❦ Transplant Perennial Plants. ❧

You may transplant perennial plants with success, provided it be done at the beginning of the month. Most of the sorts will succeed at this season, particularly golden rods, Michaelmas daisies, perennial asters, perennial sun-flowers, Canterbury bells, columbines, Greek valerian, scabiouses, campanulas, catchfly, rose campion, rockets, lychnises, bachelors buttons, sweet williams, pinks, carnations, polyanthuses, primroses, double daisies, double camomile, thrift, London pride, gentianellas, and some others.

Remember to take up the plants with balls of earth about their roots, if possible, and plant them again immediately in the places where they are to remain.

Water them well as soon as planted, and repeat the operation frequently in dry weather. By this means the plants will all flower this year, each at its respective season.

∞ Dress the Pots Containing Perennial Plants. ଓ

Those parts of perennial plants which were not dressed in March, must now be done in the following manner.

Loosen the earth on the top, and round the sides of the pot; take out the loose earth, and clear away all the decayed leaves from the plant: when this is done, fill the pots again with rich new earth, and give the plants a gentle watering.

This dressing will be very beneficial to the plants, and should be done the beginning of the month, if omitted in March.

Remember also to water all the plants that are in pots, in dry weather. This should be done frequently. or the plants will miscarry.

Fritillaria

∞ Tender Annual Plants. ଓ

A new hot-bed should now be made for the reception of the tender annuals sown in February.

By tender annuals, we mean cockscombs, tricolars, double balsams, globe amaranthus, the egg plant, the double stramonium, and the sicoides, or ice plant.

Where these curious plants are desired to blow in any tolerable degree of perfection, they must now be brought forward by the assistance of a regular and proper degree of artificial heat; and if that circumstance be duly attended to, there is no danger of the plants proving strong, and their flowers being large and beautiful.

Balsam
Impatiens

The bed for this purpose should be full two feet thick, and made of the best hot dung well prepared.

Set the frame upon the bed; and when the burning heat is over, lay on the earth, which must be light and dry, not sifted, but very well broken with the spade and hands, and laid six or seven inches thick on every part of the bed.

In about twenty-four hours after the earth has been laid on the bed, it will be in a proper condition to receive the plants, which must then be taken out of their old bed, with a ball of earth about their roots, and planted in the new bed full six inches apart, every way. Give them a little water as soon as they are planted, to settle the earth about their roots; put on the glasses, and when the sun is so powerful as to cause the plants to flag, throw a single mat over the glasses, continuing this practice till they have taken root.

Remember to raise the glasses a little every day, that the steam from the dung may pass off freely; and if you perceive any quantity of steam in the bed, let one corner of the glasses be raised at night, hanging a mat before the opening.

As soon as you perceive the plants have taken root, and begin to push, let them have plenty of free air every day, in mild and calm weather; for nothing strengthens plants more than a free circulation of air. But the glasses must be shut down every night, provided there be no steam in the bed and a mat thrown over the glasses.

Cockscomb
Celosia argentea

Remember also to refresh them frequently with water, giving them a little at a time; for this will greatly improve their growth.

You must be careful to observe, that when the plants are grown so high as almost to touch the glasses, the frame must be raised about six inches, at the bottom, in order to give them room to shoot; continuing to raise the frame in proportion to the growth of the plants.

But you must remember to close up the vacant space at the bottom every time you raise the frame, by nailing mats at the bottom, that no air may enter but at the proper place. Multiplying or drawing frames are very useful for this purpose, as they may be raised to the height desired without any trouble or danger of injuring the plants, by an admission of too much air at the bottom. A drawing frame may be made in the following manner.

Gentian
Gentiana

Let two, three, or more different frames be made of the same length and breadth, each about nine or ten inches deep except the frame for the glasses, which must be twelve inches deep in front, and eighteen at the back. Let all these be made to fit one another in a very exact manner, so as to be easily fixed upon the top of one another, and, when fixed in that manner together, to appear as one frame.

The very nature of the construction will sufficiently shew the manner in which they are to be used; it is this:

Let the frame containing the glasses be first placed upon the bed; when the plants have almost reached the glasses, let the frame be taken up, and one of the shallow frames placed in its stead, fixing the frame with the lights upon it.

By the addition of this frame, there will be ten inches more room for the plants to shoot; and when they have filled that space, let another frame be added, observing always to place the frame containing the lights uppermost.

About the middle of this month, another hot bed must be prepared for those cockscombs, tricolars, and other plants of that kind, sown in March.

This bed must be at least twenty inches thick of dung, a frame fixed on it, and, when the burning heat is over, covered with dry earth five or six inches deep.

Pansy
Viola tricolor

The plants are to be pricked into this bed at the distance of three or four inches from one another. When this is done, give the plants a gentle watering; put on the glasses, and shade them from the sun, till they are well rooted.

Remember to raise the glasses every day as occasion requires, to let out the steam, and give the plants fresh air.

The same management, in every respect, must be pursued for these, as for those sown in February, and which has been already laid down.

❧ Hardier Kinds of Annual Plants. ❧

Some of the more hardy kinds of annual plants will now be fit to be removed, particularly the marvel of Peru, China aster, balsams of the common kinds, African marygolds, chrysanthemums, scabiouses, capsicums, and several others.

A slight hot-bed must therefore be made for these plants about the middle of this month; twenty inches of dung will be sufficient, covered with five or six inches of good earth.

When the bed is in proper condition, draw from the seed-bed some of the strongest plants, and prick them into the new bed four or five inches distant from one another, giving them a little water. Place the hoops across the bed, and let mats be drawn over them every night, and also during the day, when the weather is cold. At the same time remember, when the weather is warm, to shade the plants from the rays of the sun, till they have taken root.

African
marygold
Tagetes erecta

In this bed the plants are to remain about five weeks, when they may be taken up, with a ball of earth about their roots and planted where they are intended to flower.

ℬ Sow Chrysanthemums, Marvel of Peru, &c. ℭℛ

The seeds of chrysanthemums, marvel of Peru, African marygolds, balsams, China aster, Indian pink, and ten-week-stock, may yet be sown with success.

But it must be done the first or second week in the month, on a moderate hot-bed, often refreshed with water.

The bed must be covered with a frame, or arched over with hoops, and mats drawn over it every night in bad weather.

As soon as the plants appear, let them have plenty of fresh air, by removing the coverings entirely every mild day; remembering to cover them at night, especially in bad weather.

El Dorado
marigold
Tagetes erecta

These plants will be fit to prick out into beds of light earth, in the natural ground, about the middle of May, where they are to continue a month, or five weeks, and then taken up with balls of earth about their roots, and planted in the borders, where they are to flower.

ℬ Sow Hardy Annuals. ℭℛ

It is not yet too late to sow the seeds of hardy annuals in the borders, and other parts of the garden.

The following sorts will yet succeed, namely, convolvulus major and minor, Tangier and sweet-scented peas, nasturtiums, lupines, larkspur, flos Adonis, sweet sultan, candy tuft, dwarf lychnis, Lobel's catchfly, Venus navelwort and looking-glass, Virginia stock, snails, caterpillars, lotuses, dwarf and large annual sun-flower, lavateras, oriental mallows, and many other kinds of hardy annuals.

Nasturtium
Canaris capucine

The seeds should be sown separate, in small patches, in different parts of the borders, according to the method described in the two former months.

Remember to water the patches frequently in dry weather, both before and after the plants appear; for otherwise they will be weak, and their flowers indifferent.

After the plants have been up about a fortnight, let them be thinned, where they appear too thick, remembering to clear away the weakest, and leaving the strongest plants to flower.

Semi-double
Persian Ranunculus
Ranunculus

ᔓ Management of Tulips, Hyacinths, Ranunculuses, &c. ⌘

Tulips, hyacinths, ranunculuses, and anemonies, will now advance apace towards their bloom.

The more curious sorts of these flowers must therefore be now managed with care. They must be defended from heavy rains, and high winds; nor must the sun be suffered to shine freely upon them; the former would greatly injure the plants, and the latter cause them soon to decay.

Hoops must therefore be kept constantly over the beds and mats, or canvas, drawn over them occasionally. By this means you will not only preserve the beauty of the flowers, but also continue the bloom much longer.

Turkestan tulip
Tulipa greigii

Remember that the hoops must be pretty lofty, and nailed to stakes about three feet high, fixed at proper distances on each side of the bed.

Let the mats, or canvas, be drawn over the hoops, about nine or ten in the morning, every sunny day, and continue there till four or five in the afternoon, while the plants are in flower.

When it rains hard, or when the winds are strong, the mats must also be drawn over the hoops; otherwise the flowers will be beat down, and many of their stalks broken.

The flowers should also be sheltered every night, when there is the least appearance of bad weather.

Some of the stalks, particularly of the hyacinths, are not able to support their flowers; in this case, short sticks should be placed near each plant, and the stalk neatly fastened to it with yarn, bass, or some other soft substance.

ᔓ Carnations. ⌘

You must now support the flower-stalks of your carnations, as they will shoot apace at this season.

In order to this, let a sufficient number of handsome straight sticks, of a proper length, be procured. These sticks must be thrust down carefully, near the plants; and the flower-stems, when advanced to a proper height, fastened to them. Remember to tie

Carnations
Dianthus caryophyllus

them between the joints, that the stalks may have full liberty to shoot; and as the stalks advance higher, continue to tie them carefully to the sticks.

It will also be necessary to place sticks near such carnations as are planted in the borders, for such supports will soon be necessary.

But a further care is necessary for those carnations that are planted in pots; indeed too much attention cannot be paid them at this season. Every thing that has a tendency to encourage their growth should now be put in practice.

The pots should be kept perfectly free from weeds, and the plants from decayed leaves. The surface of the earth in the pots should be stirred now and then; for this will at once give an air of neatness to the whole, and greatly encourage the plants in their growth.

Let the plants be often watered in dry weather; every second or third day, at least; but let it be moderate. For if this necessary assistance be wanting, the flowers of the plants will be at once small, and ill-shaped.

ഓ Sow the Seeds of Carnations and Pinks. ଓ

It is not yet too late to sow the seeds of carnations and pinks; especially if it be done the first or second week in the month.

In order to this, let a small spot of rich light ground be neatly dug, and the surface laid very even. Divide this spot into beds of about three feet broad, and sow the seed of each sort separately, on the surface, pretty thick; covering the seed with fine light earth about a quarter of an inch deep.

If the weather should prove dry, these beds should be often sprinkled gently with water; and the plants will appear in about forty days after they are sown.

Double Chinese pink
Dianthus chinensis

This is not the place to give further management of these plants; but it will be resumed in the succeeding months.

ഓ Management of Auriculas. ଓ

Care must now be taken to protect the more curious sorts of auriculas from heavy rains, strong winds, and too much sun; for they will now begin to blow.

Were the sun admitted to shine freely on the plants, they would soon fade; a small shower of rain, or a blast of wind, would deprive these flowers of the meally dust which covers their surfaces, and composes a principal part of their beauty.

Let therefore the pots, as fast as the flowers open, be removed, and placed on the shelves of the stage, or where

Primrose
Primula auricula

the flowers may be occasionally protected from such weather as would effectually deface the bloom.

Remember that the top of the stage must be always covered, but the front only occasionally. In order to this, a mat or canvas should be nailed to the  front, by way of a curtain, and contrived in such a manner, that it may be let down or drawn up at pleasure. By this means the flowers may be effectually sheltered from sharp, or strong winds, and driving rain. But remember to let the curtain be let down no lower than will be sufficient to shade the plants; and never to let it remain down any longer than is absolutely necessary for the defence of the flowers.

Cowslip
Primula veris humilis

Examine the pots once every day, at least, after they are placed on the stand, to see where water is wanting, and to let that want be immediately supplied. But remember not to let the water fall on the flowers, for that would wash off their beautiful dust; and that it be always given them in moderate quantities.

Let the surface of the earth in the pots be kept perfectly neat, free from weeds, and every sort of litter; nor ever suffer any decayed leaves to remain on the plants: let them be taken away as soon as discovered.

If you intended to save any seed from your auriculas, remember to mark the plants you destine for this purpose when in full bloom. A large flower that blows regularly, and lays itself perfectly flat, should be chosen for this purpose. The colours should be lively; the eye large and bright; and the stalk tall, straight, and proportionately strong.

As soon as you have marked the flowers you intend for seed, let the pots be immediately removed off the stage, and plunged into a border where the plants can enjoy the benefit of the morning sun till about ten or eleven o'clock, but no longer.

Remember to water them frequently in dry weather; to suffer no weeds to grow either in or near the pots; nor let them at any time be too much shaded with any large growing plants.

But auriculas are not only increased from seed. They are also propagated from slips or suckers, taken from the old plants; and this is the season to take them off and plant them.

Each slip should be planted singly, in a small pot of fresh earth, and have a little water given them as soon as they are planted. The plants will take root freely, provided they are watered moderately now and then, and deposited in a shady place.

ᔕ Management of Seedling Auriculas and Polyanthuses. ᆰ

These plants, when young, are not able to bear the sun; consequently they must occasionally be shaded from it.

Let therefore the tubs, pots, or boxes, in which these plants are growing, be, about the latter end of the month, removed into the shade. But remember to chuse such a situation as is open to the morning sun till about nine o'clock, and shaded the remainder of the day. They must be often refreshed with water, in dry weather.

You may yet sow the seed of polyanthuses and auriculas, provided it be done the first week in the month; but, after that time, there is great danger of its not succeeding.

ᔕ Plant Flowering Shrubs. ᆰ

The althaea frutex, Persian lilac, bladder and scorpion senas, honey-suckles, jasmines, syringas, laburnums, and some other flowering shrubs, will yet bear transplanting, but the sooner it is done, the better; it should not exceed the first week in the month.

Honey-suckle
Lonicera
sempervirens

Remember to water them well, when they are first planted; and, if the season be dry, repeat the operation once or twice a week.

ᔕ Plant Evergreens. ᆰ

Several evergreen trees and shrubs, particularly pines, firs, cypress, junipers, and cedars; hollies, bays, yews, laurel, Portugal laurel, lauristines, phillyreas, alaturnuses, pyracanthas, cytisuses, cistuses, arbutus, evergreen cassine, and magnolias, may still be planted; but it should be done the first week in the month.

Remember to open a large hole for each tree or shrub, and, when deep enough, to loosen the ground well at the bottom. When this is done, pour into each of them a pot of water, and work up the earth and water with your spade. Then place each plant upright in its hole, and let the earth be well broken and filled in about the roots. When all is in, tread the earth gently round the stem, and form the upper part into a hollow form, to contain a proper quantity of water.

When you have not far to bring the plants, let them be taken up with balls of earth about their roots, and placed in the holes with the balls entire.

But, however that be, remember to give them a good watering as soon as planted, in order to settle the earth about their roots; and then to lay some mulch or litter on the surface of the ground round the stem of each plant; for, otherwise, the earth will dry too fast about their roots, and consequently prevent their growth, if not totally destroy them.

You must also remember to place stakes near such as require support; and to fasten the stem of the plants to them, that the wind, by blowing them to and fro, may not displace their roots.

ᔕ Plant Box and Thrift. ⊂R

Box and thrift may be transplanted for edgings to beds, or borders where wanted; both will grow freely, and the latter, if planted close and neat, will form very agreeable edging.

ᔕ Stick and Trim Flowering Plants. ⊂R

You must now carefully inspect your flowering plants, and place sticks to such as stand in need of support, before they acquire an unsightly growth.

Let the sticks be proportioned to the height of the plant, fixed firm and upright in the ground, and the stalks or stems of the plants tied neatly to them with some soft substance.

Clear away all the decayed leaves from every part of the plant, together with all the straggling and broken shoots; for these will injure the plant, render it unsightly, and prevent its growth.

Ivy-leaved
morning glory
Ipomoea purpurea

ᔕ Break Up and Turn Gravel Walks. ⊂R

Such gravel walks as were not broken up and turned in March, must now be put in order for the summer season. By turning them at this time of year, you will at once destroy the weeds and moss, and give the surface a fresh and lively appearance, which will continue the whole summer.

The method laid down in the foregoing month must be observed in turning, or laying, gravel-walks at this season. That is, it must be done in dry weather, and when you have advanced about twenty feet, to tread, rake, and roll the same regularly as you go on; for gravel never binds so well as when it is first stirred. The roller also will, at that time, have a much greater effect in making the body of the walk firm, and the surface close and even.

It will also be necessary to roll gravel walks that have either been new made, or turned very frequently, twice a week, at least; for by frequent rolling, the walks will be rendered firm and beautiful, and the growth of moss and weeds in a great measure prevented.

so Mow and Roll Grass Walks, &c. ca

This is the season for putting grass walks, lawns, and other pieces of grass in the garden, into the best order. Let the grass therefore be regularly mown, and frequently rolled. In mowing your grass, be particularly careful to cut it as close and even as possible; for the walks and lawns will have a very disagreeable appearance, if the strokes of the scythe are seen.

It will be necessary to mow your grass-walks once a week, to keep them in any tolerable order; for if you once suffer the grass to grow rank, you will find it, at once, laborious and difficult to mow it smooth and level; but if the scythe be frequently applied, the mowing will be performed with ease and exactness. Remember to roll the grass the day before you intend to cut it; for you will find the benefit of it in the morning.

Let your grass-walks be rolled frequently; for this will give the walk a very neat appearance, render the grass thick at the bottom, and greatly contribute to the ease of the mower.

Whenever you perceive any worm-casts upon your grass, let these be broken, and spread with a pliable pole, before you apply the roller; for the worm casts, when first broken and spread, will readily stick to the roller, especially if the roller be of wood. By this means the grass will be made perfectly clean, and you may mow it to a much greater degree of exactness.

so Destroy Weeds. ca

Weeds will now rise plentifully, in every part of the garden, among the plants; let them therefore be destroyed, either with the hoe or hand, before they grow larger.

Remember to keep your hoe sharp, and to take the advantage of a dry day to use it, cutting the weeds up clean below the surface. At the same time, let the ground, in the intervals between the plants, be stirred as you go on, and all the dead leaves and straggling shoots be taken away.

Rake the borders neatly with a small rake, taking away all the weeds and litter, and laying the surface very smooth and even.

MAY

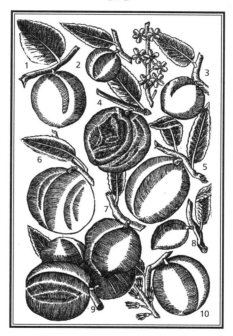

1. Apricot. *Prunus Armeniaca fine Praecocia.*
2. Nutmeg Peach. *Persica Moschatellina.*
3. Melocotone Peach. *Persica Melocotonea.*
4. Black Peach. *Persica nigra.*
5. Long Carnation Peach. *Persica Carnea longa.*
6. Queens Peach. *Persica Reginea.*
7. Peach du Troas. *Persica du Troas.*
8. Almond. *Amygdalus.*
9. Best Romane Red Nectarine. *Nucipersica rubra optima.*
10. Bastard Red Nectarine. *Nucipersica rubra altera.*

Shutters are raised and lowered to protect seedlings planted in frames.

The Works of this Month in the
KITCHEN GARDEN

❧ Cucumber Plants in Frames. ❧

Your cucumber plants under frames will now require an assiduous attendance, as they will be in full perfection for bearing.

They must be frequently, twice a week at least, refreshed with moderate waterings; for if this be omitted, many of the fruit will drop off, and the remainder prove small and ill-tasted. The best time for doing this, is about three or four o'clock in the afternoon.

Snake cucumber
Cucumis flexuosus

Air must be freely admitted to the plants every warm day; for the sun has now great power; so that, if the glasses were kept too close, the heat would destroy the plants. Let therefore the upper ends of the lights be raised every warm sunny morning, about seven or eight o'clock; and continue to raise the glasses higher, in proportion as the heat of the day increases.

But remember to shut the lights down every warm evening about six or seven o'clock; in cold evenings, shut them down an hour or two sooner.

Let the plants be shaded from the sun in very hot days, from eleven till two o'clock.

Remember to keep your glasses at a considerable distance above the plants. This distance should not be less than eight inches in front, and twelve at the back of the frame. This will give them a larger space of air, and, at the same time, lessen the fierce effects of the sun; so that there will be less danger of scorching their leaves, and parching up their roots.

Let therefore the frame be now raised to the above height, and you will soon perceive the benefit of it, by the growth of the plants.

℘ Cucumbers Under Hand or Bell-Glasses. ℃

You may now plant out cucumbers under hand or bell-glasses; and those planted at the beginning of the month, will have fruit fit for the table about the beginning of June, and continue bearing till the plants are destroyed by the cold weather.

But a slight hot bed must be made to plant them in, in order to bring them forward, at first; and it will be the best method to have all, or, at least, the greater part of these hot-beds within the ground.

Let a rich spot of ground be chosen for this purpose, and there dig a trench two feet six inches wide, and about twelve or fifteen inches deep, laying the earth thrown out along the sides of the trench.

Fill this trench with fresh horse dung, and raise it about three inches above the surface of the ground; for the bed must be, at least, fifteen or eighteen inches thick of dung.

When this is done, cover the bed with the earth that was thrown out of the trench; this must be laid eight or nine inches thick over the top of the dung, and the earth extended six inches on each side of the bed beyond the dung.

Then mark out the holes for the plants exactly in the middle of the bed, at three feet six inches from one another.

In each of these holes set two or three good plants, and give them a little water. Put on the glasses, and shade the plants from the sun till they have taken root.

The long prickly, and the long green and white Turkey cucumbers are the most proper for these plantations.

Remember to give these plants air every day in calm warm weather, by tilting up one side of the glasses, and also to refresh them now and then with moderate waterings.

But where proper plants cannot be readily procured to plant in the above bed, let some good seeds be put in; the plants will soon come up, and produce fruit at a very acceptable season.

In order to this, when the bed is made as above directed, mark out the holes for the seed about three feet and a half asunder; make the holes in the form of a shallow basin, about an inch and a half deep; and each of them about ten inches over.

In each of these holes put eight or nine good plump seeds, cover them about half an inch deep with earth, and put the hand or bell-glasses over them.

When the plants have been up about ten or twelve days, they must be thinned, leaving only four of the strongest plants in each hole; drawing, at the same time, some earth about their shanks.

These seeds, if sown the first or second week in May, and properly managed after they come up, will produce fruit fit for the table by the latter end of June.

℘ Sow Cucumbers for Pickling. ℘

The seeds intended to raise cucumbers for pickling should be sown in the natural ground, about the middle of the month; unless the season be cold, or very wet, when it will be better to defer it till the last week in May, or the beginning of June.

Let a piece of rich open ground be prepared for these seeds, divided into beds three feet broad and alleys of twelve inches broad between the beds. You may, if ground be wanting, plant rows of lettuces, savoys, or dwarf kidney-beans, between the beds.

When the beds are thus laid out, place marks for the holes exactly in the middle of the beds, three feet and a half asunder. Dig the places where the holes are to be made, and break the earth well with the spade. This being done, form the holes, with the hand, like a shal-

Long yellow Spanish cucumber
Cucumis hispanicus

low basin, about an inch and a half deep, and ten inches over; sowing in each hole eight or ten seeds, and covering them about half an inch deep with earth.

If the weather should prove hot immediately after the seed is sown, it will be necessary to sprinkle the holes with a little water; but be sure to let the sprinkling be very moderate, for too much moisture would rot the seed.

Remember to thin the plants when they have been up about a fortnight, leaving only five or six of the best and strongest plants in each hole.

It is the common practice with gardeners, where room is wanted, to sow the seed intended to raise cucumbers for pickling, between the rows of early cauliflowers, and other vegetables of that kind, allowing the same distance between the holes as above-mentioned; and as the cauliflowers will be gone by the time the cucumber plants begin to push out their runners, they will not be injured by them.

In cold wet seasons, many of the gardeners near London sow these seeds on a slight hot-bed, and remove the plants when they have been up about a week or ten days.

Their method is this:

They make a bed with new horse dung about a foot thick, adapting the breadth and length to the quantity of plants they intend to raise. This bed they cover with earth about three inches deep, drawing drills with their fingers across the bed. In these drills the seed is sown thick, and in clusters, each consisting of eight or ten good seeds; and covered with earth about half an inch deep. The seeds in the clusters almost touch one another, but a clear space of about three inches is allowed between them: the drills are about two inches asunder. The seeds being thus sown in patches, it will rise in the same manner; and when the plants are fit to be removed, they are taken up in clusters as they grow, with the earth, which will readily hang about their roots, and planted in the places where they are to produce their fruit; allotting one bunch of plants to a hole, and giving them immediately a little water. They will readily take root without flagging their leaves, and require no farther care, except a little water occasionally in dry weather.

This is a very good method in bad seasons, a very large number of plants may be raised by it, with a very little trouble.

ഔ Melons in Frames. ଔ

Your melon plants, whether under frames or bell-glasses, still require particular attention.

Some of the most early plants in the frames will shew fruit in plenty, many of which will be set, and others swelling. All the assistance, therefore, in the power of the art should be given the plants, in order to procure a full crop of fruit.

A proper degree of heat in the beds, while the fruit is setting, and some time after, is a principal thing to be remembered; for a kindly warmth is as necessary to swell the fruit after they are set, as it was to encourage the plants to produce them at first.

In order therefore to keep up this kindly warmth, your beds should be often examined; and whenever you perceive the heat to have declined considerably, let a fresh lining of well prepared hot dung be immediately applied to one or both sides of the beds, as you see occasion: for though there are often very warm days in this month, yet there are often cold nights; and, consequently, it will be necessary to preserve a due degree of heat in the beds, as many of the melons will otherwise turn yellow and fall off, and the rest neither set nor swell kindly.

At the same time the plants in frames must be allowed a good quantity of fresh air every day when the weather is calm and mild. In order to this, the upper end of the lights must be raised with props, two, or three, or four fingers breadth high, in proportion to the warmth of the day; and shut down close every evening about four or five o'clock. By this means the plants will be strengthened, and the setting and free swelling of the fruit greatly promoted.

Remember also to cover the glasses every night with mats, during this month. When the air is cold, the mats should be thrown over the glasses about five in the evening, but when warm, it will be soon enough to do this at six or seven.

Cantaloupe
Cucumis cantalupensis

When the morning is warm and sunny, let the mats be removed by six; but if the weather be cloudy, seven will be soon enough.

You must likewise remember to water your melon plants in frames, for they will require a little now and then, when the weather is warm and sunny. But let these waterings be always moderate, and not too often, for too much water would chill the young fruit, and prevent their settling. Once in ten days will therefore be often enough, and two pots of water sufficient for a three-light frame.

Let always a moderate warm day be chosen for watering your plants, and let it be done about three or four o'clock in the afternoon. Remember to

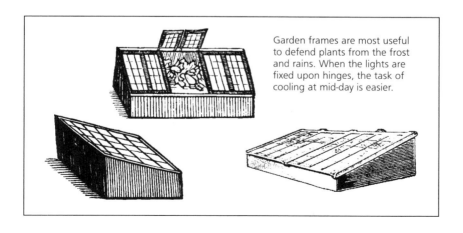

Garden frames are most useful to defend plants from the frost and rains. When the lights are fixed upon hinges, the task of cooling at mid-day is easier.

shut down the lights immediately after watering, and, if the sun shines, throw a mat over the glasses, and let it continue there an hour or two.

In watering these plants, let as little as possible touch the fruit that are about setting, or newly set. The greater part of the water should be applied towards the extreme parts of the bed; and a little only near the head, or main stem of the plant.

When the weather is very warm, you will find it of great advantage to shade the plants from the sun, during two or three hours in the hottest part of the day. Thin mats should be thrown over the glasses about eleven o'clock, and removed at two.

As the melons set, remember to place a piece of tile under each, to preserve them from the damp of the earth in the bed.

It will also be necessary to raise the frame, whenever you perceive the plants too near the glasses. This is done by placing bricks, or square pieces of wood under each corner of the frame: about six inches rise will be sufficient.

☙ Melons Under Hand and Bell Glasses. ☙

You must finish the first or second week in this month your ridges or beds for planting melons intended to be covered with hand or bell-glasses.

These ridges must be made with new horse dung, preferably as directed for making other hot beds in the two months preceding.

Let the ridges be at least a yard broad, four feet will not be too much; and full two feet thick of dung, shaken in equally, and well beat down with the fork.

If you intend to make two or more of these ridges, let the interval or space between them be four feet wide. These spaces or alleys should, in about a month or five weeks after, be filled with dung and earth; for this will greatly assist the setting of the fruit.

When your ridges are ready, cover them with rich earth, well broken with the spade, ten inches thick; mark out the holes for the plants, four feet distance from one another; and set a bell or hand glass over each, keeping the glasses close down till the earth under them is warm.

The ridges being thus prepared, bring the plants; and if they are in pots, turn them carefully out, with the ball of earth entire; make a hole in the ground where each glass stood, and place in each hole one pot of plants, with the ball of earth entire. Close the earth well about the ball, and also about the stems of the plants; pour about a quart of water into each hole, and put on the glasses.

During the first two or three days, the plants must be shaded from the sun, from eight in the morning till about four in the afternoon; but after that time let them have more and more sun every day, till they are able to bear it fully without flagging.

Remember to lift up the warmer side of the glasses every day, to give the plants fresh air; but shut them close down every night; and during this month, cover them with mats.

If any of the melon plants have filled the glasses, let the vines have liberty, about the latter end of the month, to run from under them; but they must not be trusted out before that time.

Pilgrim's gourd
Cucurbita

In order to this let each glass be raised upon props about three inches and a half high, and the ends of the vines laid out, and pegged down, at regular distances from one another.

But remember to cover the ridges with mats every night for fourteen or fifteen days at least, after they are laid out from the glasses.

ꙮ Gourds and Pumpkins. ଜ

The gourds and pumpkins which were sown on a hot-bed in April, should be planted out about the middle of this month, provided the weather be warm.

Remember to plant the orange, and other small gourds near a wall, or other fence, and when the plants begin to shoot, let their vines or runners be neatly trained, and fastened up close to the wall, pales, &c. By this means the plants, together with their fruit, will make a very agreeable appearance, during the month of July, August, and September.

If you have not the conveniency of a wall, or other fence, you may support these plants with sticks, in the following manner: let a tall firm

Pumpkin
Cucurbita pepo

stake be fixed in the ground near each plant; and, in proportions as their vines advance in length, let them be trained up carefully round the stakes.

But pumpkins, and the larger kinds of gourds, should be planted out in an open spot of ground, eight or ten feet from one another; for the vines of these sorts must run upon the ground; and where there is room, they will extend themselves to a very considerable distance.

⅋ Sow Gourds and Pumpkin. ⊂⊋

It is not yet too late to sow the seeds of gourds and pumpkins; but the sooner it is done the better.

The seeds must be sown in a hot-bed; a cucumber or melon bed already made, will answer the purpose. But if this cannot be spared, shake up two or three barrows of fresh horse dung into a bed about thirty inches square; and cover it four or five inches thick with rich earth. Sow the seeds, and cover the bed with a large hand or bell glass.

Fancy gourds
Cucurbita

As soon as the plants appear, let the sunny side of the glass be raised a little every day with a prop, to give the plants fresh air; and let them be often refreshed with water.

About the latter end of this month, or the beginning of June, the plants will have acquired rough leaves, near two inches broad, when they should be planted out in the open ground, eight or ten feet from one another.

⅋ Kidney-Beans. ⊂⊋

A full crop of kidney-beans should now be planted, to succeed those set in April.

The best and most profitable for this plantation are the speckled, and the Canterbury white dwarf sort; though any of the dwarf kinds will succeed.

They should be planted in drills two feet and a half asunder, and the beans laid two or three inches apart in the drills. Draw the earth evenly over them; and, when all are planted, let the surface of the ground be lightly and neatly raked.

Any of the running kinds of kidney-beans may also now be planted.

These are all in general surprising bearers, and therefore very profitable for a family, especially the scarlet flowering bean. There is likewise another kind, which differs in nothing from the scarlet, except in the colour of its flowers, which is white; but when fit to gather for the table cannot be distinguished from the scarlet, either in taste or manner of growth. Either of these, or any of the large white running kinds, are very proper for this plantation.

But you must remember that these, or any of the climbing kinds of kidney-beans, require more room to grow than the dwarf sorts. The drills therefore for these should be three feet and a half asunder, the beans placed five or six inches apart in the drills, and covered equally with earth about an inch and a half deep.

As soon as the plants are come up, and begin to push their runners, let some tall sticks or poles be placed to each row, for the plants to climb upon. The runners will soon take hold of the sticks, and twine themselves very naturally round them, to the height of eight or ten feet, provided the sticks are of that height.

You will derive great advantage by planting these runners at this season; for they will continue bearing till the cold weather destroys the plants.

But if you cannot procure the sticks or poles, the dwarf kinds should be planted; for the runners will not succeed without them.

♄ Sow Lettuce Seed. ♙

The seed of lettuce should be sown at two or three different times this month, that there may be a constant supply of these plants for the table.

The Coss and Silesia are the proper kinds to sow now; though the brown Dutch may be sown with success, if required.

Cabbage lettuce
Lactuca

Remember to sow the seeds in an open situation, and in a light, rich soil. Sow each sort separate, and rake in the seed with a light and even hand.

It will be necessary often to refresh the beds where the seed is sown, with water, especially if the weather proves very dry; for otherwise the seed will not grow.

♄ Transplant Lettuces. ♙

The Coss, Silesia, and other kinds of lettuce sown in the preceding month, should now be transplanted.

In order to this, let a rich spot of ground, not too much exposed to the sun, be chosen for this purpose. Let it be dug about a spade deep, the surface raked very smooth, and the plants removed to it in the evening.

They must be planted in rows ten or twelve inches asunder, and as they are set, give them some water to settle the earth about their roots.

♄ Small Salletting. ♙

Let the seeds of cresses, mustard, radish, rape and other small sallet herbs, be sown often; every five or six days at least, if a constant supply be wanted.

If the weather be hot and dry, these seeds must now be sown in a shady border, where the ground

Watercress
Nasturtium officinale

is rich and light. Draw shallow drills for this purpose, sow the seed in them tolerably thick, and cover them lightly with earth. Remember to let them have a little water every other day in dry weather.

⚬ Turnips. ⚬

Let more turnip seed be sown now: the roots will come in a very acceptable season; for they will be fit for the table by the middle or latter end of

July, and continue good for a long time.

But remember not to sow the seed in hot dry weather, for it will not then succeed. The proper time for sowing turnips, and all small seeds of that kind, is when the weather is showery; for then there is no fear of its growing.

Early white & scarlet turnips
Brassica rapa
White tipped scarlet radish
Raphanus sativus

Let the seed be sown equally pretty thick, and on an open spot of light ground. Take care also to rake it in lightly and regularly.

Those turnips which were sown the former month should now be thinned regularly, allowing seven or eight inches between plant and plant; observing, at the same time, to cut up all the weeds.

⚬ Spinach. ⚬

It is not yet too late to sow spinach, for it will succeed tolerably well, if sown in an open situation.

And if a succession of this plant be required, a little of the seed must be sown every twelve or fourteen days.

With regard to the spinach sown the preceding month, it must now be hoed and thinned, leaving the plants about five inches asunder, and cutting down all the weeds under the surface

⚬ Sow Carrots. ⚬

You may still sow carrot seed where it is required; it will grow freely, and the plants will appear soon, and be ready for the table by the latter end of July, or the beginning of August.

⚬ Dress the Beds of Carrots and Parsnips. ⚬

The beds of carrots and parsnips sown in the foregoing months, will now be advanced considerably in their growth, and should therefore be properly encouraged.

Let them therefore be cleared from weeds, and the plants separated to a proper distance from one another.

The small hoe is the best and most expeditious instrument for this purpose; for it will not only effectually destroy the weeds, and such plants as are thought improper to stand, but also greatly promote the growth of the remainder, by loosening the surface of the ground.

If you cannot use the small hoe, the work must be done by hand, or the common hoe, for the plants must, at any rate, be thinned out to proper distances, that they may have room sufficient to grow at the top, and swell at the bottom.

With regard to parsnips, they must not stand closer than six or seven inches from one another; for their roots will be both large and straight, if they have room sufficient to expand themselves.

Parsnip
Pastinaca sativa

Nor is this less necessary with regard to carrots; but in thinning these plants, the time they are intended to continue in the ground is to be considered.

If they are intended to be drawn young for the table, they should now be thinned out to four inches asunder; but if they are to remain till they attain their full growth, six or seven inches every way will be necessary.

ᔕ Management of Savoys and Cabbages. ᙢ

Those savoy and cabbage plants which are intended for winter use, must be now transplanted.

They may be set between rows of early cauliflowers; or between the wider rows of garden or kidney-beans, where room is wanting. But where there is ground unoccupied by other crops, it will be much the best method to plant out these in an open spot by themselves.

Let the rows, in which they are planted, be two feet asunder, and the plants set eighteen inches apart in the rows. Observe to plant them in moist weather, and to give each a little water immediately after planting.

Brussels sprouts
Brassica oleracea gemmifera

The earth must now be drawn up about the stems of early and other cabbages. This work is absolutely necessary, as it will greatly strengthen them, and bring them forward amazingly in their growth.

About the latter end of the month, the early plants will begin to turn their leaves for cabbaging; they should therefore be assisted in this operation, by tying the leaves together.

In order to this let some strong bass or small withies be procured, and go over the plants row by row, tying such as have begun to turn their leaves pretty much inwards. But in doing this, observe to gather the leaves of the plant up very regularly, and then tie them together with the bass or withy; but not tie them too close, for that will occasion the plants to rot.

By this means the plants will be fit to use a fortnight at least sooner than they would be if left entirely to themselves; at the same time they will be much whiter, and more tender in eating.

☙ Sow Cauliflower Seed. ☜

The cauliflower plants raised from seed sown at this season, will produce their flowers in October, and continue in great perfection the whole month of November, a season when they will be very acceptable to most families.

But the seed should not be sown before the last week in this month; for otherwise the plants will flower too soon.

Let a bed of rich earth three feet wide, in an open situation, be prepared for this purpose. Let the seed be sown equally, moderately thick, and lightly raked in with an even hand.

You should remember to shade the bed every hot sunny day, from ten to three o'clock, till the plants appear, and are all fairly come up; also to sprinkle the bed often with water in dry weather.

☙ Management of Cauliflower Plants. ☜

Your beds of early cauliflowers must be often looked over carefully, about the middle and latter end of this month; for some of the plants will then begin to shew their flowers; and as soon as these appear they should be screened from the sun and wet; for either of these would change their colour from a white to a yellow.

Remember therefore to break down three or four of the largest of the inner leaves over the flower, as soon as ever it appears in the heart of the plant.

This will answer the double purpose of shading the flower from the sun, and defending it from wet. By this simple contrivance the flower will be preserved in its natural whiteness, and at the same time be close, firm, and beautiful.

Observe to water these plants frequently in dry weather; for this will cause the heads or flowers to grow to a larger size.

If you did not transplant the young cauliflowers raised this spring from seed, let that work be done now, and the sooner in the month the better.

In order to this, let a piece of the richest ground be chosen for their reception, spread over it some good rotten dung, and dig the ground one spade deep, observing to bury the dung regularly as you proceed.

The plants must be set in this spot two feet, or two feet and a half asunder every way. Remember to water them as soon as they are planted.

You may, if you please, sow a crop of spinach on this piece of ground, between the cauliflower plants, without doing them any great injury.

ℰ❧ Sow Broccoli. ❧ℛ

The seeds for the principal crop of both the purple and white kinds of broccoli must be sown this month.

It will indeed be prudent to sow a little of the seed at two different times during the month; and if a constant supply be desired, a little of both kinds should be sown during the first week, and the second, or principal sowing between the fifteenth and twenty-fifth of the month. For the plants raised from the first sowing will, provided the weather be mild, be fit for the table by Christmas, or a little after; while the second, intended principally for spring use,

Broccoli
Brassica oleracea italica

will produce fine heads in February and March; and after the heads are gone, the stems will yield excellent sprouts in great abundance.

Remember to sow the seeds in a bed or border in an open situation, but not wholly exposed to the rays of the sun. Let each kind be sown on a separate spot, and the seeds raked in with an even hand.

ℰ❧ Bore-cole. ❧ℛ

Bore-cole, or, as it is often called Scotch-Kale, is a very useful plant, and well worth the little trouble that attends the raising of it. There are two sorts of it, the brown and the green. The plants run up

with very long stems, sometimes three, four, or five feet high, and are so very hardy, that they will survive the most severe winters; and in the months of February and March, their long stems will be loaded from the very bottom to the top with fine young shoots, which will boil and eat as tender as the best savoy.

Bore-cole
Brassica oleracea acephala

The seed should be sown the first week in this month; but if you desire the plants to grow very high, it will be better if sown about the middle of April. But whatever time be chosen, let the seed be sown on an open spot of good ground, and raked in lightly with an even hand. Remember to give the beds now and then a moderate watering in dry weather.

In about six weeks after the seed is sown, the plants will be fit to plant out in the place where they are to remain.

ଔ Beans. ଔ

Let another crop of garden beans be now planted; the white blossom and long podded beans are the most proper for this season.

If a constant succession of young beans be desired during the summer season, it will be necessary to set a few at different times this month, viz. about the third, fifteenth, and twenty-seventh.

If you are desirous of planting either the Windsor or Sandwich bean, let it be done at the beginning of the month, when either of these will often succeed tolerably well.

ଔ Peas. ଔ

Another crop of peas should also be sown now; and if a regular supply be wanted, let a few be sown twice at least in the month, if three times it will be the better, allowing about ten days between each sowing.

The marrowfats will succeed very well, if sown any time this month. The hotspur kinds sown at this season, will sometimes yield very good crops.

The dwarf kinds of peas generally succeed extremely well when sown this month. These seldom rise above two or three feet high, but are excellent bearers.

The dwarf kinds should be sown in drills two feet asunder, which will be room sufficient for them.

The earth must now be drawn up about the stems of those peas which were sown in April; for this will add strength to the plants, and greatly increase their growth.

ଔ Stick Peas. ଔ

When the peas you intend to stick are about six or seven inches high, the sticks must be added to the rows.

Remember to let your sticks be of a height adapted to the different sorts of peas; and be assured that those which have sticks to support them, will yield more than double the quantity of those which have none.

ᔓᗡ Radishes. ᦿᖇ

You may yet sow radish seed where required; but you must remember to water the bed frequently in dry weather, both before and after the plants appear.

Those radishes you intend for seed, must be transplanted when their roots are just in their prime, which will happen some time in the beginning of this month.

Let those roots which are long, perfectly straight, and whose tops are short, be chosen for this purpose; and planted on an open spot of ground in rows two feet asunder, and the plants eighteen inches apart in the rows. Remember to give a plentiful watering as soon as they are planted, to settle the earth about their roots.

Rose China winter radish
Raphanus sativus

ᔓᗡ Sow Celery. ᦿᖇ

Let the seed intended for a latter crop of celery be sown the second week in the month.

In order to this, let a bed of rich light earth be dug, and the surface laid perfectly level. When this is done, sow the seeds pretty thick, and rake them lightly into the ground.

Remember to shade the bed from ten to three o'clock, till the plants appear; for the noon tide rays of the sun would otherwise destroy the seed.

It will also be necessary to refresh the bed frequently with water in dry weather. And by this method the plants will be fit to be planted in trenches in August and September; and soon after Christmas fit for the table.

ᔓᗡ Prick Out Celery. ᦿᖇ

Prick out the plants of celery sown in March from the seed beds, about the latter end of this month.

The bed intended for the reception of these plants must be three feet and a half broad, the earth well dug, and the surface laid smooth. When the bed is thus prepared, draw out some of the best plants from the seedbed, and prick them into the other, three inches asunder every way. Give them a gentle watering, and shade them from the sun till they have taken root.

In this bed the plants are to remain till they have acquired a sufficient degree of strength, when they are to be transplanted into trenches, and there blanched for the table.

Celery
Apium graveolens dulce

໕ Sow Endive. ໕

A little endive seed should now be sown for an early crop; and if a constant supply of this plant be wanted, a small quantity should be sown at two different times this month; viz. about the middle and latter end.

The plants arising from the seed first sown will not long continue fit for use, because it will be apt to run to seed; but the plants from the second sowing will continue longer, and be fit for use at a very acceptable season.

But whatever time be chosen, the seed should be sown pretty thick, on a spot of rich ground, and raked in lightly with an even hand.

໕ Transplant Capsicums for Pickling. ໕

Red & green peppers
Capsicum annum

The capsicums sown on a hot-bed in March, should be planted out in moist weather, about the latter end of this month.

In order to this, let a spot of rich ground be chosen, well dug, and the surface raked smooth and even. When the bed is thus prepared, take up the plants, and set them in rows a foot asunder every way. Give them a gentle watering, and shade them from the sun till they have taken root.

໕ Transplant Love Apples for Soups, &c. ໕

Pear tomato
Lycopersicon pyriforme

About the middle of this month is a proper time to remove the tomatoes, or love apples, from the hot-bed in which they were raised.

As these plants are very luxuriant and rambling in their growth, they should be planted close to some wall, pale, or espalier; and when they begin to branch out, let them be nailed to the fence in the manner of a wall tree.

Remember to plant them against a wall, &c. with a south aspect, for otherwise the fruit will not ripen. The vacant spaces between the wall trees, will be sufficient for this purpose.

One stout plant in a place is enough. Let them be watered as soon as planted, and shaded from the sun till they have taken root. If you shelter them in cold nights for the first fortnight after they are transplanted, it will be of great advantage to their growth.

❧ Dress Onion Beds. ❧

The beds of onions should be now perfectly cleared from weeds, and the plants thinned out to three or four inches asunder. Remember to leave the strongest plants for a crop.

❧ Hamburg Parsley, Scorzonera, and Salsafy. ❧

Your beds of Hamburg parsley, scorzonera, and salsafy, must now be carefully cleared, and the plants thinned or hoed out to six or seven inches distance from one another.

The seeds of the two latter should now be sown for winter crops; for they are very apt, when sown early, to run to seed, before they are hardly fit for use. But those sown at this season will not run up, but be in proper order for the table by Michaelmas.

❧ Sow Pot-Herbs, &c. ❧

You may still sow parsley-seed, where it was omitted in the former months; but it must be done in a shady situation, where the sun has not too great power.

Coriander
Coriandrum sativum

At the beginning of the month a little more purslane seed should be sown, that the plants may succeed those which were sown in April.

In order to this, make choice of a spot of light rich earth in the open ground; break the clods well with the spade, and rake the surface very even. Then draw shallow drills about six inches asunder, sow the seed pretty thick in the drills, and cover it with earth. Some sow the seed on the surface, and rake it in lightly; either method will succeed, for the plants will grow freely.

If coriander be wanting, this is a proper season for sowing a little more of the seed. It should be sown in the same manner with the purslane, in shallow drills six inches asunder.

Chervil seed will still grow; if these plants therefore be wanted, let a little of the seed be sown in shallow drills and covered lightly with earth.

❧ Plant Mint. ❧

You may still make fresh beds of mint, provided it be done the first or second week in the month; but after that time you will find it very difficult to find a sufficient number of good plants.

The plants must be about six or seven inches long, drawn up carefully with their roots to them from the old buds, and planted on a spot of rich ground, in rows six inches asunder, and the plants four inches apart in the rows. Remember to give them a plentiful watering as soon as planted, to settle the earth about their roots.

☞ Plant Sage, Savory, Hyssop, &c. ☜

The slips or cuttings of sage, savory, hyssop, mastich, rosemary, lavender, may now be planted; they will grow freely.

Let such slips as have a sufficient degree of strength, and about five, six or seven inches long, be chosen for the purpose: strip off the leaves, if there be any, from the bottom; twist that part of the stalk a little, and set them about five or six inches apart, and about two thirds of them into the ground.

Remember to plant them in a shady situation, and to give them now and then a moderate watering in dry weather.

☞ Destroy Weeds. ☜

A more than common degree of care will now be necessary, with regard to destroying of weeds among the crops, in every part of the garden; for weeds are at no time more pernicious than at present. If they are suffered to grow too large, they will not only exhaust the ground, and consequently starve the plants, but also render the whole garden very disagreeable. Let it, therefore, be one of the principal works to destroy them.

Particularly, let your crops of onions, leeks, carrots, parsnips, lettuce, and other small plants that grow pretty close together, be cleaned from weeds, before they begin to spread, and over-top the plants, which they will soon do, when once they begin to run.

You should also remember that the weeds, if suffered to grow large among the small crops, will so mix and entangle themselves, that the work of weeding will be rendered at once extremely tedious, and extremely troublesome.

It will indeed be otherwise with regard to the weeds that appear between the rows of beans, peas, kidney-beans, cabbages, cauliflowers, and other crops planted in rows at a distance from one another; for their progress may then be stopped with the greatest ease; because the intervals are wide enough to admit a large hoe; and with the help of such an instrument, a person may go over a large piece of ground in a little time. And surely a task so easily performed should not be neglected, especially when it is considered that it will prove of the greatest advantage to the plants.

European beech
Fagus sylvatica

THE NURSERY

℘ Propagate Evergreens, &c. by Layers. ℘

This is a very proper season for propagating such evergreens, and other shrubs, by layers, as do not freely put out roots from any wood but the young shoots of the same summer's growth. The shoots of many shrubs of this kind will have a size proper for this purpose by the latter end of the month, and some of these should therefore be then layed down.

In order to this, let some of the more pliant branches that afford the strongest and best young shoots be brought down gently to the ground, and there firmly secured with hooked pegs. When this is done, let some of the young shoots be laid into the earth, and covered two or three inches deep with the mould, leaving about two or three inches of the top of each shoot out of the ground.

When they are thus laid in the ground, let a moderate watering be given them to settle the earth closely about the shoot, and repeated every five or six days in dry weather; but remember not to give them too much at one time, lest it rot the tender fibres when they first shoot from the wood.

℘ New Grafted and Budded Trees. ℘

You must now look carefully over your new grafted and budded trees, loosening the bandages, and taking away all the clay, for there will be no further occasion for it.

Remember not to let any shoots that rise from the stocks below the grafts remain; but let them be rubbed off as soon as they appear, for they have no other tendency than to rob the graft of its nourishment. This care must be extended to the trees that were grafted the year before; for no shoots must be suffered to remain below the graft.

ଔ Water Seedling Plants. ଔ

Umbrella pine
Sciadopitys verticillata

If the weather prove dry at this season, you must often refresh the seed-beds of all young trees and shrubs, in general, with water.

But at the same time take care not to do it too hastily, as the earth would by that means be washed away, and the tender roots of the plants would be burnt up by the rays of the sun.

Three gentle waterings every week will be sufficient, and prove highly advantageous to the plants.

ଔ Shade Seedling Plants. ଔ

Your seedling pines, cedars, cypresses, and other evergreens, should now be shaded, in hot weather, from the noon-tide rays of the sun, which will be now too powerful for them.

ଔ Water New Plantations. ଔ

If the weather proves dry, it will be necessary to water your ever-greens, and flowering shrubs, that were transplanted in March, once in five or six days, at least once a week.

At the same time, let the mulch on the surface of the ground be continued over the roots of the more curious or tender kinds of these shrubs, for this will be of the utmost service, in preventing the sun from drawing away the moisture from their roots.

ଔ Destroy Weeds. ଔ

Weeding is one of the most necessary works in the nursery at this season.

The seed-beds of all young trees and shrubs should be now carefully weeded by hand.

Nor must the weeds be suffered to grow between the rows of your young trees or shrubs. This may indeed be easily prevented, by the frequent use of a large sharp hoe; but remember to let it be done in dry days.

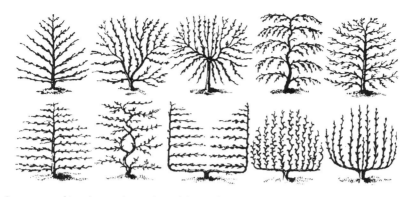

Some ways of London gardeners for training and regulating wall and espalier trees for most fruit and ease of gathering.

THE FRUIT-GARDEN

℘ Wall and Espalier Trees. ଔ

Your apricot, peach, nectarine, plum, cherry, apple and pear trees, will make strong and numerous shoots at this season; these should therefore now be properly regulated, and trained close to the wall, before they become confused.

At this same time, let all useless and ill-placed shoots be taken away. All foreright shoots, or such as are produced from the front of the branches, are of this kind; for they cannot, from the very nature of their situation, be properly trained in, and consequently become useless.

Pear 'No More'
Pyrus

But all side shoots of a moderate kind and growth, and well situated for laying in, must be left, and trained in a regular order, close to the wall.

You should be particularly careful to leave as many of the well-placed shoots of apricots, peaches, nectarines and morella cherry trees, as can be conveniently laid in; for these trees produce the principal part of their fruit upon those shoots that are one year old; that is, those which you lay in this summer, will bear fruit the next.

Pear
*Pyrus
communis*

A sufficient quantity therefore, of these shoots should be now laid in, that a proper number of the best of them may be left in the winter-pruning, and the rest taken away.

Remember that these shoots must be trained very regularly, at full length, and nailed as close as possible to the wall, or espalier. They must not, on any consideration, be shortened now, for that would cause them to produce, from their sides, a number of small useless shoots, which would

weaken and hurt the principal shoots, by forming too close a shade, so as to exclude the sun and air from having that free access to the fruit which is absolutely necessary to its proper growth. For though a slight shade is absolutely necessary to promote the growth of wall-fruit, yet too much of it is destructive.

Flanders cherry
Cerasus batavica

At the same time, it must be observed, that this caution is not extended to those parts of the wall, or espalier, that are vacant; for there some of the adjacent young shoots must now be shortened; for by this means they will put out side or lateral shoots, to supply the vacant parts.

℅ Thin Apricots, Peaches, &c. ∝

If you perceive the fruit on any of the apricot, peach, or nectarine trees too thick, let some of them be now taken away.

For it should be observed, that these trees will sometimes, in favourable seasons, set three times more fruit than their roots are able to supply with

nourishment; and if the whole, or even too many of them, were to be left, they would starve one another, and the fruit, in general, would be small and ill tasted.

Nor would the mischief end with the season, it would be extended to two or three succeeding years. For the trees, from the too great quantity of fruit, would not be able to produce shoots proper for bearing fruit the next year; and, at the same time, the trees would be so much exhausted,

Apricot
*Prunus armeniaca
fine praecocia*

that they would not recover strength sufficient to produce any proper wood before the second year after; consequently a tolerable crop could not be expected before the third year.

When therefore a tree is over-loaden with fruit, let them be now reduced to a moderate quantity; and the sooner this is done the better it will be both for the tree and the remaining fruit.

Nor should this thinning be performed in a careless manner; the branches should be regularly looked over one by one, singling out the fruit you intend to leave on each branch before you take any away.

The most promising and best shaped fruit, provided they are properly situated on the branches, should be left at such distances, that each may have sufficient room to swell, and grow freely to its full bigness, every way, without touching another; five or six inches will be sufficient room for all the middling kinds of fruit.

At the same time, some regard should be had to the strength of the branches. Suppose, for instance, the bearing shoots, or branches, to be of three different sizes, strong, middling, and weakly; you may leave three of the fairest and best placed fruit on the strong, two upon the middling, and one only on the weaker branches.

Melocotone peach
Persica melocotonea

If the above cautions, with regard to the distances between the fruit, and the nature of the branches, be observed in thinning the trees, they will doubtless bring each kind to its full perfection. At the same time the trees will shoot freely, and produce a sufficient quantity of bearing wood for the succeeding year.

The smaller kinds of fruit, such as the masculine apricots, the nutmeg-peaches, and early nutmeg-peaches, may be left closer to one another, and a greater number of them suffered to remain on the branches.

Four or five of them, for instance, may be left on the strong; three on the middling; and two on the weaker branches.

✍ Vines. ଛ

At this season your vines will shoot vigorously, and send out, besides bearing, and other useful shoots, numbers of others that are altogether useless; these should therefore be taken away, and the sooner this is done the better.

Art will greatly assist nature, in ripening grapes in an unfavourable season; and this is the time for employing it.

In order to this, the vines must now be perfectly cleared from all kinds of useless shoots; and, at the same time, all the fruit-bearing branches, and other well-placed useful shoots, should be nailed up regularly and close to the wall.

Royal muscadine grapes
Vitis rotundifolia

This work should be done before the shoots begin to entangle, or any way interfere with one another; for very great advantages attend this early dressing and regulating the vines; nor is there any other method of bringing the bunches of these fruit to any degree of perfection, but by timely nailing in the useful shoots, and clearing the vines of such as are useless.

All the bearing shoots, that is, such as have fruit upon them now, must be left, together with such other shoots as have strength, and are well situated for training, in order to produce fruit next year.

But all weak and straggling shoots, such as rise immediately from the old wood, are useless, and must be taken away, wherever they are produced; and even strong shoots that are destitute of fruit, and that rise in places where they are not wanted, or not well placed for training in to produce fruit next year, should be displaced.

When this is done, let all the bearing shoots, together with those that are useful, and produced in proper places, be nailed in regular order, close to the wall. Remember not to stop any of the shoots now, but let each, for the present, be trained up at its full length.

The shoots must not be nailed up promiscuously across each other, as is often practiced; but let every shoot be laid in strait, and clear of another, in a regular manner, so that each shoot, and every branch of fruit, may equally enjoy the advantage of the sun and free air.

After this, observe that all shoots that rise in any part of the vines must be constantly rubbed off, as soon as they appear; let not, on any account, these small shoots which commonly rise from the sides of the same summer's shoots now laid in, remain; but let these also be rubbed off, as soon as they begin to advance.

℘ Vineyards. ⊗

The vines planted in the vineyard also require a very large share of attention. All the shoots that have fruit upon them, and others that are strong and well placed for the service of another year, must now be trained up close and regularly to the stakes.

At the same time, the vines must be cleared from all useless wood, and also from all such shoots as are barren of fruit, or produced in such places, that they cannot be trained for the service of another year; let all these be rubbed off close.

Remember to keep the ground between the vines clear from weeds; a caution necessary to be observed during the whole summer season; for if weeds of any considerable size be suffered to grow near the vines, they will not only rob them of their nourishment, but also greatly retard the growth of the grapes, by keeping a continual chilly dampness about the vines. Let therefore the hoe be applied to them whenever they are found; but remember to do it in a dry day.

Examine the stakes that support the vines; let them be firmly fixed, and in their proper places; and that all the fruitful shoots, and others that are well situated, be neatly and securely fastened to them.

℘ Strawberry Plants in Blossom. ℘

Alpine strawberry
Fragaria vesca

If the weather prove dry this month, the strawberry plants, which will be now in full blossom, must be watered very frequently; thrice a week, at least; and let the waterings be sufficient to reach the roots of the plants. For if this necessary work be omitted, your crop of strawberries will be very little, and those that are produced small and ill-tasted.

℘ Examine New Grafted and New Budded Trees. ℘

Let the trees of all sorts grafted this spring be now examined, and wherever you find the graft and stock well united, take away both the clay and the bandage, for they will be then both useless.

At the same time examine the trees that were budded last summer, and take away all the shoots that rise from the stock besides the bud; for the stock should have nothing to supply with nourishment but the bud, which will therefore shoot with more vigour.

℘ Cleanse the Fruit Tree Borders. ℘

Remember to keep the borders where wall and espalier fruit trees grow very clean from weeds, for these exhaust the nourishment, prove a harbour to slugs and insects, and give the whole an unsightly appearance.

When sufficient space or a wall be not at hand, dwarf fruit trees may be trained to grow in spirals by fixing them to stakes. When the proper shape has been attained, remove the stakes.

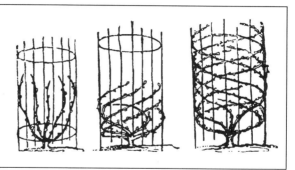

As soon, therefore, as any weeds appear, let them be eradicated, which will be easily done with a sharp hoe; but let it be done in a dry sunny day.

੪੨ Destroy Snails, Insects, &c. ੦੩

Most of the wall fruits, especially peaches, nectarines, apricots, &c. are very liable to be greatly injured by snails; let the trees therefore be looked over carefully in the morning and evening, the times when these vermin leave their holes to feed upon the fruit, when they may be easily destroyed.

If you perceive your wall trees are annoyed with any kind of insects, let them be destroyed as soon as perceived; for after they begin to attack any single branch of a tree, they will soon over-run the whole, if not prevented. The best method of destroying them is this:

Take away all the leaves that are infected with them; that is, such as are shrivelled or curled up; then strew some tobacco dust over all the branches and leaves, letting it remain there two or three days, and then wash it off, by giving the trees a thorough watering all over their branches; for if the tobacco dust was suffered to remain any longer, it would injure the trees.

A hand engine will be highly useful for watering wall trees. For by the help of this a person may stand in the walks, and, with great ease and expedition, throw the water against any part of the trees, from the bottom to the top of the wall, even supposing it fifteen or twenty feet high; and this is by far the most easy, expeditious, and effectual method of watering these trees. For the force of the water will clear the leaves and branches from dust, cob-webs, or any other filth they may have contracted; and if these waterings are repeated now and then, in very dry weather, no insects can breed upon the trees.

Experience only can fully shew the great service that wall trees, in general, receive from being watered in this manner all over their branches, in dry hot weather.

੪੨ Water New Planted Trees. ੦੩

Remember to refresh your new planted trees, whether standards or dwarfs, with water, once a week at least, in dry weather; and let them sometimes be watered all over their branches. If no mulch be laid on the surface of the ground over their roots, they should be watered moderately twice a week, in dry weather.

THE PLEASURE OR FLOWER-GARDEN

∞ Sow Ten-Week-Stocks, &c. ∞

You may still during the first or second week in this month sow ten-week-stocks, China aster, and Indian pink.

A small bed of rich light earth should be prepared for them in the natural ground, where the plants will soon come up and grow freely, if often refreshed with water, in dry weather, and sheltered in cold nights with mats.

Horned poppy
Glaucium

∞ Sow the Seeds of Hardy Annuals. ∞

The seeds of several of the sorts of annual plants, particularly lupines, sweet sultan, flos Adonis, white and purple candy tuft, Lobel's catch-fly, dwarf lychnis, dwarf poppy, Virginia stock, Venus navelwort and Venus looking-glass, snails, caterpillars, dwarf annual sun-flower, lavatera, oriental mallow, nasturtiums, convolvulus major and minor, Tangier and sweet-scented peas, may be still sown in the borders with success.

Althaea frutex
Hibiscus syriacus

But remember to sow them in small patches, in the places where you would have them flower; for none of these sorts succeed after being transplanted. Remember also to sprinkle frequently with water the patches where they are sown, in dry weather.

∞ Sow Perennial Flower Seeds. ∞

The seeds of stock july-flowers, sweet-williams, columbines, carnations, pinks, scabiouses, Canterbury-bells, pyramidal bell-flowers, holly-hocks, French honey-suckles, and some others, may still be sown with success, provided it be done the first or second week in the month.

Double sweet William
Dianthus barbatus

Let a spot of light rich ground, not too much exposed to the sun, be chosen for these seeds; break the earth well as you dig it, and divide the bed into as many parts as you intend to sow different kinds of seed.

When the bed is thus prepared and divided, let the seeds be sown as equally as possible, and raked in with an even hand. Or, which perhaps is a better method, draw off about an inch deep of earth from the surface, with the back of the rake, into the alleys, and then scatter the seed equally on the bed. This being done, draw the earth that was turned off the bed, in an even manner over the seed, and lightly smooth the surface with a rake.

By pursuing this method the plants will come up strong, and produce abundance of flowers next month.

ᴔ Transplant Biennial and Perennial Flower-Plants. ᴄᴗ

Most of the biennial and perennial flower-plants sown in March will be fit for transplanting about the third week in the month; particularly the wall-flowers, stock july-flowers, columbines, sweet-williams, single scarlet lychnis, rose campion, and catch-fly. Those also which were sown early in the

spring, as Canterbury-bells, Greek valerian, tree-primrose, foxgloves, French honey-suckles, and holly-hocks, may be transplanted about the latter end of this month.

But remember that they must be removed into the nursery beds, in order to get strength, before they are planted out for good.

In order to this, let a spot of good clean ground be

Small-leaved foxglove
Digitalis

dug, raked very even, and divided into beds three feet and a half broad.

When this is done let the plants be set in rows, six inches every way from one another, and each sort separate. As soon as they are planted, let them be moderately watered to settle the earth about their roots.

In these nursery beds they are to remain till September or October, when they must be planted out where they are to remain. They will flower, and make a very elegant appearance next summer.

ᴔ Remove Hardy Annual Plants. ᴄᴗ

The more hardy annual plants, as the African and French marigolds, chrysanthemums, marvel of Peru, China aster, Indian pink, ten-week-stock, persicarias, the common kinds of balsams, capsicums, and mignonette; purple amaranthus-es, scabiouses, egg-plants, and love-apples, may, about the middle of the month, be removed into the natural ground.

These will, if planted out into the beds, borders, and other

Iris
Iris persica

parts of the flower-garden, make a very fine appearance about two months hence.

Remember to chuse a showery time for setting these flowers; for if this be done in dry hot weather, not one in ten of the plants would succeed; about four or five o'clock in the evening is the most proper time for planting them.

You should also be careful, when you set them, to mix the different sorts, so that there may be a variety of flowers in every part.

They should be moderately watered as soon as planted, and the operation repeated every other evening till the plants have taken root.

฿ Propagate Perennial Fibrous-Rooted Plants. ଔ

The latter end of this month is a proper season for propagating perennial fibrous-rooted plants by cuttings of the young flower-stalks. The double scarlet lychnis, lychnidea, double-rockets, starwort, or the late flowering asters, and many others of that kind, will succeed very well. The method is this:

Let some of the young flower-stalks be cut off close, and divided into proper lengths, each length having three or four joints.

They must be planted in a shady border of light rich earth, about four inches asunder, and two of the joints put into the ground, leaving the rest above the surface. Close the earth well about them, and give them a moderate watering.

฿ Propagate Double Wall-Flowers. ଔ

The only method of propagating the true double kinds of wall-flowers is by slips.

These slips must have some strength, and be from three to six inches long. Let these be slipped off carefully from the mother plant in a moist or cloudy day; and the leaves from the bottom to something more than half way up the slips taken away, so that there may be two or three inches of clear stalk.

Wall-flower
'Forty Cockades'
Erysimum cheiri

Twist the stalks a little at the bottom, and plant them up to the leaves in a shady border, about four or five inches asunder, giving them a moderate watering.

By the end of September they will be well rooted, provided they are often refreshed with moderate waterings, in dry weather, when they may be taken up and planted in pots.

฿ Carnations. ଔ

You should now be careful to give your carnation plants in pots every assistance in the power of art, in order to encourage them to shoot vigorously.

Sticks should be placed to support the flower-stalks, which will now shoot apace, provided they were not placed there last month. Be sure to let the sticks be straight, and of a sufficient length. Thrust them into the

ground as close as possible to the plant, and tie the flower-stalk neatly to them in different parts.

If you perceive any decayed leaves about the plant take them away, stir the surface of the mould a little, and add a sprinkling of fine fresh earth over it; bind it close up about the plants, and immediately give the whole a moderate watering.

Pink fantasy
carnation
Dianthus

If you are desirous of having large and handsome flowers, all pods which rise from the sides of the stalks, should now be taken off, leaving none but the top buds.

Remember to shade your pots from the mid-day sun, and to water your plants every two or three days in dry weather.

ॐ Hyacinths, Tulips, &c. ॐ

Your beds of curious hyacinths, tulips, ranunculuses, and anemonies, which are now in full bloom, must be defended from the mid-day sun; and also sheltered from heavy rains, by means of hoops and mats, as directed in the former month.

The mats should be drawn over the hoops every day, when the sun shines, about nine or ten in the morning, and removed about four or five in the afternoon.

Tulip
*Tulipa dubia
major*

By this means the flowers will be preserved a considerable time in their full beauty; a fortnight at least longer, than if they were fully exposed to the sun and heavy showers of rain.

But remember to let your hoops be of a proper height; for otherwise the flower-stalks would be drawn up weak, and, in consequence of that weakness, the colours of the flowers would be faint.

ॐ Autumnal Flowering Bulbous Roots. ॐ

The leaves of such bulbous roots as blow in autumn will now be withered, and when this happens they should be taken out of the ground.

Remember to do this in dry weather, and to separate the small off-sets from the main root. When this is done, spread the roots upon a mat in the shade to dry; after which they are to be put up till about the last week in July, and then replanted.

℘ Auriculas. ☙

The pots of your auricula plants should, as the flowers fade, be immediately removed off the stand or stage, and placed upon a clean level spot where the plants can enjoy the morning sun freely, till nine or ten o'clock, but no longer. In this situation they are to remain till August.

Remember to keep both the pots and ground where they stand perfectly free from weeds; and whenever any decayed leaves appear on any part of the plants, let them be taken away immediately, and the pots often refreshed with water in dry weather.

Your tubs and boxes of seedling auriculas must now be removed to a shady place, if not done before; the place must be open to the morning sun only.

They must be frequently sprinkled with water in dry weather, and kept entirely free from weeds.

Sweet peas
Lathyrus odoratus

℘ Climbing Annual Plants. ☙

Your nasturtiums, convolvulus major, sweet-scented and Tangier peas, and others of the climbing kind, will now require support. Let sticks therefore be placed for them to climb upon as soon as they begin to run.

℘ Grass and Gravel Walks. ☙

You must now mow your lawns and grass walks often, at least once a week, if you intend to keep them in any tolerable order.

Your gravel walks should be duly rolled, especially after showers of rain; for this will make the body of the walk firm, and render the surface very close and smooth. If any weeds appear let them be immediately picked out, and no kind of litter seen upon them.

℘ Destroy Weeds. ☙

If you do not remember to destroy the weeds as soon as they appear, they will presently get a head, for they now grow very fast.

Let it therefore be a constant rule to cut them off as soon as they appear, either by the hand or hoe. If the latter be used, let it be done in dry weather, and the ground neatly raked after the operation, to draw the weeds and other litter from the surface.

JUNE

1. Closed Cabbage. *Brassica capitata.*
2. Open Cabbage. *Brassica patula.*
3. Cole Flower. *Caulis florida.*
4. Curled Savoy Colewort.
Brassica Sabaudica crispa.
5. Curled Colewort. *Caulis crispa.*
6. Cole Rape. *Rapocaulis.*
7. Changeable Curled Colewort.
Caulis crispa variata.

Potted trees complement geometric topiary. The orange trees which have wintered in the greenhouse are carted to the garden for summer.

The Works of this Month in the
KITCHEN GARDEN

ɕɔ Cucumbers in Frames. cʀ

Your cucumber plants in frames must now be well supplied with water and fresh air.

In hot weather the plants should be watered every two or three days; the best times for doing it, are about seven or eight o'clock in the morning, or four or five in the afternoon.

Let the lights be tilted up a considerable height every day, to give the plants a sufficient quantity of fresh air; but it will be advisable to shut the lights down every night, at least till the latter end of the month.

About that time also it will be proper to raise the frame high enough to let the plants run out from under it.

ɕɔ Cucumbers Under Bell-Glasses. cʀ

The cucumber plants under hand or bell-glasses, must now be suffered to run freely from under them.

Each glass should therefore be raised upon three or four props, and the vines or runners of the plants be trained out with care and regularity.

They will also require a moderate watering three times a week in dry weather.

⊗ Pickling Cucumbers. ⊗

The cucumber plants sown the latter end of last month in the natural ground for picklers, should now be thinned. Remember to do it as soon as the rough leaf in the heart of the plants begins to appear.

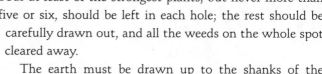

Four at least of the strongest plants, but never more than five or six, should be left in each hole; the rest should be carefully drawn out, and all the weeds on the whole spot cleared away.

The earth must be drawn up to the shanks of the remaining plants within a little of the seed leaves, and a light watering given to each hole to settle the earth. The plants after this will get strength, and grow surprisingly.

Serpent cucumber
Trichosanthes cucumerina

Remember to refresh them often with water; if the weather be very dry, let it be done every other day.

⊗ Sow Cucumbers. ⊗

You may still sow cucumber seed where required, at least any time before the fifteenth of the month.

The plants from this sowing will soon come up, begin bearing about the middle of August, and yield plenty of fruit during the remaining part of that month, and the greater part of September.

⊗ Melons in Frames. ⊗

You must still shade, during the middle of the day when the sun shines, the melon plants in frames.

This must be particularly remembered when the earth is but shallow upon the beds, or where the plants lie very near the glasses; for if they are in either of these cases, exposed to the full rays of the noontide sun, the leaves will be scorched, and the juices of the vines, roots, and young fruit exhausted. Even those that have swelled to a tolerable size, would, for want of proper nourishment, be greatly checked, and become at once stunted and ill shaped.

Let therefore some thin mats be spread over the glasses every day when the sun shines warm; but those need not be done before eleven o'clock; and the mats may be removed by two.

The thinner the mats used for this purpose are, the better, or the plants should not be darkened by too full a shade; nothing more is required than to take off part of the sun's rays, which will have the greatest tendency to promote the growth of this fruit, whatever be the size.

Remember to give the plants a constant supply of fresh air every day, by tilting the lights at the back of the frame to a considerable height.

Frequent refreshments of water will also be very ser-viceable to those plants at this season of the year, especially if the beds where they grow have but a shallow depth of earth.

Queen Anne's pocket melon
Cucumis melo dudaim

In that case the plants will, in hot weather, require to be moderately watered once a week; but care should be taken in doing this, to give very little water near the stem or head of the plants.

But where the beds are twelve or fifteen inches thick, and the earth of a loamy consistence, a very little water will be sufficient.

⟋ Melons Under Bell-Glasses. ⟍

You must now give your melons under bell-glasses free liberty to run out.

In order to which each glass should be raised and supported upon three props about two or three inches high; and the vines be laid out in a careful and regular manner.

Blenheim orange melon
Cucumis melo

It will be prudent to cover them every night with mats till about the middle or towards the latter end of the month, when the covering may be entirely laid aside, unless the weather should prove very wet; and in that case the plants should be covered occasionally.

For it should be remembered that nothing is more prejudicial to these plants than too much wet; for this not only chills the young fruit, and prevents their setting, and swelling, but also perishes many of the roots of the plants.

When therefore the weather happens at any time to be very rainy, it will be proper to defend these plants as much as possible from it; and this may be done effectually by a covering of good thick mats, or canvas, supported by hoops fixed across the bed.

ᏄᎧ Fill up the Alleys Between the Melon Ridges. ᏟᎡ

It is now time to fill up the alleys between the melon ridges, that the roots of the plants may have ground sufficient to extend themselves.

These alleys, if the beds are made wholly or a great part above the ground, must be filled up with dung, and covered with a proper thickness of earth.

If a new hot dung was used for this purpose, it would be of great advantage, as it would throw a fresh heat into the beds, which would greatly promote the setting and swelling of the fruit.

Coulommier's melon
Cucumis melo

The dung must be first laid in, and trod firmly down, raising it full as high as the dung of the beds; and then covering it with earth, till the interval be in a direct level with the surface of the beds.

ᏄᎧ Cauliflowers. ᏟᎡ

The cauliflowers sown in May should be pricked out into a nursery bed of rich earth, about the latter end of this month.

In order to this, let a bed about three feet and a half broad, in an open situation, be prepared for their reception. Then prick in the plants about three inches asunder, and give them a little water to settle the earth well about their roots; shade them from the sun till they have taken root, and, if the weather be dry, give them a little water occasionally.

In this bed the plants are to remain a month, in order to get strength, when they are to be planted out for good in the place where they are to produce their flowers.

Remember to look over your plantations of early cauliflowers now and then, in order to break down some of the inner leaves over the young heads as they appear.

ᏄᎧ Turnips. ᏟᎡ

A full crop of turnips for use in autumn should be sown some time this month.

But let it be done, if possible, in a dripping time; or, at least, when there is a prospect of rain falling soon after. Remember to sow the seed equally, and rake it in carefully with an even hand, as soon as sown.

The crop of turnips sown in May will now require hoeing, and the plants to be thinned in a regular manner.

You should remember to begin this work as soon as the turnips have gotten rough leaves about an inch broad; for then the work may be done with expedition and regularity, and prove of the greatest advantage to the growth of the plant.

Remember to leave the plants about eight inches from one another.

℘ Carrots and Parsnips. ℭ

The crops of carrots and parsnips must now be cleared from weeds; and the plants, where they stand too thick, thinned out to proper distances, that their roots may have sufficient room to grow. About six or eight inches distance between plant and plant will be sufficient.

It should be remembered, that the above distance is intended for those roots which are designed to grow to their full size; for with regard to those beds of carrots which are intended to be drawn while young, four or five inches will be a sufficient distance between them.

Carrot
Daucus carota

℘ Kidney-Beans. ℭ

Let another crop of kidney-beans be now planted, to succeed those planted last month.

Either the dwarf or climbing kinds of kidney beans, may now be planted. But the running kinds should be planted the first or second week in the month; for they do not succeed so well if planted later.

The best sorts for this purpose are the white Dutch, the scarlet blossom, and the large white kind; all these are exceeding good bearers, and equal to any kind for eating.

Remember in planting any kinds of kidney beans to allow them sufficient room; that is, let the drills for the running kinds be at least three feet and a half, or four feet asunder; and the distance between the drills for the dwarf kinds not less than two feet and a half.

If the ground be very dry at this season, it will be proper to water the drills well before you put in the beans; for this will make them rise much sooner, and with more regularity.

Let the earth be drawn up to the stems of those kidney-beans which were planted last month; this will strengthen the plants, and assist them greatly in their growth.

Sticks should also be placed to the running kinds of kidney-beans, which were planted at the beginning of last month. This should indeed be done as soon as the plants send forth their runners, for they will catch the sticks readily.

☙ Peas and Beans. ☙

You may still sow peas, and plant beans, if the season proves moist, but otherwise they will not succeed.

The small kinds of beans are most proper for planting now; none better than the white-blossom and mazagan. These will often yield plentiful crops at Michaelmas.

But the larger kinds of peas, as the marrow-fats, &c. will best answer your purpose; though a few of the best sorts of hot-spurs should be also sown.

If the weather and ground be very dry, let both your peas and beans be soaked eight or ten hours in pond or river water; and then sown or planted immediately.

Remember to allow sufficient room between the rows; for the success greatly depends upon that particular.

☙ Savoys and Cabbages. ☙

This is the proper season for planting a full crop of savoys and cabbages for winter use.

The plants should be set in rows, two feet asunder, and eighteen or twenty inches apart from one another in the rows. Some gardeners, where ground is very scarce and dear, set

Oxheart cabbage
Brassica oleracea

the savoy and cabbage plants between the rows of forward beans, early cauliflowers, and other crops of that kind, the rows of which are at a considerable distance from one another, and which will soon be off the ground. The plants will succeed by this method, nearly as well as if planted on a piece of fresh ground.

☙ Broccoli. ☙

The young broccoli plants sown in May must now be pricked out from the seed bed.

In order to this, let a piece of good mellow ground be dug, and the surface well raked. In this bed let the plants be set, about three or four inches asunder every way. Let them be watered immediately, and the operation repeated occasionally in dry weather.

In this bed they are to remain a month or five weeks, and then be planted out for good.

More broccoli seed should be sown about the second week in the month; and the plants from this sowing, will produce good heads about the beginning of March.

ﾄ Brown Cole. ﾄ

Bore-cole, brown
curled kale
*Brassica oleracea
acephala*

The plants brown or bore-cole sown in April or the beginning of last month, must be now pricked from the seed bed into a nursery bed, at the distance of four inches asunder every way. In this bed they are to remain till they have gathered strength, which will be in about a month, when they are to be planted out where they are to remain.

ﾄ Onions. ﾄ

Remember to keep your onion beds free from weeds; and whenever you perceive the plants too thick, let them be properly thinned; they should not stand nearer together than four or five inches.

But be careful in thinning your onions to leave the most promising plants behind, taking away those which are small and stunted.

ﾄ Leeks. ﾄ

Leek
Allium porrum

About the third or fourth week in the month, your leeks will be grown to a proper size for transplanting.

Let therefore a piece of ground in an open situation be prepared for that purpose, and the plants set in rows eight inches asunder, and about six inches from one another in the rows.

ﾄ Celery. ﾄ

The celery sown early last month, will about the middle of this be fit for blanching.

In order to this, let a piece of rich ground, in an open situation be chosen; and there mark out the trenches by a line, about a foot wide, allowing an interval of three feet between the trenches.

Let each trench be dug about seven or eight inches deep, laying the earth taken out equally on each side; then lay very rotten dung about two or three inches thick at the bottom of each trench, and dig the bottom neatly, burying the dung equally three or four inches deep.

The trenches being thus prepared, set the plants in a single row, exactly in the middle of the trench, about five inches asunder. As soon as they are planted, give them a little water, and repeat the operation occasionally till they have taken root.

In about a month or five weeks after the plants are set in the trenches, they will require to be earthed up, in order to render the stalks white and tender.

In order to this, the earth laid on the sides of the trenches must be broken small, and care taken to lay it gently to both sides of the plants, and not to earth them too high at first, lest you bury their hearts.

Remember to perform this work in dry weather, and, after you begin, to repeat it every fortnight or three weeks, till the plants are fit for the table.

☙ Endive. ☞

About the middle or towards the latter end of the month, some of the first sown plants will be ready for blanching.

Let therefore an open spot of ground be dug one spade deep, and the surface raked smooth.

In this bed let the endive plants be set in rows about a foot asunder every way, and some water given them immediately.

The main autumn crop of endive should be sown about the latter end of the month, in an open spot of ground, and the seed raked in equally with an even hand.

But if a constant supply of that vegetable be desired, a little of the seed should be sown at two different times this month, in the same manner as mentioned above for the autumn crop.

☙ Lettuces. ☞

Cabbage lettuce
Lactuca

It is now time to remove your lettuce plants sown in May from the seed-bed into an open spot of good ground.

But remember to do it in moist showery weather, for they will not succeed in a dry season; unless you plant them in drills about a foot from one another, and water them as soon as planted, repeating the operation frequently. For the drills will retain the water much longer than the level ground, and consequently assist the plants in their growth.

You should also sow some Coss, Silesia, and brown Dutch lettuce seed to supply the table in August and September.

ᔕᐤ Cresses, Mustard, &c. ᏣᎳ

Let a little of the seed of cresses, mustard, and other small salleting, be sown every week at least.

But remember to sow it in the shade, and to refresh the bed often with water in dry weather, both before and after the plants appear.

ᔕᐤ Mint, &c. ᏣᎳ

This is a proper season for gathering mint, and other plants that are in flower, for drying or distillation.

Remember to do it in a dry day, and when first the plants begin to flower; for they are then in the greatest perfection.

As soon as the plants are cut, let them be spread or hung up in small bundles, in a light airy room, out of the reach of the sun's rays, where they may dry gently. None of these must ever be laid in the sun to dry; for the greater part of their virtues would by this means be exhausted, and the plants rendered almost useless.

Spearmint
Mentha viridis

Pepper-mint for distilling should also be cut this month, provided the plants are in flower; but if not, let them continue till the next.

Remember to cut them in a dry day, and to let the plants be dried in the shade.

ᔕᐤ Planting Pot-Herbs, and Other Aromatic Plants. ᏣᎳ

Your young plants of thyme, savory, sweet-marjoram, and hyssop, will be ready to remove for the seed-bed about the latter end of the month, provided the weather be showery.

Let therefore a piece of ground be dug for this purpose, the surface raked smooth, and divided into beds three feet and a half broad.

In these beds let the young plants be set by a line, about six or eight inches asunder every way; and let them have a little water as soon as planted.

Burnet, borage, clary, marygold, and other herbs of that kind, sown in the spring, should be planted out.

Slips or cuttings of thyme, savory, hyssop, sage, lavender, lavender cotton, rue, rosemary, and southern-wood, may still be planted if required; for they will succeed in general, if planted in a shady situation, and now and then moderately watered.

Cardoons.

You must now remove your cardoons into the place where they are to blanch.

Remember to allow these plants a pretty deal of room, that they may be conveniently earthed up to a proper height.

In order to this, let a spot of the best ground, in an open situation, be chosen for them. In this spot plant the cardoons in rows a yard and half asunder, keeping the same distance between the plants in each row. Dig no trench, but plant them on the level ground, water them as soon as planted, and repeat the operation till they have taken root.

Watering in General.

All plants in general, which have been lately removed, should be watered in dry weather, and the operation duly performed till they have taken root.

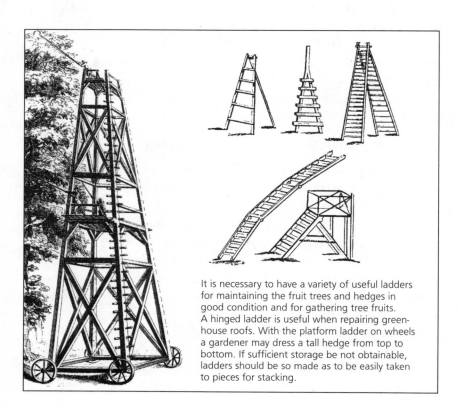

It is necessary to have a variety of useful ladders for maintaining the fruit trees and hedges in good condition and for gathering tree fruits. A hinged ladder is useful when repairing greenhouse roofs. With the platform ladder on wheels a gardener may dress a tall hedge from top to bottom. If sufficient storage be not obtainable, ladders should be so made as to be easily taken to pieces for stacking.

THE NURSERY

✂ Inoculate Peaches, Apricots, and Nectarines. ❧

You may begin, about the middle of this month, to inoculate apricots, and the early kind of peaches and nectarines.

Experience has abundantly shown that the above trees generally succeed best when budded upon plum stocks. The stocks should be raised from the stones; and when they are two or three years old, they will be of a size proper for budding.

Remember that the cuttings from whence the buds are to be taken be cut from healthy trees, such as shoot moderately free, and of the same year's growth. This being observed, the operation is performed in the following manner:

Nectarine
Prunus persica nectarina

Having provided yourself with proper cuttings, a sufficient quantity of new bass mat for bandages, and a sharp penknife, with a flat ivory haft somewhat taper, and quite thin at the end; make a cross cut with your knife in the rind in the middle of the stock, remembering to make the cut no deeper than the bark; then from the middle of the cross cut, let another be made downwards, about two inches in length, so that the two cuts together may form a T.

When this is done, take one of your cuttings or shoots and take off the bud as follows:

Begin at the lower or larger end of the shoot, and cut off all the leaves from it, but let the stalks of them continue; then about half an inch, or a little more below the said eye or bud, make a cross cut in the shoot, and placing your knife about the same distance above the eye, cut the bud, together with part of the wood. Separate immediately that part of the wood which was taken off with the bud, by placing the point of your knife between the bark and the wood at one end, and pulling off the woody part, which will part readily from the bark. This being done, examine immediately the inside of the bud to see if the eye be left; for if there appear a small hole, the eye is gone with the wood, and therefore useless; but if there be no hole, the bud is good, and is to be immediately inserted in the stock; observing, for the reception of the bud, to raise gently, with the haft of your knife, the bark of the stock downwards on each side, from the cross cut, and directly thrust the bud gently in between the bark and the wood, placing it as smooth as possible; and observing if the bud be too long for the incision in the bark of the stock, to shorten it so as to make it slip in readily, and lie perfectly close in every part.

When the bud is thus fixed, let the stock in that part be immediately bound round with a string of bass mat, beginning a little below the cut, and proceeding upwards, drawing it closely round to the top; but be sure to miss the eye of the bud, bringing the tying close to it both below and above, leaving only the very eye itself open.

About three weeks or a month after inoculation is performed, the bud will have taken with the stock, which may be known by the bud appearing plump, while those which have not will look black, and be decayed. Let therefore the bandages of those which have taken be loosened, that the sap may have free course to the bud; for were the bandages suffered to remain as first tyed, they would pinch and spoil the buds. To prevent this, therefore, all the bandages should be loosened in about three weeks, or a month at farthest after the operation.

Nothing more will be now necessary till the beginning of next March, when the head of the stock is to be cut off about a hand's breadth above the bud. The part above the bud is left to fasten the shoot to, which the bud makes next summer; for the buds never begin to shoot till the spring after budding. But the autumn following it should be cut off close, just above the bud, that the place of amputation may be the more readily barked over.

The general season to bud or inoculate is from about the middle of June till about the same time in August, according to the forwardness of the different sort of trees intended to be budded. This may be easily known by trying the buds; for when they will readily part from the wood, as already mentioned, it is then the proper season for budding that kind of fruit.

You should remember to perform this operation in moist cloudy weather, as the bud and stock being then more replete with juices than in hot dry weather, they will more readily unite.

℘ Examine the Trees That Were Budded Last Year. ଔ

The trees which were budded last year will now have made vigorous shoots, which must be supported.

In order to this, it will be proper to provide yourself with stakes about two feet long, driving one of them into the ground close to the stock of each tree that has made a vigorous shoot, and tye the shoot to the stake at two different places. This will effectually prevent its being broken or separated from the stock by the wind.

ᔥᓄ Look Over Your Grafted Trees. ᖃ

Examine your grafts; and where you perceive they have made vigorous shoots, let them be supported by tying them to stakes driven into the ground near the stocks.

ᔥᓄ Propagate Hardy Exotic Trees and Shrubs. ᖃ

Layers may now be made from many of the hardy exotic trees and shrubs, especially those of the evergreen kind.

But you must remember that only the shoots of the same summer's growth are now to be layed. The operation is performed in the following manner:

Having fixed on the plant, let such branches as are furnished well with young wood, be brought down gently to the ground, and there secured with hooked sticks. This being done, let all the young shoots on each branch be laid, covering them two three inches deep with earth; but leave at least two or three inches of the top of each shoot out of the ground.

Lime
Citrus aurantifolia

Remember to keep the earth above the layers moist, but not wet; and if this be duly observed, many of them will be well rooted by Michaelmas.

You may by this method of laying the young wood, propagate almost any trees or shrubs you desire; but it is chiefly intended for the hard wooded kinds of evergreens, and others, which do not put out roots freely from older shoots or branches; but such trees as shed their leaves, and even evergreens whose wood is soft, it is best, for the generality, not to lay them till after Michaelmas, or in February or March; choosing at these times the last summer's shoots.

Viburnum
Viburnum macrocephalum keteleeri

ᔥᓄ Transplant Pines and Firs. ᖃ

Some of your young pines and firs raised this season from seed, should, about the last week in the month, be transplanted; but before that time they will be too tender to be removed.

In order to this, let some beds about three feet broad be prepared, and the young plants be pricked into these beds, about three inches asunder every way; remembering to refresh them with water as soon as transplanted.

Silver fir
Picea pectinata

It will be necessary to shade them from the mid-day sun till they have taken root, which may easily be done by fixing hoops across the bed, and throwing mats over the bed every sunny day from ten in the morning till about three or four in the afternoon.

By this method the plants will soon take root, so that those which were pricked out at this season, will have acquired strength sufficient by Michaelmas, to enable them to endure the winter's cold much better than if they had remained in the seed bed.

℘ Shade Seedling Trees. ℃

You must remember to shade the beds of some of your seedling exotic plants from the sun in very hot weather, particularly those of the ever-green kind.

They must not however be shaded too close, or too long at a time, for that would draw the plants up weak, and make them too tender. It will be sufficient if they are shaded from about eleven in the morning till two or three in the afternoon.

℘ Water Seedling Trees. ℃

All seedling trees and shrubs must be watered in dry weather, particularly young cedars, cypress, pines, firs, junipers, bays, hollies, evergreen oaks, arbutus, and indeed all other kinds of ever-green seedling plants.

Bald cypress
cone
*Taxodium
distichum*

But be very careful not to water them too hastily, lest you wash away the earth from their roots, which are yet very small and tender. Two or three moderate waterings in a week will be sufficient, and the most proper time for it is in the evening.

℘ Water New Planted Trees. ℃

Such trees as were planted late in the spring should be watered in dry weather, once every week during the whole month.

Remember also to keep some mulch upon the surface of the ground about your new planted trees; for this will not only save some trouble in the watering, by preserving the moisture longer in the earth, but also protect their roots from the drying winds and sun; and consequently enable them to shoot with more vigour.

When, therefore, you perceive the mulch laid some time since upon the roots of new planted trees to be much wasted, let fresh be added, particularly about the choicest plants, and such as were planted late in the season.

ࠑ Weed the Seed-Beds of Young Plants. ࠇ

Remember to keep the seed-beds of young plants entirely free from weeds of every kind, for at this season of the year they rise as fast as in April or May. No labour therefore should be spared to destroy them before they grow large, especially in the beds among the seedling plants; for there they will inevitably do the greatest mischief.

Hedge trimming with long shears.

THE FRUIT-GARDEN

ᴄᴏ Apple, Pear, Plum, and Cherry Trees. ᴄᴋ

Your apple, pear, plum, and cherry trees, whether planted against walls or espaliers, will now have made strong shoots, and therefore require regulating, provided it was not done in May.

Wismer's
dessert apple
Malus

Let therefore these trees be now cleared from all useless and unnecessary shoots; let them be taken off close.

But remember to leave, at moderate distances, in every part of the tree, some of the best grown and well placed shoots; for in all probability some of these will be wanted to lay in and supply some place or other of the tree in the winter pruning. And whenever there appears an absolute want of wood, in any part of these trees, leave, if possible, some good shoots in these parts.

May cherry
*Cerasus
praecox*

When all the useless shoots are taken away, let the remaining shoots be nailed, or otherwise fastened up close to the wall or espalier, and each shoot at its full length.

ᴄᴏ Apricot, Peach, and NectarineTrees. ᴄᴋ

If any of your apricot, peach, or nectarine trees were not put in order last month, it must be done now, and the sooner the better. For where these trees are suffered to remain long in the wild confused manner they naturally grow into at this season, it will prove injurious to the trees themselves, and greatly retard the growth and ripening of the fruit.

Let therefore these wall trees be gone over as soon as possible, clearing away all the ill grown and ill-placed shoots; remember to take them off close to the place where they are produced.

At the same time be sure to leave in every part of these trees, a sufficient quantity of the best shoots for bearing next year; that is, leave all the regular and moderately growing shoots, provided they can be conveniently trained in, fastening them close to the wall in a neat manner.

Remember not to shorten any of the shoots for the reasons given last month, but lay them in, whether large or small, at full length; taking care to train them in such a manner, that their leaves may afford a moderate shade, in hot sunny days, to the fruit; for all kind of wall-fruit thrive best under a slight cover of leaves. At the same time the leaves will also prove a shelter to the fruit from the cold air of the night.

ॐ Thin Wall-Fruit. ෬

If the fruit on any of your apricot, peach, or nectarine trees were not thinned last month, let it now be done as soon as possible; observing the same method in doing it, as mentioned last month.

ॐ Vines. ෬

Let your vines, planted against walls be now looked over and regulated, unless the work was done last month.

If this be not done at the beginning of the month, it will be impossible to procure, at a proper season, large and well ripened grapes. For where the vines are suffered to run into disorder, the bunches will be small and irregular, and the grapes small and ill tasted.

Let such of the vines therefore, which were not regulated in May, be now regulated with all expedition; clearing away all useless shoots, and nailing all that are useful close to the wall in a neat and regular manner.

When this is done, let those vines which were looked over and regulated in May, be now again looked over;

Wild grapes
Vitis

clearing away all shoots in general that have been produced since last month. Be sure to rub off those small shoots which rise from the sides of the same summer shoots.

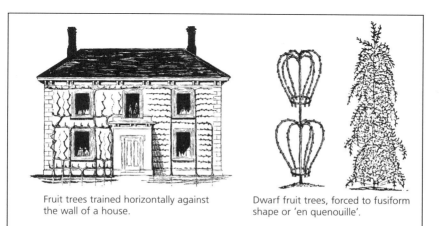

Fruit trees trained horizontally against the wall of a house.

Dwarf fruit trees, forced to fusiform shape or 'en quenouille'.

❧ Vineyards. ❧

The vines planted in vineyards will now require a considerable share of attendance, to prevent their running into confusion; and in preventing this confusion the whole success depends.

Let therefore the bearing stocks be trained to the stakes with some degree of regularity; so that every shoot may equally enjoy the benefit of the sun and free air. At the same time let all weak and straggling shoots be displaced, together with those which cannot be trained to the stakes in proper order.

It will be also very necessary to destroy the weeds whenever they grow in the vineyard; for this will be of the utmost advantage to the growth and timely ripening of the grapes.

❧ New Planted Trees. ❧

Let such fruit trees as were planted last autumn, winter, or spring, particularly standard trees, be now examined. See that they be well secured, so that they cannot be rocked about by the wind, which would disturb their roots.

At the same time take care to keep the earth well closed about the stems of new planted trees, that neither the sun or wind may have access that way to dry the earth near the roots.

The apricot, peach, and nectarine trees which were headed down in the spring, should also now be looked over. They will have made strong shoots, which should now be nailed to the wall, to secure them from the power of the wind.

❧ Budding or Inoculating. ❧

About the third or fourth week in this month, you may begin inoculating the early kinds of apricots, peaches, and nectarines.

But remember to perform the operation in cloudy weather, if possible; but if no such weather happen, let it be done in the morning or evening.

Plum stocks raised from stones, are the most proper for budding the above fruit upon; the stocks should be about two or three years old.

If the tree be intended for a dwarf, or for the wall, let the bud be inserted in the stock about six inches above the ground; but if the tree be intended for a standard, three or four feet above the earth will not be too much. But whatever height be allowed the stock, remember to make the incision for receiving the bud in a smooth part of the stock.

We have already explained the manner of performing this operation in the work of the nursery for the present month, and therefore shall not repeat it here.

℘ Plant Strawberries. ℘

If new plantations of strawberries are wanting, you may provide plants for that purpose about the middle or latter end of the month.

Let these plants be taken from such strawberry-beds as bear well, and produce large fruit. From these beds chuse a parcel of the strongest plants, and take them up carefully with their roots, which you are to trim a little, and cut off the strings from the heads of the plants.

Great Bohemia Strawberry *Fragari Bohemiea maxima*

When this is done, let them be immediately planted into a nursery-bed, prepared for them in a shady situation, about three or four inches asunder, giving them a moderate watering to settle the earth about their roots.

In this nursery-bed they are to remain till September or October, when they will have gathered sufficient strength, and be in excellent order to be removed into the bed where they are to remain; but they must then be planted a foot asunder every way.

This method is not usually practised, though much better than the common; because the plants will be much stronger by September, than any that can then be procured from the old beds.

℘ Water Old Strawberry-Beds. ℘

You must remember to water your strawberry-beds in dry weather, every two or three days from the beginning till about the middle of the month; for about that time the principal crop of most kinds of strawberries will be setting their fruit, and swelling to the respective sizes; and while the fruit are growing, they should be encouraged by keeping the earth in the beds always in a middling degree of moisture: you will soon be convinced that you have not taken this trouble in vain by the size, as well as by the quantity and quality of the fruit.

℘ Destroy Snails, &c. ℘

Be very careful to look over your fruit trees, particularly your apricot, peach, and nectarine trees, for snails every morning and evening, and especially after showers of rain; for at these times the snails leave their retreats, to feed upon the fruit.

THE PLEASURE OR FLOWER-GARDEN

℘ Carnations. ℞

You must now be very careful of your choice carnations; for towards the latter end of this month, they will begin to break their pods for flowering.

Art will be necessary to give them one of their principal beauties, that of opening regularly. Let therefore the inner cup or flower pod be cut open a little way in several places, in order to assist the opening and spreading of the petals, or flower-leaves.

This operation should be performed just as the flower begins to break the pod. A small pair of pointed scissors will be very proper for this purpose. With these let the pod be cut a little way down, from each notch or indenting at the top. But be very careful not to cut the pod too deep at first; but rather open it a little farther, if the former be not found sufficient.

You must however remember in performing this operation, to leave so much of the bottom of the pod entire, as will answer the purpose of keeping all the petals or flower-leaves regularly together.

Carnation
Dianthus caryophyllus

If you omitted to place your carnations in pots upon the stage in May, let it be done now; but you must not cover the top of the stage till the flowers are opened; and then cover must be constantly kept on, to defend them from the fierce rays of the sun, and from heavy rains.

Remember to water them three times a week at least; that is, you should repeat the operation whenever you perceive the surface of the earth in the pots to appear dry; for it should always be kept in a middling degree of moisture.

It will be also necessary, as the flower-stalks of these plants rise in height, to tye them up to the sticks. They should be tyed in several places, bringing the stalk to touch the stick: but do not tye it too strait.

℘ Transplant Carnation and Pink Seedlings. ℞

About the middle of the month, your carnation and pinks raised this year from seed, will be fit to transplant from the seed-bed into the nursery.

In order to this, let a bed or two of good earth, three feet and a half broad, be prepared, by breaking the clods well, and raking the surface even.

When the beds are thus prepared, take up your plants carefully, and set in each bed six rows of plants, by means of a line, six inches from each other in the row. As soon as they are planted, let a gentle watering be given them; and the operation be repeated once every two days at least, in dry weather, till they have taken root.

In this bed they are to remain ten or twelve weeks, when they must be removed into another, and planted a foot asunder every way.

Remember when they flower, which will be next year, to examine them very attentively, especially the carna- tions, for there will certainly be found among the whole some new and very good flowers; and these are to be then increased by layers, according to the general method.

Pink
Dianthus chinensis heddewigii

ᔓ Method of Laying Carnations, Pinks, and Double Sweet-Williams. ᔕ

About the middle of this month some of your carnations will be fit for laying, which is done in the following manner:

Provide some rich earth in a barrow or basket, a sharp penknife, and a sufficient number of small hooked pegs.

When these things are in readiness, clear away all the weeds and other litter found about the plants; stir the surface of the earth a little, and lay thereon as much of the fresh earth as will raise the surface round the plant to a sufficient height, so as readily to receive the shoots or layers.

This being done, pull off the leaves from the lower part of the shoot; let- ting those which grow upon the head of it remain, after cutting off about two inches of their tops. Then fix upon a joint about the middle of the

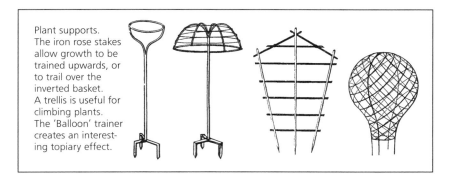

Plant supports. The iron rose stakes allow growth to be trained upwards, or to trail over the inverted basket. A trellis is useful for climbing plants. The 'Balloon' trainer creates an interest- ing topiary effect.

shoot, and placing the knife on the under side of it slit the shoot from that joint, rather more than half way up towards the next above.

When you have proceeded thus far, make an opening in the earth, and lay the shoot immediately, securing it there with one of the hooked sticks. Remember to raise the shoot gently up, so as to make the head of it stand as upright as possible, and see that the slit be open. Then cover up the body with more of the same mould; and in that manner proceed till they all are layed.

Sweet William
Dianthus barbatus

But remember, as soon as all the shoots belonging to one plant are layed, to give them a gentle watering, which will settle the earth regularly about all the layers. The waterings must be repeated in dry weather; but let them always be moderate, otherwise there will be great danger of disturbing, or washing away the earth from the layers.

These layers in about six weeks time, will be finely rooted, and must then be taken off from the old roots and planted, some of the best into small pots, and the rest into nursery-beds, where they are to remain till October; at which time they may be taken up with balls of earth about their roots, and planted in the borders.

ℰ Method of Propagating Carnations and Pinks by Cuttings. ℛ

Besides the above method of increasing carnations and pinks, especially the latter, there is another, which the gardeners call pipeing. It is performed in the following manner:

About the middle or latter end of this month, the plants will have made proper shoots for this operation. Let therefore the upper parts of the shoots intended for this purpose be taken off; and if the cutting, or, as the gardeners call it, the pipeing, hath two points when taken off, it is sufficient: some take them off with a knife, cutting them close above a joint; but it is much better to take them off with the hand only; the method is this: Take the head of the shoot between the ends of the fingers and thumb of the right hand, holding the lower part of the shoot with the left; then pulling the head of the shoot gently, it will readily part and come out of its socket, about the third joint from the top.

Having by this means procured a sufficient quantity of shoots, let their tops be trimmed pretty short, and if the bottom of the cutting appear ragged, let that be cut even; and having prepared a bed, or pots, of light rich earth, broken very fine, and the surface made very smooth, take the cuttings, one by one, between your fingers and thumb, and thrust them gently near half way into the earth, putting them about an inch, or an inch and a half, distant from one another.

Remember, in planting, to make no hole to receive the cutting, but only thrust the end gently into the earth; for it will make way for itself; and, as soon as a quantity is planted, to give them a gentle watering.

It will be necessary to shade them from the sun, from nine in the morning till about five or six in the evening. And if these cuttings can be conveniently covered with glasses, it will prove of the greatest advantage; they will then take root freely, and be fit for transplanting a fortnight or three weeks sooner than if they were fully exposed to the open air.

But however that be, remember to refresh them frequently with water, so as to keep the earth about them a little moist.

ഔ Transplant Chrysanthemums, French and African Marygolds, &c. cx

You may now, when the weather is showery, transplant chrysanthemums, French and African marygolds, persicarias, tree and purple amaranthuses, scabiouses, egg-plants, stramonium, palma Christi, love-apple, tobacco plants, marvel of Peru, balsams, capsicums, China asters, Indian pinks, tenweek-stocks, the large convolvulus, and several others.

In order to this, let them be carefully taken up with balls, or, at least, with as much earth as will readily hang about their roots; and in that manner let them be planted in the beds, borders, or other parts of the garden. Remember, when you plant them, to close the earth well about their roots and stems, and immediately to give

French marygold
Tagetes patula

every plant a little water, repeating it occasionally till they have all fairly taken root.

As they advance in height, let the larger kinds be properly supported with sticks; for great part of the beauty of these flowers consists in their having fair and upright stems; they must therefore be properly trained and supported.

ഔ Tender Annuals. cx

You must often refresh your tender annuals, such as cockscombs, tricolars, globes, double balsams, double stramoniums, &c. with water. They will require it three times a week at least; but let it always be moderate.

They must also be allowed a large quantity of fresh air every day, which must be given them by tilting up the lights with props, or sliding them a little way open.

Those balsams, cockscombs, tricolars, &c. which are grown to any tolerable size, and are pretty strong, may, about the last week of this month, be brought into the open air; but those which are small and weakly, should remain under the glasses a week or two longer.

℘ Propagate Fibrous-Rooted Plants. ⊂ℛ

This is a proper season for propagating perennial fibrous-rooted plants, which is done by setting the flower stalks.

The double sweet-williams, double scarlet lychnis, lychnideas, and several other sorts of perennial plants of that tribe, may be increased by this method, which is performed in the following manner:

Let some of the stoutest flower stems be cut off close to the head of the plant, and these cuttings divided into lengths, each containing two or three joints.

Your cuttings being thus prepared, plant them about four inches asunder in a shady border; remember to put two joints of the cuttings into the ground, and to give them immediately a little water.

Haage lychnis
Lychnis

If you cover these cuttings with hand-glasses, it will greatly assist them in taking root.

℘ Transplant Autumnal Flowering Bulbs. ⊂ℛ

All those bulbous and tuberous-rooted plants which grow in autumn, may now be taken up and transplanted; particularly colchicums, autumnal crocuses, hyacinths, narcissuses, and other flowering plants of this kind, whose leaves are now decayed.

Remember, when you take up the roots, to remove all the offsets. After which, they may be either planted again immediately, or kept out of the ground till the first or second week in August. But if they are not planted at that season, they will not blow in autumn with any degree of strength.

Hyacinth
Hyancinthus

The leaves of your calcamens will be also now decayed; let the roots therefore be taken up, parted, and planted again in fresh mould. They generally flower in February or March, according to their situation.

℘ Transplant Seedling Plants. ℃

Your wall-flowers, stock july-flowers, sweet-williams, and columbines, sown in March or April, should be now transplanted into nursery beds about six inches asunder, and have a good watering given them, to settle the earth about their roots.

In this bed the plants are to remain till about Michaelmas, and then removed into the borders, &c. where they are intended to remain. Their flowers will make an elegant appearance next summer.

Hollyhocks, tree-primrose, fox-gloves, pyramidal campanulas, Canterbury-bells, Greek valerian, single rose campion, rockets, scarlet lychnis, and other perennial plants sown in the spring, should be now transplanted into nursery beds about six inches apart.

Wall-flower
Erysimum cheiri

In these beds they are to remain till they become strong and handsome plants, which will be about September or October, when they are to be taken up and planted out, where they are to remain to flower.

And if they are judiciously placed in different parts of the garden, they will make a very elegant appearance next summer, when they will all flower.

℘ Take up the Roots of Tulips, Jonquils, Crown Imperials, &c. ℃

Some time this month the leaves of your tulips, jonquils, &c. will begin to decay; and when this happens, it is a proper time to take the roots out of the ground.

Remember to do this in dry weather, and to spread them thinly upon mats, laid in the shade, to dry, as soon as they are taken out of the ground.

As soon as they are thoroughly dry, and somewhat hardened, let them be very well cleaned, and all the off-sets separated from the large roots. When this is done, let them be put up, each sort by itself, in bags or boxes, till September, October, or November, when they are to be all re-planted.

By this method of taking up the choicest bulbous roots of any kind, as soon as their leaves decay, they are prevented from exhausting themselves too much, which many sorts would do, were they permitted to remain in the earth; because they would soon put out new fibres, and consequently set all the roots a growing at an unseasonable time of the year.

Besides, it is necessary to take up all kinds of bulbous roots once every year, in order to separate the small off-sets from each of the principal; particularly tulips, jonquils, hyacinths, and others of the choicer kinds of bulbs; and there is no time so proper to take them up, as when the leaves and flower stalks of the different kinds begin to decay; for then the roots are in a state of rest; but if permitted to remain three weeks or a month after that period, they will put out fresh fibres, and the root would begin to form the bud for the next year's bloom; and if they were then to be taken up, would, in some measure, check the next year's flower; that is, it would not blow so large as it would, had it been taken up immediately at the decay of the leaves.

❧ Guernsey Lily Roots. ❧

The leaves of the Guernsey and Belladonna lily roots will be now decayed, and consequently it is a proper season to take up the roots.

As soon as they are taken up, and the off-sets taken from them, they should be planted singly in beds of earth newly dug, or in pots filled with new compost; for this will greatly encourage them to shoot, and consequently increase the largeness and beauty of their flowers.

Lily
Lilium elegans

❧ Ranunculus and Anemonie Roots. ❧

As the leaves of the ranunculus and anemone roots will now begin to wither, they should be taken up.

But a considerable deal of care is necessary in taking these roots out of the ground; and it should always be done in a dry day, when the ground is pretty dry.

When the roots are taken up, they should be dried in the shade, and preserved in a dry place till the season for planting them arrives.

Anemonie
Hepatica trifolia caerulea

❧ Hyacinth Roots. ❧

As soon as the hyacinths are past flowering, and their leaves begin to decay, let the roots be taken up, at least all those of the fine double kind.

As soon as these roots are taken up, they should be immediately committed to the ground again, though in a different manner; they must be laid side-ways into a bed of light earth, covering the roots, but leaving the stalks and leaves out of the ground.

In this bed the roots are to lie for some time, in order to swell and harden, which they will do sufficiently by the time the stalks and leaves are perfectly decayed.

The method of preparing the bed, and laying the roots, is this:

Let a bed of light earth be dug one spade deep. When this is done, rake the earth up from each side of the bed towards the middle, so as to form an easy rounding kind of ridge from one end to the other of the bed.

In this ridge of earth the roots are to be laid, observing that they are not now to be placed with their bottoms downward; but each root must be laid fairly on its side, with the stalks and leaves hanging out.

In the above position, let them be laid in two or three rows on each side of the ridge; placing the roots about two inches asunder in the rows, and covering the roots equally with earth.

When the roots have laid in this bed about twenty days, they will be fully swelled, and thoroughly ripened; when they must be taken out of the ground in a dry day, well cleaned, and then spread upon a mat in a dry shady place. In about ten or twelve days after this, they must be put up into boxes till September or October.

ꙴ Auricula Plants. ꙮ

If you omitted last month to place any of your auricula plants growing in pots in a shady situation, let it be done now.

But remember to water the pots frequently in dry weather, and to keep both the pots and the place where they stand, free from weeds.

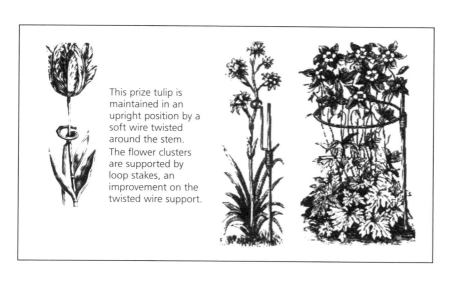

This prize tulip is maintained in an upright position by a soft wire twisted around the stem. The flower clusters are supported by loop stakes, an improvement on the twisted wire support.

ﮨ Support and Trim Flowering Plants. ﮨ

You should be very careful to see that every one of your tall growing plants be properly supported with sticks. For nothing gives plants a better appearance than their standing firmly in their places, and their being trained neatly with straight and upright stems.

At the same visit your plants, trimming such as stand in need of it.

All straggling, broken, and decayed shoots, together with all ragged or decayed leaves, should be taken away.

Cut down the flower-stems of such perennial plants as are past flowering. But, in doing this, remember to let the stems be cut off close to the head of the plant; and, at the same time, to clear the plant from all dead leaves. Unless you intend to save the seeds; for then it will be necessary to leave, for the purpose, some of the principal flower-stems, cutting off all such as are weak and straggling.

ﮨ Management of Evergreens and Flowering Shrubs. ﮨ

Weigela
Weigela florida

Examine your clumps or quarters of evergreens and flowering shrubs; and wherever you find any of them to have made any disorderly shoots, let them be reduced to order, either by shortening them, or cutting them off close.

At the same time, remember to keep the whole exceeding neat, and free from weeds.

ﮨ Cut Box Edgings. ﮨ

About the middle of this month is a proper season for cutting box edgings, provided the weather be moist; for it should never be done in dry weather.

These edgings should never be suffered to grow above three inches high, nor more than two broad. Remember to cut them very neat and even.

ﮨ Clear the Borders From Weeds. ﮨ

Be very careful to keep your borders free from weeds, and all kinds of litter. For if you permit the weeds to remain on any of the borders, especially those near walks, they will give the whole a very unsightly appearance. If the hoe be used for this purpose, let it be done in a dry day; and after the weeds are cut up clean below the surface of the ground, let the whole border be neatly raked.

℘ Mow Grass-Walks and Lawns. ℘

As soon as ever you perceive the grass to be grown of an unsightly length, let the walks and lawns be mown. They will, in general, require this labour once a week, which will keep them in tolerable good order.

At the same time, the edges of grass-walks and lawns should be kept cut very close; for this will add greatly to their neatness and beauty.

℘ Gravel Walks. ℘

You should also remember to keep your gravel-walks extremely neat and clean at this season.

The principal walks should be rolled at least twice a week, with an iron or stone roller. The former is much the best, as it will be drawn with more ease, and render the surface of the gravel smoother than any other.

JULY

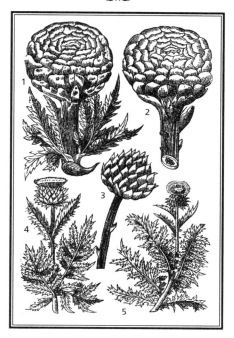

1. Red Artichoke. *Cynara satina rubra.*
2. White Artichoke. *Cynara satina alba.*
3. French Artichoke. *Cynara patula.*
4. Thistle Artichoke. *Cynara silvestris.*
5. Cardoon. *Carduus esculentus.*

Here are four individual gardens of formal beds enclosed by thick hedges. A wooden fence, against which shrubs are trained, contains the gardens and arbours; galleries border all.

The Works of this Month in the
KITCHEN GARDEN

↭ Cucumbers. ↭

Your cucumber plants will now demand attention, particularly those which are planted under hand or bell-glasses.

They will now be in full bearing, and therefore must be well supplied with water in dry weather. They should have a moderate watering once every other day.

If this be complied with, and the beds kept entirely free from weeds, the plants will continue to bear handsome and well-tasted fruit till the middle of September.

Antilles cucumber
Cucumis sativus

↭ Cucumbers for Pickling. ↭

The cucumber plants sown in the natural ground for picklers will also require some care.

You must remember to lay out their vines in regular order, as they begin to advance: and if the ground between the holes of these plants was not dug last month, let it be done now; and as you proceed in the digging, let the vines be laid out in a neat manner, at regular distances. At the same time, let some earth be laid between the plants, pressing it down gently, in order to part, and make them spread different ways, according as you would have them run. Remember also to draw the earth up round each hole, in order to form a basin for holding the water given them in dry weather; for they will require frequent waterings.

෨ Melons. ෬

The melon plants, whose fruit are now beginning to ripen, will require particular regard.

Very little water must now be given these plants, for too much moisture would spoil the fine taste of the melons. They must, however, in very dry and hot weather, be moderately watered now and then. But regard must always be had to the nature of the earth, and its depth upon the beds. Where there is a considerable depth of good loam, we mean twelve or fourteen inches, the plants should not, when their fruit is full grown, be allowed any more water; for good loam, where it is of a tolerable depth, will retain a moderate and proper degree of moisture for a long time.

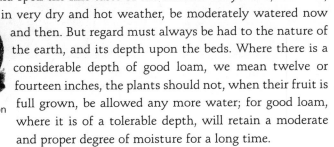

Superior musk melon
*Cucumis melo
reticulatus*

But such melons which grow in common light earth, and where there is, at the same time, but a moderate depth of it upon the beds, the plants will, in very hot weather, still require water; but then it must be done with moderation, and not repeated above once a week.

෨ Protect Melons from Heavy Rains. ෬

If the weather should be very wet at this season, which sometimes happens, your melon plants must be occasionally protected.

This may be done without any difficulty, where the plants grow under frames; but it will be different with regard to those planted out under hand or bell-glasses. All possible means must, however, be used to shelter them, when the weather happens to be uncommonly wet; for these plants will be now full of fruit.

In order to this, let the fruit, at least as many of them as are swelled, be put under their own bell-glasses; or, where there are any spare glasses, let them be placed over the fruit.

Watermelon
Citrullus lanatus

Another method is to place hoops over the ridges or beds, about sixteen or eighteen inches from one another; and when it rains very hard, let some large and thick mats be drawn over the hoops; or, which will be still better, pieces of painted canvas.

But whatever covering be used, remember that it is not to remain any longer than just to defend the plants from heavy rains; for a free circulation of air will be now absolutely necessary.

ᔥ Savoys and Cabbages. ଔ

Let a spot of good ground, in an open situation, be now prepared for a principal crop of savoys, and winter cabbages.

As soon as the ground is dug and raked, let the plants be set at eighteen or twenty inches asunder every way.

Midsummer cabbage
Brassica capitata

ᔥ Broccoli. ଔ

You must now remove your broccoli plants intended for a full crop into the place where they are to remain.

Let a piece of the best ground be chosen for this purpose, and the plants set in rows two feet asunder, and about twenty inches apart in the rows. Give them a little water as soon as they are planted; and if the weather should prove dry, let the waterings be repeated once every two or three days, till the plants have all taken root.

But these plants should, if possible, be planted out in a showery time, which will prove an advantage to the plants, and also save considerable trouble in the watering.

You should now sow a little broccoli-seed for the last time this season: it should be done before the end of the second week in the month.

In order to this, let a rich spot of ground, where the sun has not too much power, be chosen; and after the seed is sown, let the bed be often sprinkled with water, in dry weather; for this will both assist the plants in their springing and growth.

About the latter end of August, the plants sown now, will be ready to plant out for good, and produce heads in April, or the beginning of May.

ᔥ Cauliflowers. ଔ

You must now plant out the cauliflower plants sown in May for the autumnal crop, where they are to remain.

Remember to chuse a showery time for this work; and to plant them in rows two feet asunder every way. Let them be watered as soon as planted, and the watering frequently repeated, in dry weather, till they have taken root.

୨ Kidney-Beans. ଓ

Kidney-beans, either of the dwarf or running kind, may now be planted for a late crop.

But remember to let the seeds be in the ground before the end of the first week in the month; otherwise they will not succeed. You should also remember to plant them where they may be sheltered from the nipping morning frosts, which too often happen in September; for this crop will continue bearing, if the weather continues any thing mild, till October.

The following caution likewise should be observed in planting these beans.

If the weather, at the time of planting, be very hot, and the ground very dry, it will be proper to soak the beans in rain, river, or pond water, about six or seven hours before they are set. But remember to plant them as soon as ever they are taken out of the water. The drills also should be watered before the beans are dropped into them.

This soaking of the beans is only necessary when the weather is very hot, and the ground very dry; for, at other times, it will be better to let the drills only be watered, and the beans immediately planted.

୨ Sow Onions. ଓ

This last week in this month, but not before, you may sow onions to stand the winter.

Let therefore a rich spot of ground, in a sheltered situation, be dug, and divided into beds three feet and a half, or four feet broad. Sow 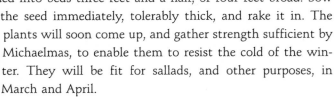 the seed immediately, tolerably thick, and rake it in. The plants will soon come up, and gather strength sufficient by Michaelmas, to enable them to resist the cold of the winter. They will be fit for sallads, and other purposes, in March and April.

Extra early
red onion
Allium cepa

Remember when the plants are come up to let them be weeded in time; for, otherwise, the weeds, which will rise with the onions, will soon get the start of them, and destroy the whole crop.

❧ Sow Turnips. ❧

Turnips for autumn and winter use may be sown any time this month. But, if possible, let it be sown in a showery time, for a little rain will now be of the utmost advantage to the seed.

Remember not to sow the seeds too thick, but as regularly as possible; the same care will also be necessary in raking in the seed; let it be done lightly, and with an even hand.

Those turnips which were sown in June must now be hoed; but let this be done in dry weather; at the same time cut down all the weeds, and thin out the plants to seven or eight inches distance.

Orange jelly
turnip
Brassica rapa

❧ Sow Winter Spinach. ❧

The best sorts of spinach for sowing at this season, are the prickly-seeded kinds; these being more hardy than the other sorts, and consequently better able to endure the cold of the winter.

Near the latter end of the month, let a clean well situated spot be neatly dug; and as soon as the ground is ready, let the seed be sown. Remember not to sow it too thick, but as equal as possible; and to rake it in with an even hand. Some tread the ground as soon as the seed is sown, and then rake the surface smooth and even. Either method will succeed, and perhaps almost equally.

❧ Sow Turnip-Rooted Radishes. ❧

These are two sorts of the turnip-rooted radish, the one black, and the other white, and are generally called the black and white Spanish radish.

Between the tenth and twenty-fourth of this month, will be a very proper time for sowing the seeds of either. But remember to chuse an open spot of ground for this purpose.

Soon after the plants are come up, they should be hoed out to five inches distance, that their roots may have room to swell. They will be ready to draw for the table about Michaelmas, and will continue good, especially the black sort, till Christmas, unless the frost be very severe; in which case they should be drawn out of the earth, and preserved in sand.

Yellow Malta
turnip radish
*Raphanus
sativus*

℘ Sow Common Radishes. ℭ

If these plants are wanted, as in some families they are, some of the seed may be sown the last week in this month, but not before. The plants will soon come up, and be ready to draw for the table by the first or second week in September.

℘ Sow Coleworts. ℭ

This is the very best season in the whole year for sowing coleworts. They are very useful in families, as they will supply the table in the spring, when the savoys and other greens of that kind are over.

But remember not to sow this seed before the twenty-fourth of the month, when an open spot of rich ground should be prepared for its reception, and divided into beds four feet wide. In those beds let the seed be sown moderately thick, and raked in lightly with an even hand.

In about a week after sowing, the plants will come up, and by the middle of September be strong enough to be transplanted; when they are to be set in rows a foot asunder, and eight inches apart in the rows.

℘ Sow Endive. ℭ

You may now sow some endive for the principal winter crop. But it must be sown the first week in the month, or it will not succeed.

Let the seed be sown tolerably thin, in a rich open spot of ground, and lightly raked in with an even hand.

Remember to water the bed frequently in dry weather; for this will be of great service in bringing up the plants soon, and also in causing them to rise regularly.

Broad-leaved endive
Cichorium endiva

℘ Sow Small Salleting. ℭ

Cresses, mustard, radish, and other small sallad herbs, may now be sown if required.

But remember to sow the seeds, each sort separate, in shady border, in shallow drills. If the weather be dry, there will be a necessity for daily watering the bed, or the plants will not rise regularly.

If a constant supply of these small salleting herbs be wanting, a little of the seed should be sown once every week.

℘ Sow Carrots. ℆

A little carrot-seed may be sown the first or second week in the month, in order to raise some young carrots for the table in autumn; about Michaelmas they will be fit to draw, and continue very fine all October and November.

℘ Sow Lettuce. ℆

The Coss, Silesia, or Dutch lettuce are most proper to be sown at this season.

About the first or second week in the month, let a spot of rich ground be dug, and the seed sown on it immediately. The plants will be fit for the table in the beginning of September.

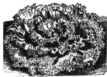

Green fringed
salamander lettuce
Lactuca sativa

And if a little more seed be sown on another spot of ground the last week in the month, a regular supply of lettuce will be continued till November, if the weather be favourable.

℘ Transplant Endive. ℆

A parcel of the strongest endive plants must be now removed to supply the table in autumn.

But you must remember that endive requires a good soil, well dug, and the surface sufficiently raked.

As soon as a spot of ground is thus prepared, let your plants be set in it, a foot distant from each other every way. They must be watered as soon as planted; and the waterings repeated every other day in dry weather, till the plants have taken root.

℘ Transplant Celery. ℆

You must now prepare your trenches for planting out a good crop of celery.

In order to this let an open spot of rich ground be chosen, and well cleared from weeds. When this is done, mark out the trenches about a foot broad, allowing an interval of three feet and a half between the trenches. Let each trench be dug about a spade deep, and the earth that comes out laid neatly in the interval between the trenches, remembering to spread it as even as possible.

When this is done, let some good rotten dung be laid at the bottom of the trench, and dug in.

This being performed, chuse a sufficient number of the strongest of your plants, trim the ends of their roots, and cut off about two inches of the tops of their leaves, and then plant them in the trenches.

Remember that one row only must be planted in each trench, and that this row be directly in the middle of it. Four or five inches will be a sufficient distance between plant and plant, but some water must be given them immediately, and the waterings repeated occasionally in dry weather, till the plants have taken root.

℘ Transplant Lettuces. ℂℛ

The Coss, Silesia, common cabbage, and brown Dutch lettuces, sown last month, should now be transplanted.

In order to this let a spot of the richest ground be chosen, well dunged, and the surface raked very even.

When the ground is ready, put in the plants by a line, at the distance of twelve inches from one another.

Give them a little water as soon as they are planted, and repeat the operation occasionally, till they have all taken root.

℘ Transplant Leeks. ℂℛ

You should make choice of a good piece of ground for transplanting your leeks, as that will prove of the utmost advantage to the plants, especially if a little rotten dung be spread on the surface and dug in.

When the ground is properly prepared, let it be divided into beds four feet broad. Then take up your leeks, choosing the strongest plants, and trim their roots and tops of their leaves. When this is done, let them be planted in rows, six inches apart every way.

Leek
Allium porrum

℘ Artichokes. ℂℛ

Your artichoke plants, which will now soon come into use, must be ordered in the following manner:

If you desire to have large artichokes, you must, in order to encourage the main head, cut off all the suckers or small heads which are produced from the sides of the stems, and these in some families are dressed for the table.

You must also remember that as soon as the principal head or artichoke is cut, let the stem be immediately broken down close to the ground. This practice is indeed too often disregarded; but this is utterly wrong, for the stems, if permitted to remain, would greatly impoverish the roots, and injure them much more than is generally imagined.

℘ Plant Sage, Hyssop, &c. ℭ

You may still plant the slips of sage, hyssop, winter savory, and other herbs of that kind, for they will yet succeed.

The slips must be about six or seven inches long, planted in a shady border, and often refreshed with water in dry weather.

Remember to chuse such slips as have strength, and to put them two thirds of their length, at least, into the earth.

Hyssop
Hyssopus officinalis

℘ Pull Onions. ℭ

About the latter end of this month, examine your forwardest crops of onions; and when their leaves begin to wither, it is a proper time to take the roots out of the ground.

It is not indeed very common that these roots are fit to be taken up this month; but when they are, let them be managed in the following manner:

Take them up in dry weather; and as you take them out of the earth, pull off their leaves, four or five inches of the stalk only to be left to each onion. As soon as they are taken up, let them be spread to harden upon a clean, dry, spot of ground; and let them lay there twelve or fourteen days, remembering to turn them once every two or three days at least, that they may dry and harden regularly.

Yellow Danvers onion
Allium cepa

When these have laid their proper time, they must be gathered up in a dry day, well cleared from earth and all loose outer skins, and carried into the house, where they must be spread thin upon the floor of a dry airy room.

Remember to keep the windows of the room constantly open in dry weather, for about a week or ten days after the onions are housed; but after that time no more air should be admitted through the windows; nothing then being wanting but to turn them now and then, picking out all the decayed roots.

❧ Pull Garlick and Shallots. ☙

When the leaves of your garlick and shallots begin to wither, it is time to take the roots out of the ground. This will happen to the most forward plants some time this month, when they should be taken up, and dried in the shade, nearly in the same manner as above directed for onions.

❧ Gather Seeds. ☙

As your seeds ripen, let them be gathered; but remember to do it in very dry weather.

As soon as the pods, or seed-vessels are cut from the stalk, let them be spread immediately in a dry place, where a free current of air may be admitted to them. In this situation let them lie a fortnight or three weeks; when they may be beaten out of their pods, and preserved in bags or boxes for use.

Asafoetida
Ferula assa-foetida

❧ Gather Herbs for Drying. ☙

Baum, mint, hyssop, winter savory, thyme, &c. should be gathered, in order to be dried for winter use, some time this month.

But remember to let this be done when the plants are in flower; for then they are in the highest perfection. Remember also to cut them in dry

weather, and to spread or hang them up in small bundles, in a dry airy place, shaded from the sun. In this situation let them remain and dry gently; for they must never be dried in the sun.

❧ Gather Herbs to Distil. ☙

Many of the herbs proper for distillation will be now in flower, and consequently proper to be cut for distillation. It will perhaps be unnecessary to mention, that they should be cut in a dry day; unless they are intended to be distilled

Hops
Ostrya
Theophrasti

by what is called a cold still, when they should be gathered in the morning with the dew about them.

❧ Gather Camomile Flowers. ☙

About the latter end of this month, some of your camomile flowers, together with those of marigold and lavender, will be fit to be gathered.

But remember to do it in a dry day, and to spread them out thinly to dry in a shady place. When they are sufficiently dry, put them up in paper bags for use.

✿ Clear the Ground from Stalks, Weeds, &c. ❧

As many of your plants will now have done bearing, let the ground be cleared from their leaves, weeds, or any other kind of rubbish.

Pull up also the stalks and haulm of cauliflowers, beans, peas, &c. as are past bearing; together with other plants that are past service, and clear them entirely off the ground.

When this is done the ground will have a neat appearance, and be in a proper condition to be dug, for receiving an autumn or winter's crop.

Nor is the elegance of the appearance all the advantage that will flow from this trouble; the ground will be in much better condition to receive the intended crops than if the stalks, haulm, weeds, and other rubbish, had been suffered to continue; for they would have exhausted a very considerable part of its substance.

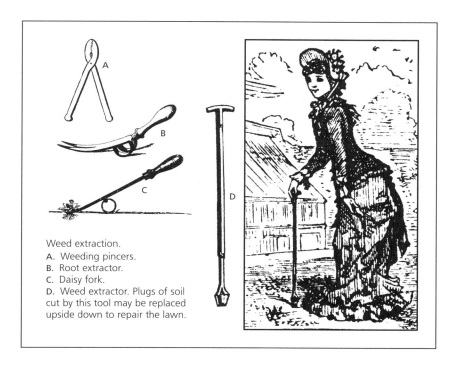

Weed extraction.
A. Weeding pincers.
B. Root extractor.
C. Daisy fork.
D. Weed extractor. Plugs of soil cut by this tool may be replaced upside down to repair the lawn.

Peach
Prunus persica

THE NURSERY

❧ Bud Apricots, Peaches, and Nectarines. ❧

This is the principal season for budding apricots, peaches, and nectarines; but remember to do it upon plum-stocks, which are the best adapted to these kinds of fruit. These stocks should be raised by sowing the stones of plums; and they will be fit for budding in the third year of their growth.

With regard to the manner of performing the operation of budding, we have fully described it in the work of the nursery of the foregoing month.

❧ Bud Plums, Pears, Cherries, &c. ❧

Plums, pears, cherries, &c. may also now be budded on their proper stocks. Plums, for instance, succeed best when budded on plum-stocks, raised by sowing the stones; pears when budded upon quince or pear-stocks, raised by sowing the kernels; and cherries when budded on cherry-stocks, raised from sowing the stones.

In performing this operation, regard must be had to the nature of the intended tree. If it be designed for a wall or espalier, the budding should be performed in a smooth part of the stock, about five or six inches above the ground; because the tree will then readily furnish the wall or espalier with bearing wood from the very bottom.

Brown pear
Pyrus

But if it be intended for a standard, the budding should be performed considerably higher, three, four, or even six feet from the ground. You must also remember to chuse stocks that are grown to a proper size; otherwise they will not have substance sufficient for receiving the buds at a sufficient height from the ground.

ᔕ Bud Jasmines. ᙏ

The budding of jasmines is the most certain method of raising the more curious kinds; and this is the proper season for performing the operation.

The common white jasmine is the proper stock to bud the more curious kinds upon; and it should be done the first or second week in the month.

ᔕ Examine New Grafted and New Budded Trees. ᙏ

Look over all your new grafted trees, and displace all such shoots as are at any time produced from the stocks below the graft, or bud; for these would rob the latter of their nourishment.

At the same time observe, where any of the grafts or buds have made vigorous shoots, to let every one of these shoots be supported with a firm stake.

Service tree
Sorbus latifolia

ᔕ Transplant Seedling Firs and Pines. ᙏ

Whenever you find your young firs or pines stand too close in their seed-beds, let them be transplanted now. For though they will now require a little more care than when transplanted next spring; yet they will succeed very well, provided they are properly watered and shaded from the sun.

Let therefore beds be prepared, about three feet broad, the ground well broken, and the surface raked very even. Into these beds let the plants where they stand too thick in their seed-beds be transplanted, and watered immediately.

Remember to shade the plants every day from the sun till they have taken root; for otherwise they will be burnt up and destroyed. Let them also be supplied with water till they have taken root. The waterings should be moderate, and often repeated in dry weather.

If this method be observed, they will soon take root, and by Michaelmas have gained sufficient strength to endure the winter's cold. Indeed they generally do better than those which are suffered to remain in the seed-bed till March.

Swiss pine
Pinus cembra

Pine
Pinus

☙ Water the Seed-Beds of Young Plants. ଓ

You must still continue to water the seed-beds of all young shrubs once in two or three days at least, during the dry weather.

This will prove of the utmost advantage to the young plants, provided the watering be always moderate; for if the water be poured on the beds too hastily, or given in too great a quantity at one time, it will greatly injure, if not totally destroy the plants.

☙ Destroy Weeds. ଓ

As soon as ever you perceive any weeds in the seed-beds of your young plants, let them be destroyed; for nothing is so destructive to young seedling plants as weeds. These will do the young plants more injury in two or three weeks, than they will be able to recover in a twelvemonth.

But it is not enough that the beds alone be kept free from weeds; every part of the nursery must be the same; for this will be at once an advantage to the young plants, and give the whole a pleasing appearance.

When weeds appear between the rows of transplanted trees, they may be expeditiously destroyed by the application of a good sharp hoe in dry days.

Above all, be very careful that none of the weeds in any part of the nursery perfect their seeds; for whenever this is permitted, the seeds will fall upon the ground, and lay a foundation for a seven year's crop at least. Many of them also, by their particular form and appurtenances, will be wasted to a great distance from the mother plant, and fill the nursery with disagreeable inhabitants.

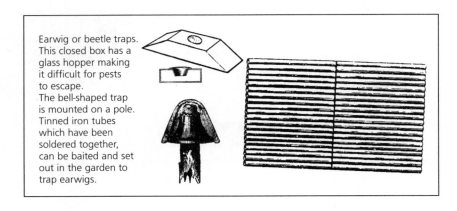

Earwig or beetle traps. This closed box has a glass hopper making it difficult for pests to escape.
The bell-shaped trap is mounted on a pole. Tinned iron tubes which have been soldered together, can be baited and set out in the garden to trap earwigs.

THE FRUIT-GARDEN

∞ Budding. ∞

This is a proper season for inoculating or budding fruit trees.

You must remember to bud each sort upon its proper stock. Thus apricots, peaches, and nectarines, flourish best upon plum-stocks; and generally make the strongest and most lasting trees when budded upon stocks raised from plum-stones.

Portugal quince
Cydonia oblonga

Pears should be budded upon quince or pear-stocks, raised from the seeds of the respective trees. Cherries are generally budded upon cherry stocks raised from the stones.

If any of your cherries, pears, or plums, grafted in the spring have miscarried, they may now be budded with the same kind of fruit; for the trees equally succeed either by grafting or budding.

You should remember to perform this operation in cloudy weather; at least early in the morning, or in the evening after four o'clock; for the great power of the midday sun is apt to dry the cuttings so much, that the buds will not easily part from the wood.

Cherry
Cerasus

When the trees are intended for the wall or espalier, the budding must be performed above four or five inches above the ground; but if they are designed for standards, four, five, or six feet will not be too much.

As we have already in the work of the nursery for June, described the method of performing this operation, it will be unnecessary to repeat it here; but it may not be amiss to add, that budding may also be performed upon trees that bear fruit.

If therefore you have either wall or espalier trees that produce fruit of a different kind than what you desire, you may bud them with the sort more agreeable; but remember to perform the operation on shoots of the same summer's growth.

Summer Bon
Chretien pear
Pyrus

You may even put several buds into one and the same tree, by which means the wall or espalier will be soon covered with the desired kinds, and the trees will, in two or three years after budding, begin to bear fruit.

⋈ Wall Trees. ⋈

If any of your wall trees have not yet received their summer pruning and nailing, let it now be done as soon as possible, otherwise the fruit upon those trees will be both small and ill tasted, in comparison of what they would have been, had not this work been neglected.

Nor is this all, the trees themselves will likewise suffer; particularly the apricots, peaches, nectarines, and other, which produce the greater part of their fruit on wood of one year old.

If therefore any trees remain unpruned, let it be done the first week in the month, remembering to clear away all the luxuriant wood, and to displace all foreright or otherwise ill-placed shoots. At the same leaving, and nailing close to the wall as many of the well-placed moderate growing shoots as can be conveniently laid in; especially of the apricot, peach, and nectarine trees. Remember not to shorten any of the shoots at this season; but let them all be laid in at full length.

With regard to those trees which were dressed and nailed during the two preceding months, let them now be again looked over, to see if all the shoots laid in last month keep firm in their places; and whatever seems amiss let it be rectified; at the same time observing to displace all the straggling shoots produced since the last pruning.

⋈ Vines. ⋈

You must now look over your vines once more, in order to clear them from such shoots as have been produced since last month. By pursuing this method, of rubbing off all the shoots as soon as they appear, your bunches

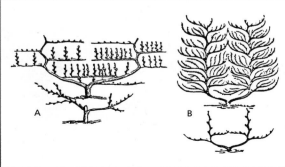

Training of wall trees.
A. Horizontal training with the screw stem is most used for pear and apple trees. The screw causes buds to push at the right place for horizontal shoots.
B. Training in a wavy pattern allows branches bearing fruit to be more densely placed.

of grapes will be large and well grown; every bunch will ripen regularly, and three weeks sooner at least, than where the vines were neglected, and permitted to be over-run with useless shoots.

๕ว Fig Trees. ଔ

This is a proper season for beginning to nail your fig trees to the wall or espalier. Remember not to top or shorten any of the shoots, but to lay in as many of them as you conveniently can, in a strait and regular manner.

๕ว Destroy Snails. ଔ

You must continue your assiduity with regard to destroying snails; for they will otherwise greatly damage your choicest wall fruits. Let the trees therefore be often looked over, early in the morning, and at the close of the evening, especially after showers of rain.

๕ว Destroy Wasps, Hornets, &c. ଔ

Wasps, hornets, and other insects of that kind will now devour many of your choicest fruits, if not carefully prevented. Let therefore a sufficient number of phials filled with sugar water, be hung upon the branches of the trees, before they begin to attack the fruit.

By this means the greater part of your choicest fruits will be preserved; for the smell of the liquor will entice these insects into the phials, where they will be drowned. But it will be necessary to look over your phials often, in order to empty the insects they may contain, and to replenish the phials with a fresh quantity of the above sweetened water.

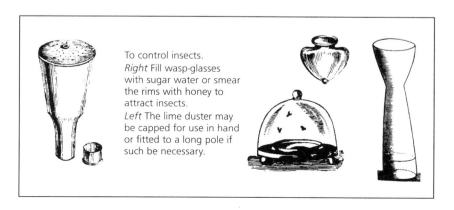

To control insects.
Right Fill wasp-glasses with sugar water or smear the rims with honey to attract insects.
Left The lime duster may be capped for use in hand or fitted to a long pole if such be necessary.

THE PLEASURE OR FLOWER-GARDEN

೧ Management of Choice Carnations. ଓ

Your choice carnations will still require a considerable degree of attention. Their flower pods, as they begin to break, must be assisted by opening the pods deeper according to the manner directed in the preceding month; this is very necessary to promote their regular spreading, in which one of the principal beauties of choice carnations consists.

Remember to refresh the pots duly with water; in very hot weather they will require a little once every other day. Remember also to protect them, when in bloom, from wet and the mid-day sun.

The best method is to have the top of the stage covered with a light covering, supported at a convenient height, that it may neither hide the flowers, nor draw them up weak. In order to this, let a light frame of lattice-work, resembling the roof of a house, be made, of the breadth and length of the stage; and let this be covered with painted canvas, or oiled paper. This roof should be supported by posts fixed up in proper parts of the stage; and of a sufficient height to admit the flowers being viewed with pleasure, and at the same time to defend the flowers from wet, and the scorching rays of the sun.

∞ Lay Carnations and Double Sweet-Williams. ∞

You may continue to lay carnations and double sweet-williams, during the whole month; but the sooner it is done the better. The same method laid down in the preceding month must be pursued.

Remember to refresh your layers often with water in dry weather; and where you perceive any of them have started from their places, let them be again pegged down in their proper position.

∞ Transplant Carnation Layers. ∞

At the latter end of this month, many of the carnation layers that were laid about the middle of June, will be sufficiently rooted for transplantation.

Let them therefore be looked over, and let such as have shot out tolerable roots, be carefully separated from the mother plant. They should be cut off close to the slit part of the layer, and planted immediately after cutting off the tops of the leaves.

They may either be planted in small pots, or beds of rich earth. If in the former, the pots must be left in a shady place, and the plants moderately watered from time to time, till they have taken fresh root. In these pots they are to remain till March, and then removed into larger pots, where they are intended to blow.

Carnation
Dianthus caryophyllus

The beds, in which the layers of common carnations are generally planted, should be three feet broad, the earth well dug, and the surface raked very even. In these beds the layers must be set as soon as taken from the mother plant, in rows five or six inches asunder, and watered as soon as planted.

In these beds they are to remain till October, when they are to be taken up with balls of earth about their roots, and planted in the borders where they are to flower. But remember, during the interval, to weed and water the beds occasionally.

∞ Management of Tender Annuals. ∞

Let your cockscombs, tricolars, double-balsams, and other curious annuals, kept till this season under glasses, be now brought out; remembering to clean the plants from all decayed leaves, to stir the earth a little at the top of the pots, and to add a sprinkling of sifted earth over it.

Remember also to support every plant with a stick of a proper height, fixed in each pot, and to let the stem of the plant be tied neatly to it in different places.

When this is done, let a moderate quantity of water be gently poured over the head of the plant. This will at once refresh the plant, cleanse the leaves from dust, and give it a very lively appearance.

Remember to place them where they are to remain, and to supply the plants duly with water in dry weather.

ﾞ Transplant Common Annuals. ﾞ

If any of your common annuals still remain in the seed or nursery-beds, let them be transplanted at the beginning of this month. But remember to take them up with balls of earth about their roots, and to plant them in the places where they are to remain.

Sweet peas
Lathyrus odoratus

As soon as they are planted, let them be refreshed with water, and such as have long stems be supported with stakes.

ﾞ Remove Perennial Plants. ﾞ

All your perennial and biennial plants, particularly wall-flowers, stock july-flowers, sweet-williams, columbines, Canterbury and pyramidal bell-flowers, Greek valerian, tree primrose, single scarlet lychnis, rose campions, French honey-suckles, hollyhocks, &c. that still remain in their seed beds, must now be removed into nursery beds.

In order to this, let some beds of rich earth, three feet and a half broad, be now prepared; and the plants taken up and set immediately, each sort separate, in the nursery-beds. Each bed will contain six rows, and the plants must be set about six inches asunder in the rows.

Bell flower
Campanula pyramidalis

Remember to water the plants as soon as they are set, and to repeat the waterings occasionally, till they have taken root.

ﾞ Transplant Seedling Auriculas and Polyanthuses. ﾞ

It is now time to remove your seedling auriculas and polyanthuses from their seed-beds.

In order to this, let a spot of ground, well defended from the mid-day sun, be chosen, neatly dug, and the surface raked very even.

This being done, let the plants be taken up, and immediately set, about four inches asunder every way in these beds, closing the earth well about them, and refreshing them gently with water.

Remember to keep the beds clear from weeds, and to refresh them with water every two or three days, in dry weather, during the summer season.

℘ Propagate Scarlet Lychnis, &c. ℆

You may still propagate scarlet lychnis, and other plants of that kind, by cuttings, in the manner laid down in June. But remember to do it at the beginning of the month, lest they have not time sufficient to shoot out proper roots before the cold weather comes on.

℘ Management of Auricula Plants in Pots. ℆

Examine often your choice auricula plants in pots, taking away all dead leaves as fast as they appear, and pulling up every weed.

Remember not to omit watering your plants pretty frequently in dry weather.

Primrose
Primula auricula

℘ Take Up Bulbous Roots. ℆

Your crown imperials, red lilies, bulbous irises, and narcissuses, with several others of the same kind, will be now past flowering, and their leaves in a decaying state. Let them therefore be taken up in a dry time, and after separating the off-sets from the principal, the latter may be either planted again immediately, or properly dried, cleaned, and preserved, till October or November, and then planted regularly in the borders.

The small off-sets should be planted by themselves in a nursery-bed, for a year or two, to gather strength, and then be planted among other bulbous roots in beds or borders.

Lily
*Lilium auratum
vittatum*

℘ Trim Flowering Shrubs and Evergreens. ℆

Let all the rude straggling branches on your flowering shrubs and evergreens, be now cut off with a knife. By this means the head of each plant will be formed in a regular manner, and every shrub stand separate and distinct.

Firethorn
Pyracantha coccinea

ఴ Support Flowering Plants. ⌘

Look over your flowering plants, and wherever you perceive a support necessary, let a stake be fixed in the earth, and the stem of the plant tied to it.

If this be done early, few of your plants will be broken by the wind or rain, which would otherwise be the fate of many.

ఴ Cut Down Decayed Flower Stems. ⌘

Many of your perennial fibrous-rooted plants will now be past their bloom; let their stems therefore be cut down close to the head of the plant, and all the dead leaves cleared away.

ఴ Clip Hedges. ⌘

If you would have your hedges perfectly neat, they should be clipped at the beginning of this month, and a second time about the middle of August, but if you think one clipping sufficient, it will be better to defer it till the latter end of this month, or the beginning of August.

Asparagus-shaped
trillium
Trillium

ఴ Cut Box Edgings. ⌘

Your box edgings that were not trimmed last month, must be trimmed now. But remember to do it in a moist time; for when box is cut in dry weather, it will turn brown, and make a very unsightly appearance.

Box edgings should never be suffered to grow higher than three or four inches, nor broader than two and a half.

ఴ Destroy Weeds in the Borders. ⌘

Remember to keep your borders, especially those next the walks, entirely free from weeds; and be sure not to let any of them ripen their seed in any part of the garden.

As soon as you have hoed the borders, let them be immediately raked, in order to draw off the weeds and all other litter; for this will make a surface smooth and even, and give the whole a neat and pleasing appearance.

℘ Mow Grass-Walks and Lawns. ℜ

Your grass-walks and lawns should be regularly mown about once a week, which will keep the grass in general in tolerable, good order.

Remember, likewise, to roll your grass now and then; for this will be a great addition to the beauty of the plats and walks, and, at the same time, render the surface firm and even.

℘ Gravel-Walks. ℜ

Your gravel-walks will require some care. They must be rolled twice a week, at least, if they are intended to be kept any thing neat. Nor must any weeds be suffered to grow, or any sort of litter be seen upon them.

AUGUST

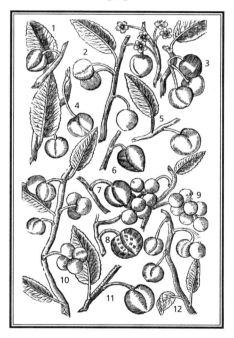

1. May Cherry. *Cerasus praecox.*
2. Flanders Cherry. *Cerasus Batavica.*
3. White Cherry. *Cerasus Hispanica fine alba.*
4. Great Leafed Cherry. *Cerasus platophyllos.*
5. Luke Wards Cherry. *Cerasus Luca Wardi.*
6. Naples Cherry. *Cerasus Neapolitana.*
7. Heart Cherry. *Cerasus Cordata.*
8. Bignarre or Spotted Cherry. *Cerasus maculata.*
9. Wild Cluster Cherry. *Cerasus avium racemosa.*
10. Flanders Cluster Cherry. *Cerasus Corymbisera.*
11. Archdukes Cherry. *Cerasus Archiducis.*
12. Dwarf Cherry. *Chamacerasus.*

Regular lawn rolling maintains overall smoothness, and flattens worm casts prior to scything of grass.

The Works of this Month in the
KITCHEN GARDEN

℘ Cucumber Plants. ℘

Your cucumber plants will, at this season, demand particular attention, especially those which are sown in the open ground, to produce fruit for pickling.

These plants must be well supplied with water in dry weather; they will require it three or four times a week, at least. And it should be remembered, that the quantity of fruit will greatly depend on this circumstance.

Cucumber
Cucumis sativus

The young fruit should be gathered about three times a week; for when once the fruit have attained a proper size, they will soon be too large for pickling. Let the vines be carefully looked over, in a regular manner, every other day.

℘ Ripening Melons. ℘

It will be necessary to take particular care of your ripening melons; for if too much rain should happen to fall at this time, it would, in a great measure, destroy the fruit, unless properly defended. Let, therefore, both the roots and fruit be sheltered by the methods mentioned last month.

᎒ Sow Winter Spinach. ᎒

If the seed for a full crop of spinach was not sown last month, it must be done at the beginning of this.

Let therefore a piece of rich ground, that lies tolerably dry in winter, be neatly dug, the seed sown immediately, trod in, and the surface raked even.

As soon as the plants have got leaves about an inch broad, let them be thinned and cleared from weeds. This may be done either by hand or hoe, observing to thin the plants regularly, leaving them at about four inches from one another. This will give them proper room to spread, and gather strength sufficient to enable them to endure the cold.

It should also be remembered, that when spinach is allowed room to spread itself regularly, the plants will produce very large and thick leaves, far superior to those found on plants crowded too near one another.

᎒ Sow Cabbage Seed. ᎒

Between the sixth and twelfth of this month, is a proper season for sowing early cabbage seed, particularly the sugar loaf, or early Battersea kinds.

In order to this, let an open spot of rich ground be dug, and divided into beds three feet and a half broad. Sow the seed moderately thick, and rake it in lightly with an even hand.

Other kinds of cabbage seed, particularly that of the long sided cabbage, may also be sown at the beginning of the month.

Kohlrabi
Brassica oleracea gongylodes

᎒ Sow Cauliflowers. ᎒

Between the eighteenth and twentieth of this month, a little cauliflower seed should be sown for raising plants to produce an early crop next summer; and about a week after sow for the main crop.

The plants raised from the first sowing should be planted out for good about the latter end of October, under hand or bell-glasses. Some of the plants may, at the same time, be set under a south wall, where they will often endure the winter without any other shelter.

With regard to the plants raised from the second sowing, and intended for the main crop, they should, for their more certain preservation, be planted under frames about the last week in October, and continue there during the whole winter.

The seed must be sown in a spot of clean rich ground, neatly dug, and divided into beds three feet and a half broad. As soon as the seed is sown, let it be raked in very carefully; or about a quarter of an inch thick of light earth be sifted over it. In dry weather, the bed must be moderately watered from time to time, both before and after the plants appear. By this means the plants will soon come up, rise equally, and all take a regular growth.

℘ Transplant Broccoli. ℞

At the beginning of this month, let a spot of open ground be prepared for planting out the second crop of broccoli. If some rotten dung be spread over the ground, and well dug in, it will prove of the greatest advantage to the plants.

These broccoli plants should be planted in rows two feet asunder, and twenty inches apart in the rows. Remember to give them a little water as soon as planted.

With regard to the broccoli planted out last month, you must now remember to draw the earth about their stems; for this will greatly strengthen them, and promote their growth.

℘ Transplant Savoys. ℞

This is a very good season for transplanting savoys, for the plants will be in excellent order for the table soon after Christmas. Let them be set in rows eighteen or twenty inches asunder, and the same distance be allowed between the plants in the rows.

℘ Transplant Celery. ℞

More celery must be transplanted at this season. Let there-fore an open spot of ground be chosen, and the trenches prepared in the manner directed last month. In these trench-es, let the plants (after trimming the ends of their roots, and cutting off the tops of their leaves) be set four or five inches distant, in a single row along the middle of each trench. Remember to water them as soon as they are planted, and, if the weather prove dry, to repeat the operation every evening, till the plants have taken root.

Turnip-rooted
celery
*Apium
graveolens
rapaceum*

℘ Earth up Celery. ℞

As your celery planted in the trenches during the two last months advances in height, let it be earthed up. But remember to do this in dry weather, and when the plants are also dry. The earth must be well broken, and then laid up lightly to the plants.

They must be earthed up to a proper height on each side; but, at the same time, particular care must be taken not to break down their leaves, or bury their hearts.

ℓ Transplant Endive. ℣

Another parcel of endive must be now transplanted. In order to which, let an open spot of ground be properly dug. When this is done, draw up some of the strongest plants, trim the extremities of their roots, take off the tops of their leaves, and plant them twelve inches from one another every way.

Remember to water them as soon as planted, and, if the weather be dry, to repeat the waterings every two or three days, till the plants have taken root.

ℓ Blanch Endive. ℣

Towards the latter end of this month, the endive planted out in June will be full grown, and should therefore be tied up to promote their blanching.

When the weather is dry, let the plants be examined, and the leaves of such as are proper for blanching be tied up with fresh bass. Remember to gather the leaves up regularly in your hand, and to tie them together in a neat manner, but not too straight.

ℓ Sow Turnips. ℣

A late crop of turnips may still be sown; and if it be done the first or second week in the month, there will be very little danger of success; but after that time it is not prudent to sow turnips, for they generally miscarry.

ℓ Hoe and Thin Turnips. ℣

The turnips sown last month must now be hoed and thinned. But take the advantage of dry days, and do it before the plants are too far advanced in their growth: the time may be known by examining the plants; for when their rough leaves are the breadth of a man's thumb, the work may be done with expedition and regularity. Six or eight inches should be allowed between the plants.

Early strap-
leaved turnip
Brassica rapa

ℓ Sow Onions. ℣

If you omitted to sow for spring onions last month, let it be done at the beginning of this; by the second week at farthest.

In order to this, let a clean dry spot of ground be neatly dug, and divided into beds three feet and a half, or four feet broad. On these beds let the seed be sown tolerably thick, but as equal as possible, and raked in with a very even hand, that the plants may rise regularly in all parts of the beds.

It will be prudent to sow, at the same time, a little Welsh onion-seed, that if the former should be destroyed by the frost, the latter, which will survive almost the severest winter, may supply its place.

The Welsh seed should be sown in the same manner as the English; so that the instructions given for the latter will be equally sufficient for the former.

ᔕ Take Up Onions. ᘓ

Examine your crops of onions; and when you perceive their leaves begin to fall, and wither, the roots have acquired their full growth, and must therefore be taken out of the ground. But remember to do this in dry weather, and to spread them immediately in the shade to dry, as directed last month.

ᔕ Take Up Garlick and Shallots. ᘓ

Your crops of garlick and shallots must also be taken out of the ground when their roots have acquired their full growth, which is known by their leaves, which always begin to wither as soon as the roots have done drawing nourishment.

Garlick
Allium sativum

ᔕ Sow Carrots. ᘓ

About the third or fourth week in this month, but not before, a little carrot seed may be sown, in order to raise plants for spring use. Let the seed be sown in beds, not too thick, and raked in regularly. The plants raised from this sowing will supply the table in the spring.

ᔕ Sow Radishes. ᘓ

A little radish seed, of the salmon or scarlet kind, may be sown at two different times this month; about the middle, and towards the latter end. The plants from the former will be fit to draw about the middle of September, and those from the latter about Michaelmas, and continue tolerably good all October.

Remember to sow the seed in an open spot of ground, and to water the bed now and then in dry weather.

᎒᎒ Sow Lettuce Seed. ᎒᎒

A small quantity of the seeds of Coss, Silesia, brown Dutch, and common lettuce, should be sown at two different times this month. Let the first sowing be performed before the tenth of the month, and the second between the eighteenth and twenty-fourth. The plants from the first will supply the table in October and November, but the plants from the second are to be removed into warm borders, in order to stand the winter, and supply the table in April and May.

Remember to sow the seeds of each sort separate, to rake them in evenly, and to water the beds now and then in dry weather.

Some of the plants raised from the seed of the second sowing, particularly the brown Dutch and cabbage lettuce, may when fit, be planted in shallow frames, where they must be covered every night, and in all wet, or other bad cold weather, with the glasses: in hard frost they must also have coverings of the dry straw, fern, &c. laid over the glasses, and about the outsides of the frames. By this means they will be tolerably well cabbaged by February, when they will be considered as a very great rarity.

᎒᎒ Transplant Lettuces. ᎒᎒

Some of the lettuces sown last month, to supply the table in autumn, must be now transplanted.

In order to this, let a spot of rich ground, in a dry situation, be prepared, and the lettuces planted in it immediately, ten or twelve inches asunder every way. Remember to water them as soon as planted, and to repeat the operation occasionally, in dry weather, till they have taken root.

᎒᎒ Sow Small Salleting. ᎒᎒

A small quantity of the seeds of mustard, radish, cresses, rape, and turnip, should be sown once every week, if a regular supply of some salleting herbs be wanting.

A shady border must be chosen for this purpose, where the seeds are to be sown, each sort separate, in shallow drills, and covered with dry earth about a quarter of an inch thick. Remember to water them occasionally in dry weather.

᎒᎒ Thin Colewort Plants. ᎒᎒

About the middle, or latter end of the month, look over your colewort plants sown last month; and wherever you perceive they stand too thick, let some of them be drawn out, and transplanted in rows twelve inches asunder, and the plants six inches apart in the rows.

By this means, the plants remaining in the seed-bed will have more room to grow, and those taken up and transplanted will be fit for use three or four weeks sooner than if they had been left in the seed-bed till next month.

℘ Clean Asparagus Beds. ℭ

Remember to clear your beds of asparagus from weeds and litter of every kind, particularly those that were planted last March or April.

At the same time, let the seedling asparagus sown in the spring be kept very clean: a careful hand-weeding will best answer this purpose.

℘ Examine Artichoke Plants. ℭ

Your artichoke plants set in March or April must be now examined, as many of them will be in fruit; and besides the principal, or top artichoke, there will rise many small heads, or suckers, from the sides of the stems; but all these should be displaced, if you desire the principal head to be large. It will, however, be necessary to take these off before they exceed the size of an egg, otherwise they will have exhausted too much of the strength of the root; and, consequently, render the principal head proportionably smaller.

It may not be amiss to repeat the caution mentioned last month, of breaking down the stems of the artichokes when you cut the fruit.

℘ Propagate Sweet Herbs. ℭ

The slips of many of the aromatic herbs, particularly those of sage, hyssop, mastich, marjoram, lavender, rue, and rosemary, may still be planted, for they will succeed, if planted in the beginning of the month.

The slips must be from six to nine inches long, and planted in a shady border. Remember to put two-thirds of the slip into the ground, and to water occasionally in dry weather.

Marjoram
Origanum
marjorana

℘ Trim Aromatic Herbs. ℭ

The decayed flower-stems of hyssop, savory, lavenders and other aromatic plants of that kind, should be cut down, and all the straggling and other young shoots should be shortened at the beginning of this month.

But remember to do this in a moist time, if possible. The flower stems, and young shoots, should be cut pretty close, with a pair of garden shears. This will make them put out numbers of fresh short shoots, so that they will form close snug heads before winter, and appear neat during that dreary season.

ഇ Gather Herbs to Dry and Distil. ଔ

Let the herbs intended to serve the family in the winter be cut down in a dry day, and spread to dry in an airy room, out of reach of the sun. When thoroughly dried, let them be tied in bunches, and hung up in a dry room for use.

This is also the season for cutting down many plants for distillation. But remember to do it when they are in flower, for then they are in their full prime.

Basil
Ocimum

ഇ Gather Seeds. ଔ

As young seeds ripen, let the heads or pods be gathered in a dry day; and as soon as they are cut let them be spread on mats or cloths, to dry and harden, in a shady place, where no rain can touch them. In about a fortnight the heads or pods will sufficiently dry, and the seed should therefore then be beaten or rubbed out, and well cleaned.

When you have thus procured clean seed, let it be spread upon cloths in a dry but shady place, for a day or two, to harden, and then put up in bags or boxes for use.

Single parsley
Selinum dulce

ഇ Destroy Weeds. ଔ

You must be very careful, at this season to destroy the weeds, among all your crops. Be sure never to let them get to any great head; nor any of them ever ripen their seed. This care must be extended to every part of the garden, whether cropped or not.

By this means you will keep the weeds under; for it should be remembered that every weed suffered to ripen its seed, will lay a foundation for hundreds the year to come. No care therefore should be wanting to destroy them before they arrive at maturity.

In open spots, and wherever there is room to use a hoe, this is easily done; but remember to let your hoe be sharp, and let it be done in a dry day.

When you have hoed down the weeds, do not suffer them to lie on the ground where they grow, but rake them up, and carry them away.

White Oak
Quercus alba

THE NURSERY

ᔓ Transplant Seedlings. ᔕ

Examine the buds of your seedling plants, particularly those of the pine, fir, and box; and wherever you perceive the plants crowded too close together, let some of them be drawn up and transplanted, observing the same directions that were given last month. For though this is not the season for making a general transplantation; yet where the plants stand too close together, some of them should be removed, otherwise they will spoil one another.

ᔓ Prepare Ground for Transplanting. ᔕ

About the latter end of this month, it will be time to begin trenching such pieces of ground as are intended to be planted in autumn, with any kind of trees or shrubs. The ground should be well dug and laid up in high ridges, that it may enjoy every possible advantage from the rains, sun, and dews.

Remember to keep the whole spot free from weeds; cutting them up with the hoe as soon as they appear, and carrying them off the ground.

ᔓ Trim Evergreen and Forest Trees. ᔕ

This is a proper season for trimming evergreens and such other shrubs in the nursery, that appear to want it. Remember to cut away the vigorous shoots, or to shorten them so as to form a more regular head.

At the same time examine your forest trees, and wherever you perceive they have made any vigorous shoots from their stems near the roots, let such shoots be cut off close.

❧ Bud Fruit Trees. ∝

The operation of budding may still be performed on some sorts of fruit trees, provided it be done at the beginning of the month.

You must also now look over the stocks that were budded three weeks or a month before, in order to untye the bass, that the parts about the bud may not be pinched.

❧ Weed and Water Seedling Plants. ∝

Remember to keep your beds of seedling plants entirely free from weeds; and to water them occasionally in dry weather.

Let the spaces between the rows of all kinds of young trees and shrubs be destroyed. Remember to do this work in dry days; and then the weeds are so cut down with the hoe, to rake them up, and carry them away; for otherwise many of the larger weeds would take fresh root, and grow up again.

Plum
Prunus

THE FRUIT-GARDEN

❧ Wall Trees. ∝

Your peach, nectarine, and other trees of that kind still require attention. It will be necessary to look them once more carefully over, and wherever you find any of the branches displaced by the wind or other accident, to nail them again in a neat and secure manner.

At the same time take away all the straggling shoots that have been lately produced, for they will only tend to hinder the ripening of the fruit.

❧ Vines. ∝

You must once more look over your vines, whether planted in vineyards, or against walls, in order to displace every shoot that has been lately produced, whether from the old or young wood; for they are all not only entirely useless, but will tend greatly to retard the growth and ripening of the fruit.

At the same time examine carefully all the bearing or other proper shoots; and wherever you perceive any of them started from their places, fasten them again to the wall or stakes, in their proper direction. By this means, every bunch of fruit will ripen equally, for every one will enjoy equally the advantages of the sun and air.

It will also be proper to examine the fruit, and wherever you find the branches entangled either with one another or with the shoots, let them be relieved, so that every bunch may hang in its proper position.

ɛɔ Fig Trees. ଓ

The figs will be now full grown and begin to ripen; consequently a proper share of the sun will be necessary to give them a flavour.

In order to this, let all the young shoots be low laid in close to the wall, taking care to use the knife at this season as little as possible. Let therefore no shoots, except those which are produced foreright, be now cut off; laying in all the fair growing side-shoots to produce fruit next year. And as these trees produce their fruit upon none but shoots of one year old,

Figs
Ficus carica

it is the safest way to leave enough of them at this season; for all that are not wanted to lay in at the general season of pruning, may then be cut away.

But whatever you do with regard to these shoots, be sure not to shorten them; they must be laid in at their full length, for the shoots of these trees must never be shortened.

Remember to lay them in regularly, not across one another, and to secure them properly, for the broad leaves of these trees give the wind and rain great power over them.

ɛɔ Bud Trees. ଓ

You may still perform the operation of budding with success, provided it be done at the beginning of the month. The same method my be pursued as is given in the work of the nursery for June.

Apple
Malus bertini

ɛɔ Examine Budded Trees. ଓ

It will be necessary to look over your trees that have been budded about three weeks or a month, in order to loosen the bandage; for if this be neglected, the motion of the sap will be greatly impeded, the parts about the bud will swell irregularly, and four out of five of the buds will miscarry.

At the same time remember to examine the part of the stock below the bud, and rub off all the shoots produced in that part.

❧ Defend Wall Fruit From Birds, Insects, &c. ☙

Your choice wall-fruit will still want your care to defend it from birds, insects, &c.

The former may be effectually kept off by fixing up nets before the trees whose fruit they are fond of. This precaution therefore should not be omitted; particularly with regard to grapes, figs, and late cherries.

Raspberry
Rubus idaeus

With regard to wasps, flies, and hornets, the best method is that mentioned last month, namely, by fixing phials filled with sugar-water, on proper parts of the tree; for the sweetness of the water will allure the insects from the fruit, and induce them to crawl into the bottles, where they will be drowned.

❧ Cleanse the Borders About Fruit Trees. ☙

No weeds should be suffered to grow, or litter of any kind to lie, on fruit tree borders.

The keeping these borders clean will be attended with a double advantage; the trees will not be deprived of their nourishment; and at the same time, the clean smooth surface of the ground will reflect the sun's heat upon the tree, and

Heart cherry
Cerasus cordata

consequently promote the ripening, and improve the flavour of the fruit. Add to this, the agreeable pleasure the eye will receive from the neatness of the borders.

❧ Destroy Weeds. ☙

Remember to destroy all the weeds between the rows of vines in the vineyard; let them be cut down as soon as they appear; and when this is done, let them, together with all other kind of litter, be taken away.

This will greatly promote the growth and ripening of the grapes; for a perfectly clean surface in a vineyard, answers in some degree the purpose of a wall, by reflecting the sun's heat upon the vines and fruit.

But were the weeds permitted to grow, no heat could be reflected from the surface. On the contrary, a moist vapour would arise from the intervals between the rows, which would greatly retard the growth and ripening of the grapes; besides robbing the roots of great part of their nourishment.

Border Pinks
*Dianthus chinensis
heddewigii*

THE PLEASURE OR
FLOWER-GARDEN

℘ Management of Carnations and Sweet William Layers. ℘

All those carnation layers that were layed five or six weeks ago, will now be well rooted, and should therefore be cut from the original root, and transplanted into beds or pots. The choicest kinds should be planted in pots, that they may be more easily defended from the cold of the winter.

In order to this, let a quantity of penny or half penny pots be procured, and filled with good earth. This being done, take off the layers, trim their tops a little, cut off the bottom of the stalk close to the slit part, plant one layer in each pot, and immediately give it a little water.

When all are planted place the pots in a shady situation, and water them occasionally till they have all fairly taken root.

As soon as you perceive the plants are firmly rooted, let the pots be removed into a more open situation, and there remain till the latter end of October. At that time a bed of

Double Sweet
William
*Dianthus
barbatus*

dry compost should be prepared, of the breadth and length of a common frame: the bed must be composed of dry and light earth well mixed with coal ashes, and raised at least four inches above the level of the ground. When the bed is thus prepared put on the frame, and plunge the pots up to their rims in the compost, and as near together as may be; for here the plants are to remain all the winter, and to be defended in severe frosts, snow, and heavy rains with glasses; but in dry and mild weather the glasses must be taken away.

By this means the plants will be effectually preserved from frost, which cannot enter at the sides of the pots to hurt the roots.

If a frame and glasses be wanting, the pots may be plunged in a bed prepared as above, and effectually defended by fixing hoops across the bed, and covering them with thick mats in bad weather.

In this bed the plants are to remain till the latter end of February, or the beginning of March, when they are to be turned out of the small pots with balls of earth about their roots, and planted in larger, where they are to blow.

With regard to the common carnation layers intended to blow in the borders, they should be managed as follows:

As soon as the layers are well rooted, they are to be separated from the old roots, and trimmed as above directed; and then planted in a bed or border of rich earth. They should be set at least six inches asunder every way, watered immediately, and the operation repeated occasionally till they have taken root. Remember also to shade them from the sun till they are well rooted.

In this bed or border the layers are to remain till October; and then transplanted into the borders where they are to flower.

The layers of double sweet-williams that were layed five or six weeks ago, must be now taken from the old roots, and managed in the same manner as the layers of carnations.

℘ Propagate Fibrous-Rooted Plants. cx

This is a proper season to increase many of the double flowering fibrous rooted plants, particularly the double rose campion and catchfly, double scarlet lychnis, and double rocket, double ragged robin, bachelors button,

&c. by parting their roots, which is done in the following manner:

Where the plants have grown into large fruits, let the whole of each root be taken entirely out of the earth. When this is done let it be divided, taking care that every plant or slip so separated, be properly furnished with roots.

The root being thus parted into several slips or distinct plants, let the ends of the roots of every such slip or plant be cut off, and

Dwarf Haage lychnis
Lychnis

all the dead and broken leaves taken away.

As soon as your plants are thus prepared, let them be planted in a shady border, or where they can be occasionally shaded with mats, about six inches apart. Remember to close the earth well about them, and to give them a little water. Some of the strongest slips may be immediately planted again in the borders.

They will soon take root, if occasionally watered, and by the latter end of October have acquired strength sufficient to be removed, when they are to be taken up with balls of earth about their roots, and planted some in pots, and the rest in borders: they will all flower next summer.

℘ Sow the Seeds of Auriculas and Polyanthuses. ℘

Auricula and polyanthus seed may now be sown, in boxes or large pots. Let therefore some pots or boxes be filled with light earth, about the middle or latter end of the month. On the surface of this mould let the seed be sown pretty thick, and covered about a quarter of an inch deep.

Remember to place your pots or boxes where the seed may have the benefit of the morning sun, and let them continue there till the latter end of next month, when they are to be removed into a situation where the mid day sun may shine upon them.

Cowslip
*Primula veris
humilis*

℘ Sow the Seeds of Bulbous-Rooted Flowers. ℘

About the latter end of the month you may sow the seeds of tulips, hyacinths, narcissuses, irises, crown imperials, fritillarias, lilies, martagons, crocuses, and other bulbous-rooted flowers.

It will be much the better method to sow these seeds in boxes, rather than in beds, because the former may easily be removed to any situation. These boxes should be about fifteen or eighteen inches broad, and ten or twelve deep, and filled within half an inch of the top with fine rich earth raked very fine and even.

On the surface of this earth let the seed be sown moderately thick, and covered about half an inch deep with sifted earth.

Lily
Lilium candidum

When the seed is thus sown, let the boxes be removed into a shady situation, and, if the weather proves dry, lightly watered now and then. In this place they are to continue till the latter end of September, when they must be removed into a warmer situation.

But if you have not boxes for this purpose, the seed may be sown in beds of light earth, about three feet broad, and situated in a dry and warm part of the garden.

You must however remember to defend the plants, whether sown in beds or boxes, from severe frosts and snows, by laying dry litter on the surface of the beds, and outside of the boxes.

About the latter end of next March the plants will begin to appear, and must be kept clear from weeds, and refreshed often with water in dry weather.

ᔑᓄ Sow the Seeds of Anemonies, Ranunculuses, &c. ⊗

Cyclamen
Cyclamen persicum

The seeds of anemonies, ranunculuses, and spring cyclamens may now be sown; but it should be done in boxes or wide-mouth pots, filled with rich light earth.

The seeds should be sown pretty thick on the surface, and covered about a quarter of an inch thick with sifted earth.

ᔑᓄ Remove Bulbous Roots. ⊗

The roots of crown imperials, martagons, red lilies, bulbous and Persian irises, narcissuses, spring crocuses, jonquils, and fritillarias, may now be taken up, and the off-sets separated from them.

Jonquil
Narcissus jonquilla

When this is done the principal roots may either be planted again in their proper places, or dried, cleaned, and put up till October, and then planted.

With regard to their off-sets, the best of them at least should be planted in nursery-beds, each sort separate, and remain there a year or two.

ᔑᓄ Transplant Perennials. ⊗

The seedling wall stocks, sweet-williams, columbines, scabiouses, and other perennial and biennial plants, which still remain in the seed-bed, must be now transplanted into nursery beds.

But remember to let it be done in moist weather, and the sooner in the month the better; because the plants will have more time to root and get strength before winter.

Scabious
Scabiosa

Let them be planted in beds about six inches distance from one another every way, and directly watered.

After standing about two months, they must be transplanted from these beds into the places where they are to remain.

❦ Trim Flowering Plants. ⊙

Remember to look over all your flowering plants, and wherever you perceive any branches advance in an irregular and straggling manner, let them be either cut off close, or shortened. And where the shoots of different branches interfere with one another, let them be shortened, that every branch may stand single; for flowers always appear to greater advantage when they stand clear of each other, than when they are blended together.

Let the main stems be well supported with stakes, and all the withered and decayed leaves pulled off.

African marigold
Tagetes erecta

All the shoots produced near the ground by strong branching annual flowers, such as French and African marigolds, &c. should be cut away, and a foot at least of clear stalk left above the surface. By this means the plants will form handsome and regular heads, and the flowers will have more liberty to grow, and shew themselves to much greater advantage.

❦ Gather Flower Seeds. ⊙

The seeds of such flowers as are now ripe should be gathered in a dry day; and spread to dry in an airy shady place.

As soon as they are sufficiently hardened let them be beat or rubbed out, and preserved for use in bags or boxes.

❦ Cleanse the Borders from Weeds, &c. ⊙

Remember to keep the borders exceeding neat, and free from weeds. In order to which they should be frequently gone over with a sharp hoe, to loosen the ground, and cut up the weeds as they appear.

Sunflower
*Helianthus
decapetalus
multiflorus*

When this is done, let them be neatly raked, in order to draw off all the weeds and other litter, and to lay the surface smooth and even.

❦ Clip Hedges. ⊙

This is the most proper season for clipping your hedges of holly, yew, hornbeam, elm, lime, thorn, &c. provided you trim them but once in the year, for they will not now push out any more branches of consequence this summer.

And those which were clipped about the beginning or middle of last month, will want clipping again about the middle or latter end of this.

ℰ Cut Box and Thrift Edgings. ℭ

This is also a proper season for cutting box and thrift edgings; but remember to do it in moist weather, and not to let those of box grow too broad.

The decayed flower stalks of your thrift edging should now be cut off, and where the sides have grown uneven they should be reduced to order with a pair of garden shears, ground very sharp at the points.

ℰ Water Annual and Perennial Plants. ℭ

Double daisy
Bellis perennis

Remember to water your annual and perennial plants frequently in dry weather: those of the former preserved in pots, will require it three or four times a week.

At the same time let all the dead leaves on your annual plants be taken off; and the stalks of those perennial plants that have done blowing be cut down, a little of the old earth taken from the surface and replaced with fresh, and the pots set in a shady place.

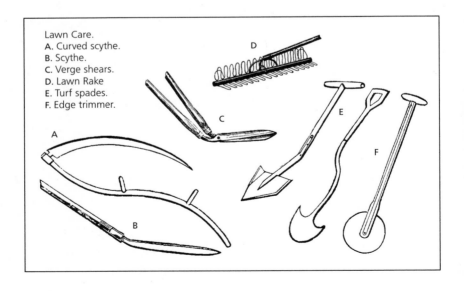

Lawn Care.
A. Curved scythe.
B. Scythe.
C. Verge shears.
D. Lawn Rake
E. Turf spades.
F. Edge trimmer.

❧ Mow Grass Walks and Lawns. ❧

It will be necessary to continue the mowing of grass walks and lawns, once a week at least.

It will be also necessary to pole and roll them frequently; for otherwise the worm-casts and other protuberances on the surface will greatly impair their beauty.

❧ Gravel Walks. ❧

Remember to keep your gravel walks entirely free from weeds and other litter, and to roll them twice a week at least.

SEPTEMBER

1. Skirrets. *Sisarum.*
2. Parsnip. *Pastinaca latifolia.*
3. Carrot. *Daucus carota.*
4. Turnip. *Rapum.*
5. Navews. *Napus sativus.*
6. Black Radish. *Raphanus niger.*
7. Common Radish. *Raphanus vulgaris.*

Some gardeners favour setting out strawberries on a mound of rich soil.

The Works of this Month in the
KITCHEN GARDEN

∞ Cauliflowers. ∞

About the middle or latter end of the month it will be time to remove the cauliflower plants sown in August, into a nursery-bed.

In order to which let a bed be made in the manner described last month, in a well sheltered part of the garden open to the sun, for their reception.

As soon as the bed is finished, draw up some of the best plants from the seed-bed, clear them from decayed or damaged leaves, and plant them in rows about three inches asunder, allowing the same distance between the plants in the rows. Remember not to plant them so deep as to bury their hearts, for that would inevitably destroy them.

Give the plants a little water to settle the earth about their roots, as soon as they are set; but be sure not to pour the water upon them too hastily, lest you break their leaves, or wash the earth into their hearts.

The plants being thus set, put on the frame and glasses for a few days till the plants have taken root, remembering to shade the plants from the rays of the sun; when the glasses are to be removed, and only applied in very heavy rains, during an interval of a month at least.

℘ Michaelmas Cauliflowers. ⊂⋧

About the end of this month, some of the cauliflowers planted out in July for a Michaelmas crop, will begin to show their flowers. The plants must therefore be encouraged as much as possible, by hoeing between, and drawing the earth up round the stem of each plant, and keeping them entirely free from weeds.

At the same time remember if the weather proves dry, to form the earth like a basin round each plant, and pour water therein; for this will so greatly encourage their growth, that they will produce large heads in October and November. Whereas their heads would have been small at the proper season, had the plants been denied a sufficient degree of moisture.

℘ Broccoli. ⊂⋧

Broccoli
Brassica oleracea botrytis

During the first or second week in this month, your last crop of broccoli must be transplanted into the place where they are to produce their heads.

In order to this, let a rich spot of ground be dug for these plants in a warm situation, and the broccoli planted in rows a foot and a half asunder, allowing the same distance between the plants in the rows.

With regard to the broccoli planted out in the preceding month, they want no other care than that of hoeing the ground, and destroying the weeds between the rows, and of drawing up the earth round the stems of the plants.

℘ Cabbage Plants. ⊂⋧

Early Wakefield
cabbage
Brassica capitata

About the middle of this month, the cabbage-plants sown the second week in August, for an early crop next summer, must be pricked out into the nursery-beds.

Let, therefore, a piece of good ground, in a sheltered situation, be dug for that purpose, and laid out in beds three feet and a half wide.

When the beds are ready, thin out the best plants regularly in the seed-bed, leaving the smaller for a fortnight longer; and plant them in rows length-ways of the bed, about four inches asunder, leaving an interval of six inches between the rows. Remember to close the ground well about their stems, and to leave the surface smooth between the plants.

As soon as the plants are set, give them a little water, and if the weather be dry, repeat the watering two or three times during the first week or ten days, when the plants will have taken good root.

ᔥ Coleworts. ᔥ

Some time in the beginning of this month many of the forwardest of the colewort plants sown the latter end of July, will be fit to plant out into the places where they are to remain.

Let therefore a piece of ground be dug for their reception, in a part of the garden where the cutting winds in the winter have the least power; and there planted in rows ten or twelve inches asunder, and the plants six or eight inches apart in the rows.

Colewort
Brassica oleracea
acephala

ᔥ Turnips. ᔥ

The turnips sown the preceding month must now be hoed out regularly, leaving them about eight inches distant from one another.

Your hoe should be sharp, and of a middle size, that the weeds may be cut up clean.

ᔥ Spinach. ᔥ

The spinach sown in August must now be cleared and thinned out regularly, to the distance of four or five inches, either by the hand or hoe. But remember to leave the strongest plants, and to clear the whole bed perfectly from weeds.

If you omitted to sow spinach last month, it may still be done, provided it be not deferred longer than the middle of the month. It will succeed tolerably well, if the seed be sown in a rich warm soil.

ᔥ Onions. ᔥ

Your beds of onions sown the beginning or middle of August will now want weeding; for the weeds must never be suffered to get the start of the plants. This work must be done very carefully, and entirely by hand; otherwise many of the young plants will be drawn up with the weeds. But the onions need only be thinned, at present, except in those places where they rise in clusters.

Trebons onions
Allium cepa

⊗ Lettuces. ⊗

Towards the latter end of this month, the different sorts of lettuces sown in August, for spring use, should be planted out where they are to continue.

Let therefore a warm border, under a south wall, or other fence, be prepared for their reception; observing, when you dig the ground, to lay the border somewhat sloping to the sun, and afterwards to rake the surface smooth and even.

When the border is thus prepared, let some of the best plants be drawn out of the seed-bed, and after trimming the ends of their roots a little, and picking off all the broken or decayed leaves, let them be planted in rows length-ways of the border, about four or five inches asunder, allowing the same distance between the plants in the rows.

If the greater part of these plants survive the winter, near one half of them may be removed in the spring, and planted in a more open exposure; while the rest may remain in the border to cabbage early.

It is not yet too late to sow a little lettuce-seed for spring use, provided it be done in a rich spot of ground during the first week in the month.

⊗ Small Salleting. ⊗

The seeds of cresses, mustard, radish, and rape, should be sown every week or ten days, in rich, light earth, and in a warm situation.

The seeds should be sown in shallow drills, and covered about a quarter of an inch deep with light earth. The seed sown the last week in the month, must be covered with a frame and glasses during the nights, if the weather be cold.

Mustard green
Brassica hirta

⊗ Celery. ⊗

A late crop of celery, for spring use, should be planted out about the middle of this month.

In order to this, let some trenches about twelve inches wide, and five or six deep, be dug, leaving an interval of two feet and a half between the trenches.

Take up the celery plants, trim their roots and tops, and plant one row in each trench, about four or five inches asunder.

℘ Earth up Celery. ℭ

The rows of celery planted in trenches during the former months, must be earthed up. Remember to do it when the plants are dry, to break the earth well, and to lay it properly to the plants, without breaking the stalks, or burying the hearts.

℘ Plant Endive. ℭ

At the beginning of this month some endive must be planted out on a dry spot, in a warm situation, for winter use. Let the plants be a foot distant from one another every way.

℘ Blanch Endive. ℭ

Let the leaves of endive be tied together, when both the weather and plants are dry, in order to blanch it; observing to tie up such plants only as have arrived at, or near, their full growth. The leaves must be gathered up evenly in the hand, and tied together with a string of bass.

℘ Cardoons. ℭ

By the beginning of this month your cardoons will be advanced to a sufficient height for blanching. Let therefore their leaves be gathered up, and tied closely and regularly together with hay-bands; beginning at the bottom, and winding the bands of hay pretty close together about the plants, as high as you intend to earth them.

When this is done, let the earth be well broke, and laid up about the plants as high as they are tied.

Cardoon
*Cynara
cardunculus*

℘ Mushrooms. ℭ

This is the season for beginning to prepare the dung, in order to make mushroom beds.

But it will be necessary, before the beds are made, to be provided with a proper quantity of the spawn, in order to plant in the bed.

The spawn of mushrooms, from which only they are propagated, looks like a white mouldiness shooting out in long strings. It is frequently found among the dung of old hot-beds, or in dung-hills, especially where much litter has been mixed with the dung, and the wet has not penetrated so as to rot it. It may also be procured by mixing some long stable-dung, which has not been thrown up in a heap to ferment, with strong earth, and then laying this mixture under cover, where it cannot be wet, and where the air may be excluded from it as much as possible; for the more effectually it is kept from air, the sooner will the spawn be produced.

Common mushroom
Agaricus campestris

It will generally appear in about two months, if the heap has not laid so close together as to heat (for that will destroy the spawn); and especially if it has been well covered with old thatch or litter, which has lain so long abroad, as to have lost the power of fermenting.

These are expedients by which the spawn of mushrooms may be procured almost at any time, by those who have not mushroom-beds in their gardens, and consequently cannot collect it from their remains: for there are only two months in the year when it can be gathered from downs or pastures; namely, in August and September, when mushrooms spring up naturally in many of these places.

To procure this spawn, the ground should be opened about the roots of mushrooms, and such earth as is there found full of small white knots, which are the off-sets, or young mushrooms, should be carefully gathered up, so as not to break either the lumps, or the earth about them. This spawn should be kept dry till you have occasion to use it; for the drier it is, the better it will take to the bed, as has been remarkably experienced by Mr. Miller, who declares that he never saw those plants produced so soon, or in so great plenty, as from a parcel of their spawn, which had lain near the oven of a stove for upwards of four months, and was become so dry, that he despaired of its success.

When a proper quantity of the spawn is procured, let the beds be made of dung, plentifully intermixed with litter, but not thrown in a heap to ferment. The best dung for this purpose, is that which has lain spread abroad for a month or longer.

Horse mushroom
Agaricus arvenis

The breadth of these beds should be about two feet and a half at the bottom, and their length proportioned to the quantity of mushrooms intended to be raised.

These beds must be made on the surface of a dry spot of ground, by spreading upon it first a layer of dung, about a foot thick, and upon this about four inches deep of strong earth; then a couch of dung about ten inches thick, and upon that another layer of earth, contracting the surface of the bed all the way till it terminates like the ridge of a house. This may be done with three layers of dung, and as many of earth.

When the bed is finished, it should be covered with litter, or old thatch, as well to prevent its drying, also keep out the wet; and after it has remained eight or ten days in this situation, it will be of a proper temperature for receiving the spawn.

The bed being thus in readiness, the thatch or litter should be taken off, the sides of the bed smoothed, and a covering of rich dry earth laid all over it about an inch thick.

Upon this the spawn should be placed, by laying it in lumps about two or three inches asunder, in such a manner as to prevent their slipping down; and then the whole covered gently with the same light earth as was used before, about half an inch deep.

The covering of litter should then be replaced over the bed, so thick, as to secure it from wet, and prevent the drying.

Parasol mushroom
Agaricus procerus

If the weather be temperate, and the spawn placed in the beds about the middle of the month, the mushrooms will come up about the middle of October. Sometimes, indeed, the beds will not yield any mushrooms for near six months after their being planted: but the gardener should not be discouraged at this disappointment; for they will then produce uncommon quantities, and continue in perfection for a long time.

The great art in managing these beds, consists in keeping them constantly in a due degree of moisture, and, above all, not to suffer them to receive too much wet; for that would inevitably destroy the spawn of the mushrooms.

St.George's
mushroom
Agaricus gambosus

The mushrooms produced from these beds have a much finer flavour than any gathered in the fields; and if the above directions are observed, they may be had in plenty during the whole year: for each single bed will continue good for seven months at least; and yield great quantities, if the spawn takes kindly.

You should remember, when any of these beds are destroyed, to take away the spawn, and lay it up in a dry place till the proper season for using it arrives, which should not be sooner than five or six weeks, that it may have time to dry well before it is put into a new bed; for, otherwise, there will be some danger of its succeeding.

THE NURSERY

᎙ Dig and Trench the Ground for New Plantations. ᎙

This is the season for digging and trenching the ground where you intend to plant out a nursery of young stocks for fruit trees; and also where you intend to plant out young forest trees, or any kind of hardy shrubs.

᎙ Transplanting. ᎙

You may begin to transplant about the last week in the month many of the more hardy kinds of trees and shrubs, whose leaves are then decayed, especially if the weather be something moist.

But if the weather should be very dry, you must be sure to give them a plentiful watering as soon as they are transplanted.

Laurustinus
viburnum
Viburnum tinus

Several advantages attend the transplanting of trees soon after the leaves decay; they will have time to take root before the frost is severe enough to prevent it; and by the next summer they will be so well established, that the drought of that season cannot hurt them.

It should, however, be remembered, that such trees only should be now transplanted, whose leaves are absolutely decayed; for with regard to the rest, they must continue some time longer before they are removed.

᎙ Transplant Fruit Trees. ᎙

All those fruit trees whose leaves are not decayed, may also be transplanted at the latter end of this month. But be sure to give them some water, if the weather be dry.

᎙ Transplant Stocks to Bud or Graft Upon. ᎙

During the last week in this month, the stocks raised for budding or grafting different kinds of fruit upon, may be transplanted into the places where they are to remain.

᎙ Transplant Evergreens. ᎙

Mock privet
Phillyrea

Laurels, Portugal laurels, laurustinus, arbutus, phillyreas, and several other kinds of evergreen, may be transplanted about the middle, or towards the latter end, of the month; for they will then take root freely; but remember to give them some water soon after they are planted.

℘ Propagate Trees and Shrubs by Cuttings. ℘

Gooseberry and currant trees may be propagated by cuttings, about the middle or latter end of the month. They will indeed succeed, if the cuttings are planted any time between the middle of this month, and the latter end of February; but those planted in this, or the succeeding month, generally make the finest trees.

Remember that the cuttings, either of the gooseberry or currant tree, must be taken from the same year's shoots, and be from ten to fifteen inches in length: they should be planted in a shady border.

Honey-suckles may also be propagated from cuttings, about the latter end of the month.

Red currant
Ribes rubra

The cuttings should be from strong shoots ten or twelve inches in length, and planted in rows about a foot asunder, and six or eight inches apart in the rows. Each cutting must be set about half way into the earth.

The laurel and Portugal laurel may be propagated by cuttings any time this month; but the cuttings must be planted in a shady border.

Let the cuttings be taken from the moderate growing shoots of the same year's growth, remembering to cut off with each shoot two or three inches of the last year's wood; for this will render the success more certain.

Honey-suckle
Lonicera flexuosa

When you have provided yourself with a sufficient number of cuttings, take off all the leaves from the bottom half way up the shoot; plant them in a shady border, putting each cutting as far into the earth as it is stripped of its leaves, and give them a little water as soon as planted.

℘ Destroy Weeds. ℘

Remember to hoe the intervals between the rows of all kinds of trees and shrubs, during dry weather, in order to destroy all the weeds before the autumn rains begin.

Indeed every part of the nursery should be kept as free from weeds as possible, for they will grow very fast at this season.

THE FRUIT-GARDEN

❧ Plant Strawberries. ☙

Any time this month is a proper season to plant strawberries, provided the weather be moist; but if the weather be very hot and dry, it will be

proper to defer the work till the middle or latter end of the month.

The beds intended for these plants should be four feet broad, and four rows should be planted in each bed; allowing an interval or alley of eighteen or twenty inches broad,

Strawberries
Fragaria

between the beds, for the convenience of going in to weed, water, and gather the fruit.

❧ Vines. ☙

Look over your vines once more, to see that the fruit equally enjoy the benefit of the sun and air. And wherever you perceive any of the bunches to be too much shaded, let some of the leaves be taken off; loosening and disentangling any of the bunches that may be confined, either by the branches or other bunches.

At the same time, if you perceive the vines have made any shoots since they were last looked over, let them be rubbed off close; for they are not only useless, but will also draw away part of the nourishment from the fruit.

❧ Peaches, Nectarines, &c. ☙

Let your peach, nectarine, and other wall trees be again examined; and wherever you perceive any of the branches to be loose, or project from the wall, let them be fastened up in their proper places. By this means the branches will be in no danger of being broken by the wind, and, at the same time, the fruit will enjoy the benefit of the sun to ripen it.

If you perceive any of the fruit to be too much covered with leaves, let some of them be displaced. But remember that this is only to be practised where they are uncommonly thick, for a sufficient quantity of

Peach
Persica davidiana

leaves is absolutely necessary to the growth and ripening of the fruit.

℘ Destroy Wasps. &c.

You must still continue your phials of sugared water, in order to catch the wasps, flies, &c. which will otherwise devour the finest of your fruit; especially your grapes.

The best method indeed of securing the latter, is to put the finest and ripest bunches into bags made for that purpose; these will be an effectual security both against insects and birds.

Your figs will also require phials of sweetened water to be hung up in different parts of the trees; for wasps, hornets, flies, &c. are very fond of this fruit.

℘ Gather Apples and Pears. ℘

Many sorts of your apples and pears will be fit for gathering about the middle or latter end of this month.

But remember to let this work be done in dry weather, and when the fruit are perfectly dry, otherwise they will soon rot. They will begin to drop apace from the trees, when they have attained their full maturity; and whenever this happens, let the fruit be gathered.

℘ Make Preparations for Planting. ℘

Towards the latter end of this month, you may begin to prepare the ground where you intend to make new plantations.

If an entire new border for wall trees be designed, let the ground be prepared in the manner mentioned in the introduction to this Kalendar.

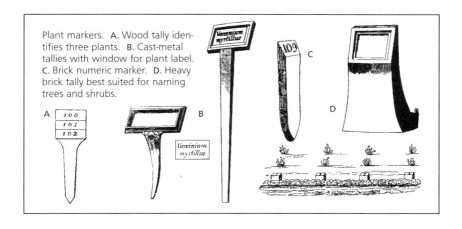

Plant markers. **A**. Wood tally identifies three plants. **B**. Cast-metal tallies with window for plant label. **C**. Brick numeric marker. **D**. Heavy brick tally best suited for naming trees and shrubs.

Starflower
Triteleia uniflora

THE PLEASURE OR FLOWER-GARDEN

℘ Sow Anemonie and Ranunculus Seed. ❧

It is not yet too late to sow anemonie and ranunculus seed, provided it be done at the beginning of the month.

In order to this, let some pots, boxes, or tubs, be filled with rich light earth, and the surface laid very even. Sow the seed, each sort separate, pretty thick on the surface, and cover it with light fine earth about a quarter of an inch thick.

℘ Sow the Seeds of Bulbous-Rooted Flowers. ❧

The seeds of tulips, hyacinths, crown imperials, fritillarias, and many other bulbous-rooted flowers, may yet be sown either in beds or boxes; for they will succeed in either.

The earth must be rich and light, broken very fine, and the surface laid very smooth and even.

Crocus
Crocus imperati

When the earth is thus prepared, let the seeds be sown on the surface, each sort separately, and covered with light sifted earth about half an inch thick.

℘ Sow Auricula Seed. ❧

You may still sow the seeds of auriculas in large pots or boxes, filled with rich earth, broken very fine, and the surface made very smooth and even.

The seed should be sown pretty thick on the surface, and covered with light rich earth about a quarter of an inch thick.

As soon as the seeds are sown, the pots or boxes should be placed out of the reach of the mid-day sun, till towards the latter end of the month, and then removed into a warmer situation.

ഔ Propagate Fibrous-Rooted Plants. cഃ

This is a proper season for increasing rose campion, scarlet lychnis, campanulas, catch-flies, and other fibrous rooted plants by slips.

These plants generally grow in tufts; and where this happens, let the whole be entirely taken up, parted, and some of the best slips planted again in the borders where they are to flower; while the smaller slips are planted in a nursery bed to get strength: remember to water them as soon as planted.

In the same manner you may part the roots of daisies, polyanthuses, double camomile, thrift, gentianella, saxifrage, and London pride. Let these likewise, where they are increased to large bunches, be taken up, divided, and then planted in a shady border, about five or six inches asunder.

The double rocket, double ragged robin, double bachelor's button, double feverfew, leonurus, bell-flower, and all other fibrous-rooted plants that are past flowering, may now be propagated by parting their roots; but it will be better if done about the beginning of the month.

ഔ Transplant Peonies, and Other Knot-Rooted Plants. cഃ

This is a proper season for transplanting peonies, the different sorts of flag irises, monkshood, traxinella, and other plants of that kind.

The roots are to be taken up and parted, and then planted again in places where they are to continue.

Peony 'Lady Branwell'
Paeonia

ഔ Transplant Hardy Shrubs and Trees. cഃ

You may begin, about the latter end of this month, to transplant most kinds of hardy shrubs and trees; for they will then succeed, and have time sufficient to take good root before the cold weather comes on. But remember to give them a plentiful watering as soon as transplanted.

ഔ Plant Hyacinth and Tulip Roots. cഃ

About the latter end of this month will be a proper time for planting your choice hyacinth and tulip roots.

In order to which, let beds be prepared at least a fortnight before the roots are planted; especially if you stir the earth to the depth of two feet, as is often practised by those who are curious in these kinds of flowers. But if this be thought too much, let the ground be dug one spade deep and one shovelling, and, at the same time, the soil remarkably well broken and divided.

When the ground is thus prepared, let it be parted into beds three feet and a half or four feet broad, laying the earth in a rounding form, highest in the middle.

Four or five rows of these roots are then to be planted in each bed, allowing nine inches between row and row, and the same distance between the roots; for nothing is of greater advantage to these flowers, than giving them sufficient room.

It will be necessary to bury these roots so deep in the ground, that their crowns may be at least four or five inches below the surface of the bed.

∞ Plant Ranunculuses and Anemonies. ∞

About the middle or latter end of this month it will also be time to prepare the ground for planting the finest sorts of your anemonies and ranunculuses.

Buttercup
*Ranunculus
montanus*

If you intend these roots in beds by themselves, let the beds be about three feet and a half or four feet broad, laying them somewhat rounding, as was mentioned above with regard to those intended for hyacinths and tulips.

When the beds are ready, let the roots be planted in them at six inches every way from one another; and about two or three inches deep.

The above distances are considerably greater than what is commonly allowed for these flowers; but room is of the utmost advantage to them; for the flowers will be much larger, and show themselves to much greater advantage, than when they are placed closer together. At the same time they will produce much larger off-sets, and consequently increase must faster.

∞ Plant Box. ∞

About the middle of this month is a very proper season for beginning to plant box, where new edgings are wanted, for it will then take root freely; but remember to give the box a plentiful watering as soon as the edgings are planted.

This is also a very proper time for repairing any box edgings formerly planted; or removing them where they have grown thick and clumsy. In order to which, the edging should be taken up, the roots parted, and a proper quantity of the box be slipped, trimmed, and immediately planted down again in a close but thin edging.

In a month after planting the box will be well rooted, and the edgings will appear neat during the whole winter.

ᔕ Transplant Carnations, and Other Perennial Plants. ᙢ

Towards the latter end of this month, some of your strongest carnations, pinks, sweet-williams, seedling wall-flowers, stock-july flowers, columbines, and other perennial plants, sown in June, or beginning of summer, may be transplanted into the borders.

But it will be proper to take advantage of dripping weather for transplanting them at this season.

At the same time many of those which were pricked out from the seed-bed into nursery beds, two or three months ago, may now be safely taken up with balls of earth about their roots, and planted where they are intended to remain. By this practise the plants will hardly feel their removal. But do not forget to give each plant as soon as removed a moderate watering; for this will at once nourish the plants, and close the earth about their roots.

Dwarf hybrid columbine
Aquilegia vulgaris

ᔕ Management of Carnations Layers. ᙢ

Your carnation layers must now be taken care of. If any of them still remain on the old plants, let them be transplanted some time before the middle of the month, that they may have time to take good root before the winter.

You may plant the choicest kinds of these layers in small pots, in order to their being more easily protected during the severe weather in the winter. But the common sorts may be planted in nursery-beds in a warm situation; and some of the strongest layers may be planted out at once into the borders where they are intended to flower.

With regard to those layers that were planted in pots or beds during the former month, let them be watered now and then, if the weather proves dry; and be sure to keep them entirely free from weeds.

ᔕ Management of Auricula Plants in Pots. ᙢ

All your auricula plants in pots will now require attention, particularly those that were shifted last month. If the weather proves very dry, they must be moderately watered now and then: on the contrary, if a great deal of rain falls, they must be defended from it; for too much wet will rot their roots.

Let therefore the pots containing your choicer plants be placed together in a bed arched over with hoops; and when the weather is excessively wet, let thick mats or canvas be drawn over the hoops to defend the plants. By this method the plants will be much better protected from wet than by that commonly made use of, namely, to lay the pots down on one side. But if a convenience of this kind cannot be had, the pots must be laid down on one side, that the plants may not receive too much moisture, which would destroy them.

℘ Clear Away Decayed Flower Stalks. ℛ

Remember to go round your borders frequently, cutting down the stems of such plants as are past flowering: these should never be suffered to stand long after their bloom is over, for dead stems have very unsightly appearance among plants, whether growing or in bloom.

℘ Trim Flowering Plants. ℛ

Examine frequently your plants in general, and cut off all straggling or irregular branches, together with those that are weak and dangling, and all dead or damaged leaves.

At the same time tye up to stakes such plants as have been thrown down by the winds or too much wet. This will give an air of neatness to the whole, and greatly improve the elegant appearance of your flowering plants.

Jerusalem sage
Pulmonaria saccharata

℘ Cut Box Edgings. ℛ

If you omitted to clip your box edgings during the two preceding months, let it be done now, and the sooner the better, that the box may have time to recover, before the winter comes on.

℘ Clip Hedges. ℛ

All your hedges that still remain unclipped, must now be finished; nor should it be deferred beyond the middle of the month, for the shoots will soon acquire too great a degree of hardness.

Remember to keep your shears in the best order; for otherwise the work will be tedious, and badly performed.

Let the sides of the hedges of all sorts be trimmed as straight as possible, and in such a manner, that the hedge may run

Broom
Cytisus

somewhat tapering from the bottom to the top; for the former should always be broader than the latter. With regard to the top, the utmost care should be taken to cut it very straight and even.

✌ Clean Borders. ✌

Take particular care to keep your borders, especially those near the principal walks, always very neat and clean. Neither weeds, dead leaves, nor any other litter should ever appear on those borders.

✌ Mow Grass Walks and Lawns. ✌

Let your grass walks and lawns be mowed frequently, otherwise they will have a disagreeable appearance; nor will it hardly be possible to mow the grass with any degree of truth, it if be once suffered to grow very rank and rough.

Remember also to keep the edges of all the grass, bordering upon gravel walks, very close and neat. These edges should be cut once a fortnight during the summer season.

✌ Roll Gravel Walks. ✌

It will be necessary, if you would have your gravel walks look well, to roll them at least twice a week. Nor should you suffer any weeds or other litter to be seen upon them.

OCTOBER

1. Bugloss.
Lingua bouis sine Buglossum luteum.
2. Arrach. *Atriplex sine olus aureum.*
3. Blites. *Blitium.*
4. Beets. *Beta.*
5. Alexanders. *Hipposelinum sine olus atrum.*
6. Sweet Parsley. *Selinum dulce.*

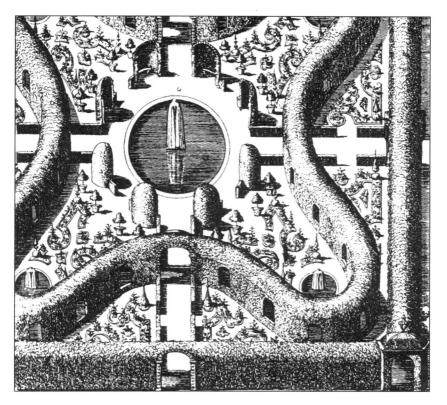

A French garden design much copied in English gardens. Galleries of hornbeam form one tunnel around the garden perimeter, and another tunnel, with look-out windows, within.

The Works of this Month in the
KITCHEN GARDEN

ꜱꝋ Cauliflower Plants. ꝗ

Those cauliflower plants which were planted last month under frames, should about the latter end of this month, be planted out under hand or bell-glasses; but unless the weather should prove very wet and cold, they need not be covered at all with the glasses; and even in the day-time of heavy rains, let the plants have air by tilting up the glasses.

During the last week of this month, some of your best cauliflower plants should be removed into the place where they are to remain. But as they are to be covered with hand or bell glasses, two or three of the plants are to be put under each glass.

The ground for these plants should be rich and light, situated in a warm part of the garden, where water is not apt to stand in winter.

Before the ground is dug, let some good rotten dung be spread upon the surface, and then dug spade deep, taking care to break the clods very well, and to bury the dung equally.

When this is done, let the ground be divided into beds three feet wide, allowing a foot and a half between the beds for the conveniency of putting on, raising, or taking off the glasses.

The beds being thus laid out, stretch your line along the middle of each bed from one end to the other, and at every three feet put in two or three plants, within four or five inches of each other, and close the earth well about their roots and stems, giving them a moderate watering to settle the earth about their roots.

As soon as the planting is finished, bring your hand or bell-glasses, and place one of them over each clump of plants every night, removing them in the morning while the weather continues mild and dry.

But when the weather is extremely wet, the glasses must not be taken entirely off; they must be only raised two or three inches on the warmest side, and supported in that position with props, to admit air to the plants: in frosty weather they must be kept close.

If you have not hand or bell-glasses, you may remove some of your plants into a warm border, where they will, if the winter be mild, produce tolerable heads in the spring.

ᏎᎡ Cabbage Plants. ᏣᎡ

A few of your early cabbage plants may be removed into the beds where they are to cabbage next summer, about the middle or latter end of

Cabbage
Brassica oleracea capitata

the month.

In order to this, let some good rotten dung be spread over the surface, and ground dug one spade deep, remembering to bury the dung properly in the bottom of the trench.

When the ground is ready, let the plants be set in rows two feet asunder, and the same distance apart in the rows.

As it often happens that cabbage plants removed early into an open exposure, are, in severe winters, killed by the frost, it will be prudent to let some of the early cabbage plants remain in nursery beds made in a warm situation, till January or February, that you may have plants to supply any defects in the former, or even to form new plantations.

Let therefore all your cabbage plants that still remain in their seed-beds, be now removed into nursery-beds at the beginning of this month, that they may have time to get strength before the severe weather begins. And remember to let the beds be made in a warm situation, and to set the plants about five or six inches asunder.

℘ Broccoli. ℘

Let the ground between and about the broccoli plants which were set late be loosened with a hoe, and some of the earth drawn up about their stems; for this will be of the utmost advantage to them, provided it be done early in the month.

℘ Beans. ℘

A few mazagan beans may be planted any time this month, for an early crop in the succeeding summer.

But remember to plant them in a warm border under a south wall or other fence, in rows two feet and a half asunder, dropping the beans two or three inches apart in the rows.

Many gardeners in planting early beans, chuse first to sow the beans pretty thick in a bed of rich earth, and transplant them into the borders when they are come up to a sufficient height. The method is this:

Let a bed of good rich earth, about four feet broad, situated in a warm corner of the garden, be well dug. Then draw off the surface of the earth to the depth of an inch and a half, or two inches, from every part of the bed equally. This being done scatter the beans about an inch asunder, and immediately cover them with the earth drawn off the bed.

When the beans are come up, and grown about two inches high, they should be transplanted in mild weather into warm borders, in

String beans
Phaseolus vulgaris

rows two feet and a half asunder, and two or three inches apart in the rows. Remember to close the earth well about their roots, and there will be no danger of their growing freely.

Experience has shewn, that beans transplanted in the above manner, will come a week or ten days sooner than those planted in the place where they are to remain; provided both are set the same day.

At the same time there will be less danger of their being injured by the frost, as they may, from being crowded together in the seed-bed, be more easily protected by covering them when the weather is very severe.

℘ Peas. ca

About the first or second week in this month, a few peas should be sown for an early crop. The earliest hotspur is the most proper sort to be sown at this season; but remember to make choice of such seeds as are plump and sound.

They should be sown in a warm border under a south wall, in drills two feet asunder, and the peas placed pretty close together in the drills, but as regular as possible, and covered immediately with earth an inch and a half or two inches deep.

℘ Lettuces. ca

Those lettuces which were sown about the middle of September, in order to be covered with frames or hand-glasses, should be removed, about the middle of this month, into the places where they are to remain.

In order to this, a spot of light rich earth, in a warm situation, and fully exposed to the mid-day sun, should be chosen, and a bed proportioned to the size of a cucumber or melon frame marked out; the surface laid somewhat sloping to the sun, and raked very smooth and even.

When the bed is thus prepared, let the lettuces be planted not too deep in the earth, about two inches distant every way. Let them have a little water as soon as planted and let the surface between the plants be made perfectly smooth.

The plants being thus set in the bed, put on the frame, and, when the weather is wet and frosty, cover it with the lights. By this precaution there will be no doubt of these plants surviving the cold of winter, notwithstanding those which were planted in borders are destroyed.

About the middle of this month will be also a very proper time to transplant those lettuces which were sown about the latter end of August or the beginning of September into the places where they are to remain.

But you must remember to chuse a warm border for their reception; and then, if the weather proves mild, they will cabbage early in the spring.

ᔅᔓ Spinach. ᔕᔓ

Remember to keep your winter spinach perfectly clean from weeds; for if the latter are suffered to grow at this season of the year, they will soon overrun, and totally destroy the plants.

If you neglected to thin your spinach last month, let it be done at the beginning of this; remembering to clear away the weaker, and to leave the stronger plants at the distance of four or five inches from one another.

Spinach
Spinacia oleracea

ᔅᔓ Endive. ᔕᔓ

You must remember, provided the weather be dry, to tye up some endive plants every week for blanching.

In order to this, let such plants be chosen as are quite or nearly full grown; to let the leaves be regularly and closely gathered up in the hand, and tyed neatly together with a piece of strong bass.

At the same time let the earth be drawn up round each plant almost to the tops of the leaves; for this will at once promote the blanching, and render the plants exceedingly white and tender.

ᔅᔓ Earth Up Celery. ᔕᔓ

As your celery plants advance in height they must be duly earthed up, that they may be thoroughly branched before they are attacked by severe frosts.

Let therefore every advantage of dry weather be taken, in order to earth them up to a proper height. At the same time remember to break the clods of the earth very well, and to lay it up to the plants, without breaking their leaves or burying their hearts.

ᔅᔓ Earth Up Cardoons. ᔕᔓ

Remember to earth up your cardoons when both the weather and the leaves of the plants are dry, in the manner mentioned the foregoing month.

ᔅᔓ Sow Carrot Seed. ᔕᔓ

About the last week in this month, a little carrot seed should be sown on a warm border; as it is very probable a few of the plants, at least, will survive the frost, and consequently produce young carrots very early in the spring.

Half-long Luc carrot
Daucus carota

ဢ Sow Radish Seed. ⊘

Olive scarlet, olive white, and French breakfast radishes
Raphanus sativus

A little radish seed should also be sown about the middle of the month, in a warm border; for if the weather be any thing mild, the plants will be fit for drawing early in the spring. Let the seed be sown pretty thick, and raked in with an even hand.

ဢ Sow Small Salleting. ⊘

A small quantity of the seeds of mustard, cresses, radish, rape, and lettuce, should be sown every week; but that sown about the latter end of the month should be defended by a frame and glasses.

In order to this, let a bed of light rich earth, in a warm situation fronting the south, be dug, and proportioned to one of the shallowest garden frames. Let the earth be broken very fine, and laid a little sloping towards the south.

When the surface is raked very even, let shallow drills be drawn from the back to the front of the frame, about two or three inches asunder. In these drills let the seed be sown pretty thick, and covered with earth about a quarter of an inch deep.

The glasses must be put on every night, and continued also in the daytime, when the weather is very cold or wet.

ဢ Dress Asparagus Beds. ⊘

The stalks of your asparagus must be cut down, and the beds properly dressed some time this month.

Remember to cut down the stalks or haulm within two or three inches at least, of the surface of the beds, and immediately to carry it off the ground.

When this is done, cut up all the weeds with a sharp hoe, and draw them off into the alleys, which are to be marked out with a line and spade, about eighteen or twenty inches wide.

The beds being thus cleared, let the alleys be dug one spade deep, spreading the earth, or at least the greater part of it, neatly over the beds, observing, as you advance in digging, to bury the weeds taken off the beds in the bottom of the trench, and to cover them a proper depth with earth.

If you intent to manure your asparagus beds, this is also the proper season to do it; but the dung, which must be applied before the alleys are dug, should be very good and very rotten. None is more proper than the dung of old cucumber and melon beds. This must be spread over the surface, as the haulm and weeds are cleared away: let it be well broken, and laid of an equal thickness on every part of the beds. When this is done, let the alleys be dug as above directed, and a proper quantity of the earth spread upon the dung.

You may plant a row of cabbages or coleworts in each alley, five or six inches apart in the row. And these will generally survive very severe frosts, when all those planted in an open or level spot will be destroyed.

∾ Clear the Beds of Aromatic Plants. ∾

Your beds of sage, savory, thyme, hyssop, mint, baum, tarragon, tansey, sorrel, &c. must now be dressed in the following manner:

Let all the stalks, or decayed flower stems, be cut close to the heads of the plants, or the surface of the ground; the beds well cleared from weeds and other litter, and the whole carried off the ground.

When this is done, let the earth be dug lightly between such of the plants as will bear it, either with a spade or trowel. At the same time let the alleys be dug, and a little of the earth spread upon the beds. If a little rotten dung had been scattered over the beds before they had been dug, it would have been of great advantage to the plants.

Sage of virtue
*Salvia minor
primata*

The beds of mint and pepper-mint, will not admit of digging; but let them be well cleared from weeds, a little rotten dung spread over the surface, and some of the earth from the alleys thrown over the dung.

By this means the roots will, in some measure, be protected from the frost; and the rain, by washing down the salts in the dung and earth, will greatly enrich the beds, and strengthen the plants.

∾ Dung and Trench Ground. ∾

The parts of the kitchen-garden now unoccupied should be dunged and trenched, that it may receive every possible advantage from the sun and air. By this means the soil will be greatly enriched, and consequently produce much larger crops in the spring, than it would if suffered to have lain neglected till it was wanted.

William the Conqueror's oak in Windsor Park
Quercus

THE NURSERY

ഔ Sow Haws, Holly Berries, &c. ⊗

This is the season for sowing haws, holly, hips, and yew-berries.

In order to which, let beds of three feet and a half, or four feet wide, be prepared: the berries of each sort separately sown on the surface, and covered near an inch deep with earth.

Many bury their haws and holly-berries a whole year in the earth, before they sow them, for they seldom come up before the spring twelvemonth after they are sown. The method is this:

European holly
Ilex aquifolium

They mark out in some part of the nursery, where the ground is firm and dry, a trench about two feet wide, dig it twelve inches deep, and make the bottom very even and level. In this trench they lay the berries of an equal thickness and cover them with earth six inches deep, at least.

In this manner they are suffered to lie a twelvemonth, when they are taken up and sown in beds as above directed.

℘ Sow Acorns. ❧

About the latter end of this month your acorns must be sown, for, if kept much longer out of the ground, they will begin to sprout.

Penduncled or common oak *Quercus robur pedunculata*

They should be sown in beds about four feet wide, and covered an inch deep with earth.

℘ Sow Plum-Stones. ❧

This is a very proper season for sowing plum-stones, to raise a supply of stocks for the purpose of budding and grafting.

In order to this, let beds about four feet broad be dug, the stones spread, not too thick, as equally as possible on the surface, and covered a full inch deep with earth.

If you scatter some dry short litter over the surface of the beds as soon as they are planted, it will prove of great service.

Some preserve these stones till about the middle of February, and then plant them in beds as above directed. The method they take to preserve the stones is this:

They procure a strong close box or tub, and cover the bottom three inches deep with sand. When this is done, they scatter on it a parcel of the stones, covering them two inches deep with sand; upon this covering they scatter another parcel of the stones, covering them in the same manner, and so proceed till the tub or box is full. By this artifice the vegetative faculty of the stones is preserved, and they may be sown any time in February, when the weather is favourable.

℘ Sow Beech-Mast, &c. ❧

This is the best season in the whole year for sowing beech-mast, and maple seed.

Let therefore a bed four feet broad be prepared for each of these seeds; the earth well broken, and the surface laid very smooth.

When this is done, let the seeds be sown pretty thick on the surface, and covered with earth about an inch deep.

℘ Propagate Trees and Shrubs by Layers. ❧

About the middle of this month, you may begin to propagate the hardier kind of forest trees, and flowering shrubs, by layers. The method is this:

Dig the ground round the tree or shrub you intend to propagate. When this is done, bring the branches down, lay them in the earth, and fasten them down with forked or hooked sticks. Then cover the body of the shoots three or four inches deep with earth, leaving the tops three or four inches above the ground.

Limes, elms, and other forest trees, will succeed extremely well by this method; but it will be necessary to cut down the tree, from which the layers are intended to be taken, near the ground, that it may produce shoots or branches at a height proper for this operation.

℘ Propagate Trees and Shrubs by Cuttings. ⊗

Many of the hardy kinds of trees and shrubs may be propagated by cuttings; and this is a very proper season for doing it.

Honey-suckles, gooseberry and currant trees are better raised by cuttings than by any other method. The manner of performing this operation has been fully described in the works of the nursery for last month.

Hall's Japan
honey-suckle
Lonicera japonica
'Halliana'

℘ Transplant Layers. ⊗

Those layers which were laid down last year must now be taken off, and planted in an open spot of ground, in rows eighteen inches asunder, and twelve inches apart in the rows.

℘ Transplant Hardy Trees and Shrubs. ⊗

You may, any time this month, transplant all sorts of hardy trees and shrubs; and by next summer they will have fixed themselves firmly. This will be of great advantage; for they will require very little trouble in watering.

℘ Transplant Stocks to Bud and Graft upon. ⊗

This is a very proper season for transplanting all kinds of stocks intended for budding or grafting the different sorts of fruit upon.

They should be planted in rows two feet and a half asunder, and twelve or fifteen inches be allowed between the stocks in each row.

℘ Transplant Laurels. ⊗

Laurels, Portugal laurels, laurustinus, and other evergreens of that kind, may be transplanted with safety at the beginning of the month.

Walnut tree
Juglans

THE FRUIT-GARDEN

℘ Prune and Nail Peach, Apricot, and Nectarine Trees. ℘

As soon as the leaves of your peach, apricot, and nectarine trees are dropped, which will happen about the latter end of this month, you may begin to prune and nail them.

Remember to unnail the greater part of the small branches, before you begin to prune; because you will have room to use your knife with greater facility, and, at the same time, may examine with more convenience the several shoots, and consequently be better able to judge which are proper to be taken off, and which to remain.

You must be careful to leave at equal and regular distances, and in every part of the tree, a proper supply of the last summer's shoots, that every part of the wall, from the bottom to the top of the tree, may be regularly furnished with them; for these, and these only, are the shoots that will bear the fruit next season.

At the same time, remember to cut out all the old wood, as it becomes useless; we mean such branches as advance a great way, and are not furnished with young wood.

But though a sufficient number of the young shoots are to be left, yet they must not be crowded, or left too close together. Let them therefore be carefully examined, and where you perceive they stand too thick, let some of them be taken away. In doing this, remember to leave the most promising and best placed shoots for the purpose of bearing, and to leave them at due and regular distances from one another; five or six inches will be a proper interval between them, if the tree be in good health. Those which you take away must be cut off close.

When you have taken away all the useless shoots, you must shorten those you intend to preserve; for by this means they will next summer produce, besides their fruit, a proper supply of bearing shoots for the year after.

But in doing this, remember to shorten every one in proportion to its growth, and original length: for instance, a shoot of about twelve inches must be reduced to about eight inches, one of fifteen or sixteen to ten, and a shoot of twenty to fourteen; and so on in proportion to their different lengths. In a word, you should cut away about one third of the length of every shoot.

A difference must, however, be made with regard to those nectarine and apricot trees which produce very strong and vigorous shoots; for these must be left about five or six inches asunder, and not more than one fourth of their original length must be cut off; indeed some of the most vigorous shoots should be but very little shortened, and others not at all. For the more wood you cut out of a vigorous tree, and the more shoots are shortened, the more vigorously will the tree shoot. This, therefore, is the only method of pruning a vigorous shooting tree, in order to its producing such moderate shoots as are necessary for their bearing fruit.

If the above observations be well understood, the gardener will be at no loss in pruning apricot, peach, and nectarine trees, in proportion to their different growths.

But it will be necessary to observe, that where any of the shoots left to bear have produced any smaller shoots from their sides, they must be cut off close to the principal shoot; for these will be entirely useless; they will produce neither good wood, nor good fruit.

In shortening the bearing shoots, you should remember to cut them off at a leaf bud, or, as some call it, a double bud, if possible. A leaf, or double bud, is where two buds appear upon the same eye. Every one of these eyes will generally produce a good shoot next year; it is therefore necessary, in shortening the shoots, to cut them at or near such an eye, in order that each may produce a good shoot next year for its leader; for where there is a fair leading shoot produced at or near the extremity of a bearing branch, such a shoot will generally yield fair and well tasted fruit.

With regard to the apricot tree, in particular, it should be observed, that there are often on the two years old branches short shoots, or natural spurs, about an inch or two in length, and, frequently, on each of these spurs several blossom buds. Some cut these spurs entirely away; but this is bad practice; for they generally produce handsome and well tasted fruit. But, at the same time, such only of these spurs which are well placed, and promise, by their blossom buds, to bear fruit, should be spared; such as advance considerably in a foreright direction, together with such as are destitute of blossom buds, should be cut off close to the branch.

Remember, as soon as you have finished pruning one tree, to nail it close to the wall in a proper manner, before you begin the next; and not leave it, as many do, till all the trees on the wall are pruned. Some, indeed, direct them to be left unnailed till March; but by this method many of the branches will be injured by the winds, and the blossom buds so much swelled by the time of nailing them, that many of them will unavoidably be displaced in the operation.

You should observe great exactness in nailing your trees: the branches must not any where be nailed across one another; but every branch laid in entirely clear of the rest, and about four, five, or six inches distant, according to the condition of the tree. At the same time, let all the branches be laid perfectly straight, and close to the wall.

The rolling platform is most useful for trimming tall hedges, especially those bordering the long avenues in formal landscapes.

‏ℰᴑ‎ Transplant Fruit Trees. ‏CR‎

Most sorts of fruit trees may be safely transplanted about the latter end of this month.

In the introduction to this Kalendar, we have given full directions for making borders, and mentioned the distances that are necessary between the trees of different sorts of fruit, and therefore it will be needless to say any thing on that subject here.

‏ℰᴑ‎ Propagate Gooseberry and Currant Trees by Cuttings. ‏CR‎

This is a very proper season for propagating gooseberry and currant trees by cuttings; and it should be remembered, that the trees raised from cuttings always produce larger and better tasted fruit, than those which are raised from suckers.

Black currant
Ribes nigrum

These cuttings must be shoots of the last summer's growth, taken from healthy trees, and such as are remarkable for bearing the finest fruit of their kind.

When a proper number of these shoots are provided, let them be shortened to about ten, twelve, or fifteen inches in length; and planted in a shady border, in rows across the border, ten or twelve inches asunder. Each cutting must be set near half its length into the earth.

‏ℰᴑ‎ Prune Gooseberry and Currant Trees. ‏CR‎

About the latter end of this month, your gooseberry and currant trees may be pruned. In doing which, observe to keep their branches thin, and at regular distances from one another. The heart of the trees also must be kept open and free from wood, and the branches nowhere suffered to cross one another.

At the same time, remember to take away all suckers from the roots, and to train up each tree with a single stem.

It is natural for these trees to produce numbers of young shoots every summer, many of which should be now taken away; but be sure to leave, at proper distances, some of the best placed, and most regular grown shoots, for a succession of young bearing wood, to supply the place of such branches as are past bearing good fruit; remembering, at the same time, to cut shorter, or remove entirely, some of the older branches, in order to make room for those which are young, and promise to bear better fruit.

You should also remember, in shortening the last summer's shoots, not to cut off more than one third of their length; and where the shoot is very vigorous, one fourth will be sufficient; for if they are shortened much more than this, their vigour will be so greatly increased, that they will next year fill the tree with so many useless shoots as will prove prejudicial to the fruit.

❧ Transplant Gooseberry and Currant Trees. ☙

About the middle, or towards the latter end of this month, will be a proper season for transplanting gooseberry and currant trees.

If these shrubs are intended to be set in a spot by themselves, let them be planted in rows eight feet asunder; and let six feet, at least, be allowed between plant and plant in the rows. This will give room to dig and hoe the ground between the shrubs; and the berries will grow very large, and ripen properly.

Fay's
currant
Ribes

But if they are intended to be set in single rows round the quarters of the kitchen garden, they should be planted eight or nine feet distant from one another.

❧ Plant Strawberries. ☙

Where new plantations of strawberries are wanting, they may be made any time this month, but the sooner the better.

In order to this, let some of the best rotten dung be spread over the surface of the ground where you intend to plant your strawberries, and then neatly dug, remembering to bury your dung in a proper manner.

When the piece is thus prepared, let it be divided into beds four feet broad, leaving an interval of eighteen inches for an alley between the beds, and rake the surface very smooth.

Parry strawberry
Fragaria

The beds being thus in readiness, chuse a parcel of the strongest plants produced last summer, and take them up with good roots. Cut off all the runners, pull off all the dead leaves, trim the roots, and plant them in four rows length-ways of the bed. Consequently the rows will be one foot asunder; and the same distance should be allowed between each plant in the rows.

Remember to close the earth well about every plant, and to give each of them a little water as soon as they are set.

❧ Dress Strawberry Beds. ☙

It will be necessary to give your strawberry beds their winter's dressing some time this month; but remember to chuse a dry day for it. The manner is this:

Clear away all the runners or strings close to the head of the plants; clean the beds from weeds, and let all the litter be carried away.

When this is done, let the earth in every bed, where there is room, be loosened with a small spade, trowel, or hoe, taking care not to disturb the roots. Then mark out with your line the alleys of their proper width, and dig them immediately, spreading some of the earth carefully over the beds; taking particular care to lay it neatly between, and close about every plant.

The plants should never be suffered to spread over the whole surface of the bed; they should be kept, as it were, in single bunches or heads. And by pursuing this method you will every year, when the season is kind, have a great quantity of large and well tasted fruit.

❧ Plant Raspberries. ☙

This is a very proper season for making new plantations of raspberries; but the spot intended to be planted must be in an open situation, the ground good.

The plants must also be well furnished with roots, or they will not succeed: let therefore such only be chosen.

Being furnished with a proper number of such plants, let the shoots be shortened a little, and only one strong shoot left on each root. The extremities of the roots also must be trimmed, and then planted in rows four feet asunder, and the plants set three feet apart in the rows.

❧ Prune Raspberry Plants. ☙

Experience has sufficiently shewn that three only of the last year's shoots should be left upon each root for bearing fruit the next year; these must therefore be allowed room; and, in order to this, all above that number on each root must be now removed. In doing this let them be cut off close to the surface of the ground; cutting away at the same time all the old wood, together with all the straggling branches between the rows.

When this is done, let each of the branches left to bear fruit the succeeding year be shortened, cutting off about one third or one fourth, in proportion as the shoot is less or more vigorous, of its original length.

When this is done, and all the cuttings, &c. cleared away, let the ground in the intervals and between the roots be dug, clearing away all the straggling roots between the rows, together with those that do not belong to the standing plants.

ᔕᔭ Gather Winter Apples and Pears. ᔕᔭ

This is generally the season for gathering winter apples and pears. But they will be ripe at different times; some at the beginning, some about the middle, and others not till the latter end of the month.

Apple
Malus

In order to know whether the fruit are proper to be pulled, try several of them in different parts of the tree, by turning them gently upwards: if they quit the tree easily, it is time to gather them; if not, they must remain some time longer.

You should not, however, let any of your fine eating pears hang on the trees after the middle of the month, especially if the nights are inclinable to be frosty; for if they are once touched with the frost, many of them will rot before they are fit for the table, notwithstanding all the care that can afterwards be taken of them.

Nor must any kinds of apples or pears be suffered to hang longer on the trees than the latter end of the month; for after that time they will get no good by being abroad.

But whenever you gather any of your keeping fruit, let a dry day be chosen; and before you begin to gather, let both the fruit and leaves be thoroughly dry. Between eleven and twelve is generally the best time to begin; nor should the work be continued after three or four in the afternoon.

'Winter Gray' Pear
Pyrus

Take care to pull your fruit one by one, and to lay them gently in a basket; for if they are bruised by any means, they will soon be spoiled.

Carry the fruit as soon as they are gathered into the fruitery, or other dry place, laying them carefully in heaps, each sort by itself.

In these heaps they must be suffered to lie a fortnight to sweat; which will at once improve their flavour, and make them keep the better.

After sweating in this manner, let them be wiped one by one, and laid up where they are to remain. Remember, in severe frost weather, to cover them with clean neat straw.

Tea rose
Rosa odorata

THE PLEASURE OR FLOWER-GARDEN

❧ Management of Carnation Layers. ❧

You must during the last week in this month remove your carnation layers, planted into small pots during the two last two months, into places where they can be readily defended in bad weather; a common garden frame will be very proper for this purpose; and if the earth be light and dry, let the pots be plunged into it up to the rims.

In this frame let the pots remain during the winter, observing when the weather is frosty or very wet, to cover them with the glasses; and when the cold is very severe, to throw mats over the glasses. But let them constantly enjoy the benefit of the open air, when the weather is dry and mild.

If you have not the convenience of a frame, let the pots be plunged in a bed of dry compost, arched over with hoops, and covered over with the mats or canvas in bad weather.

❧ Management of Auricula Plants. ❧

It is necessary to defend your auricula plants in pots from frost and heavy rains. In order to which many persons think it sufficient to lay the pots down on one side; but this is a very poor expedient, as several methods more effectual may be easily contrived.

A garden frame will answer the purpose with very little trouble, as the plants may be defended in bad weather by putting on the glasses. But if a frame cannot be spared, let the pots be placed close together under a warm wall, and arched over with hoops, that when the weather is very wet or frosty, canvas or mats may be thrown over them.

But whatever method be taken for the security of these choice flowers, let all the dead leaves be taken from the plants, and the earth near the surface loosened.

℘ Plant Tulips and Hyacinths. ℘

It is not yet too late to plant tulips and hyacinths, but it should be done some time this month.

Remember to dig the spot where you intend to plant them very well, and to lay the surface of the beds rounding, or in a convex form, in order to throw off the wet. The beds should be four feet broad.

Five rows of roots should be planted in a bed, about nine inches apart, and four or five inches deep. Remember to chuse a dry day for setting these roots.

If you intend to set any of these roots in the borders among other flowers, let them be planted in clumps or patches, rather than in single rows. In order to this, let a small circle seven or eight inches diameter be drawn in the border, with your finger, and set one root in the center, and three or four round the circumference; and in that manner plant a clump at about every two or three yards distance. The flowers planted in this manner will make a much more

White Roman hyacinth
Hyacinthus

pleasing appearance in the flowering season than they would, had they been planted in a single row.

But the choicest flowers should always be planted in beds by themselves, because they may be more easily sheltered from too much rain, and also shaded from the scorching rays of the sun, both of which would greatly impair their beauty.

℘ Plant Ranunculuses and Anemonies. ℘

This is also a good season for planting the roots of ranunculuses and anemonies; but remember to plant the choicer sorts in beds by themselves.

In order to which let the ground be well dug, and divided into beds four feet broad. In each of these beds let five rows of the roots be planted six inches from one another, and about two inches and a half or three inches deep. By allowing them this distance, which is greater than common, the roots will blow much stronger, and the flowers will appear to much greater advantage.

Remember to cover the beds where your finest are set, with peas-haulm, or other dry litter, in severe frosts.

With regard to the common sorts of ranunculuses and anemonies, they may be planted in clumps in the borders, where they will make a very agreeable appearance in the spring among other flowers.

෨ Plant Crocuses and Snow Drops. ෬

Let the crocus and snow-drop roots which were taken out of the ground in the summer be now planted in the borders, either in rows or in clumps. If in the former, the roots should be set six inches apart.

But they will make a much finer appearance if planted in clumps or patches. In order to which mark out a small circle about five or six inches diameter, and plant one root in the center, and four or five round the edge or circumference; two feet farther mark out another circle, and plant it in the same manner; continuing the same method to the end of the border.

Elves' snow drops
Galanthus nivalis

These roots should never be planted above three inches deep; two and a half will, in general, be sufficient.

෨ Plant Narcissuses, Jonquils, &c. ෬

Your narcissuses, jonquils, bulbous and Persian irises, fritillarias, and other bulbous roots of that kind, which were taken up when their leaves decayed in summer, should now be planted.

If they are intended to be set separate in beds, let them be planted in rows eight or nine inches asunder every way. But if they are to be planted in the common borders, let them be planted three or four together in a small circle, allowing five or six feet between each circle or clump.

෨ Plant Crown Imperials, Martagons, &c. ෬

This is likewise a proper season for planting your crown imperials, martagons, orange lilies, and other bulbous roots of that kind, which were taken out of the ground in the summer.

They should be planted in rows in the middle of a bed or border, each sort at ten or twelve feet distance from one another, intermixing them as you proceed; each root should be about three feet distance from the next.

Turk's cap lily
Lilium martagon

℘ Plant Hardy Flowering Shrubs. ℘

Roses, honey-suckles, gilder-roses, lilacs, laburnums, syringas, althæa frutex, jasmines, privets, double bramble, flowering raspberry, double blossom cherry, bladder and scorpion sena, double flowering peach, almonds, mezereons, cornelian cherry, double hawthorn, scarlet horse-chestnut, shrub cinquefoil, sumach, rock-rose, cytisuses, acacia, and other hardy flowering shrubs may be now transplanted.

But remember to plant them at such a distance, that each plant may have full room to grow and shew itself to advantage.

When it is intended to plant them in clumps, or quarters, let the plants in general be set at least five or six feet distant from one another; and such as are of a humble growth, let them not be planted promiscuously among the tall growing plants, because they would be wholly concealed from sight. Let therefore the low growing plants be set towards the front, or outside of the clump; and the taller the plants are, so much the farther back let them be planted.

Chinese lilac
Syringa chinensis

℘ Transplant Fibrous-Rooted Flowering Plants. ℘

Rose campions, sweet-williams, campanulas, catchfly, rockets, bachelors buttons, double feverfew, scarlet lychnis, lychnidea, and other fibrous-rooted perennial plants, should now be transplanted into the borders or places where they are wanted. And as these are nearly of the same height, they are very proper to be transplanted into the middle of the border. All these, especially those of the double kinds, make a very agreeable appearance at the flowering season.

But you should remember to plant some of your double rose campions, double lychnis, double sweet-williams, and the like, in pots; for as these flowers deserve particular care, they should be sheltered in severe weather.

This is also a proper season to slip and plant out where wanted, polyanthuses, double daisies, double camomile, violets, London pride, thrift hepaticas, gentianella, saxifrage, and other low growing fibrous-rooted plants. And, as they are but low, they should not be planted more than fifteen or sixteen inches from the edge of the border.

Columbines, monkshood, Canterbury bells, fox-gloves, tree primrose, Greek valerian, scabiouses, and the like plants should now be planted into the middle of the beds or borders; for they grow from two to four feet high.

Carnation
*Dianthus
caryophyllus*

Carnations and pinks, both seedlings and layers, double walls, and double stock-july flowers, should now be planted in the beds or borders.

But the Michaelmas daisies, golden rod, everlasting sun-flowers, French honey-suckles, and holly-hocks, are much better planted in clumps among flowering shrubs, than in beds or borders, unless they are planted toward the further side; and then they should be set fifteen or twenty feet distant from one another.

ℳ Plant Evergreen Trees and Shrubs. ℭℛ

You may now remove most sorts of evergreen trees and shrubs; but the sooner it is done in the month the better.

The arbutus, or strawberry tree, laurel, Portugal laurel, laurustinus, pyracanthas, phillyreas, alaturnus, bays, evergreen oaks, cytisuses, hollies and magnolias, may, particularly, be now removed with safety. These should all be planted in clumps, and four or five feet every way asunder; for at that distance each plant will have room to shoot every way regularly, and form handsome heads. At the same time you will have room to hoe, dig, and cleanse the ground about the shrubs, which will be of the greatest advantage to them.

ℳ Transplant Pines, Firs, &c. ℭℛ

Pines, firs, cedars, junipers, and cypresses, may be safely removed any time this month.

Remember to chuse for them a dry soil, and to open for every plant a hole wide enough to receive the roots freely every way; and when the holes are dug a proper depth, to let the ground be well loosened at the bottom.

When the holes are thus prepared, bring the plants, and after shortening the ends of their roots and cutting off all that are dead, broken, or damaged, place each plant upright in the holes; break the earth well, and throw it in equally, shaking the plant gently, that the earth may fall in closely among the roots and fibres. When all the earth is thrown in, tread the top gently round the plant, and give every one of them a little water.

But in planting the more tender sorts of evergreens, the plants should, if possible, be brought with balls of earth about their roots, and the plants set immediately in a hole prepared for their reception, with the balls of earth entire; and as soon as the hole is filled up, the surface should be trod gently, and each plant have a proper quantity of water.

✂ Trim Evergreens. ✃

Remember to go often at this season round your plantations of evergreens, reducing to order such as are of an irregular growth. Let all the strong straggling branches be shortened; and where the trees interfere with one another, let the branches be shortened so that every plant may stand separate.

✂ Transplant Forest Trees. ✃

The oak, elm, beech, maple, ash, lime, and plane trees, may be transplanted with safety about the middle or latter end of this month. But remember to do it in mild weather, and in a dripping time.

✂ Management of Seedling Flowers. ✃

All your seedling flowers in pots or boxes must be now removed to a warm situation, where the cutting winds have no power, and where they may enjoy the full sun all the winter. Remember to clear the pots or boxes from weeds.

With regard to your seedling flowers in beds, let them be carefully weeded, and then some light rich earth sifted over the surface to the thickness of half an inch; for this will be of the utmost service to the plants, particularly those which were not transplanted in the summer.

✂ Propagate Roses and Other Flowering Shrubs by Suckers. ✃

Roses, lilacs, and other flowering shrubs of that kind are increased by suckers from the roots; and this is a very proper season, if the weather be mild, to transplant them. They will make good plants in two years time.

✂ Prune Roses, Honey-suckles, &c. ✃

This is a very proper season to prune roses, honeysuckles, and all other sorts of flowering shrubs.

Rose
Rosa

Remember to prune them with a sharp knife, and to cut off close to the place from whence they proceed, all the strong luxuriant shoots of the last summer's growth: and where any branch advances in a straggling manner from the rest, let it be shortened, observing, if possible, to cut it close to a young shoot.

All suckers which rise from the roots should be taken away, and every shrub kept to a single stem.

As soon as the pruning is finished, let the cuttings and litter be cleared away, and the ground well dug a spade deep, cutting off all the straggling roots, and taking up all the suckers.

&o Propagate Hardy Trees and Shrubs by Layers. c@

Most of the trees or shrubs that shed their leaves in winter, may be propagated by layers, and this is a proper season for doing it on the hardy kinds. The method is this:

Dig the ground round the tree or shrub, bend down the pliable branches, lay them in the earth, and secure them with hooked or forked sticks. When this is done, let all the young shoots on each branch be laid down, and the bodies of them covered about three inches deep with earth, leaving the top of each, two, three, or four inches out of the ground.

Bramble rose
Rosa polyantha

In this manner they must remain till this time twelve-month, when they will be sufficiently rooted, and should then be transplanted.

&o Transplant Layers. c@

This is the proper season for transplanting the layers of such trees and shrubs as were layed last year. As soon as they are taken up let their roots be pruned, and afterwards planted in rows twelve inches asunder.

&o Propagate Flowering Shrubs by Cuttings. c@

Honey-suckles, laurels, and Portugal laurels and many other sorts of hardy shrubs and trees may be raised from cuttings, and this is the proper season for planting them.

Let the cuttings be chosen from the last summer's shoots, about ten or twelve inches in length, and planted in rows twelve inches asunder, and about eight inches apart in the rows.

The cuttings of laurel, and Portugal laurel, should have about two inches of the former year's wood with them.

&o Plant Box Edgings. c@

This is the best time of the year for planting box edgings; for the box will now take root freely.

If you intend your edgings should be neat, procure a sufficient quantity of short bushy box, which must be slipped or parted, and the long sticky roots cut off.

Your box being thus prepared, stretch your line along the edge of the bed or border, and let that part be made up all the way pretty firm and full; then with your spade cut a trench about six or eight inches deep on the side of the line next the walk, making the side next the line perfectly upright.

In this trench let the box be set close against the side next the line, placing the plants so near together, as to form a close compact edging, without being too thick and clumsy; and as you proceed in planting, draw the earth up to the outsides of the plants, which will fix them in the proper position. When the row is planted, let the top be cut as neat and even as possible with a pair of shears.

ᔥ Plant Thrift Edgings. ᔐ

This is also a very proper time for planting thrift; and the same method should be followed in planting thrift as in planting box. The plants, if the edging be intended to be neat, should be set so close as just to touch one another.

ᔥ Mow Grass-Walks and Lawns. ᔐ

If the grass of your walks and lawns be not well cut at this season, they will appear very rough all the winter; let your walks and lawns, therefore, be now mown as close and even as possible.

It will also be often necessary to pole your grass walks, in order to scatter the worm-casts, and then to roll them with a wooden roller. For the worm-casts being broken, and spread abroad by means of the pole, will readily stick to the rollers, and consequently give the surface of the grass a clean and neat appearance.

NOVEMBER

1. Pot Marjoram. *Marjorana major Anglica.*
2. Garden Thyme. *Thymus vulgatius.*
3. Savory. *Satureja.*
4. Hyssop. *Hyssopus.*
5. Penny-royal. *Pulegium.*
6. Common Sage. *Salvia major.*
7. Sage of Virtue. *Salvia minor primata.*

One must question the survival rate of trees transplanted in this fashion. The trees, which were excavated while in full leaf, are being stripped of foliage before replanting.

The Works of this Month in the
KITCHEN GARDEN

℘ Cauliflower Plants. ଔ

Remember to let the air have free access to your cauliflower plants set in frames, every day, by taking the glasses entirely off the frame in the mornings, except the weather be extremely wet, when the lights must be raised a considerable height, but not taken away. But let the plants be covered every night.

Whenever you perceive any dead leaves upon your plants, let them be taken away; and be sure to keep the bed perfectly free from weeds.

The same treatment will be necessary for your cauliflowers under hand or bell-glasses; and it will be of great service to the plants, if a little earth be drawn up round their stems.

You may yet plant out cauliflower plants under hand or bell-glasses; but let it be done at the beginning of the month, and the sooner the better.

ɞ Beans. ɞ

If you omitted to plant beans last month, for an early crop, let it be done at the beginning of this: but if some were planted at that time, and these are intended to succeed them, they should not be set till about the latter end of the month.

The mazagan bean is the most proper for planting at this season, because it comes in the soonest, is a great bearer, and very good for the table.

You must remember to plant your beans in a warm border, under a south wall, or other fence, and to follow the instructions given in October.

Peas
Pisum

ɞ Peas. ɞ

About the middle of this month, you should sow another crop of peas, if a regular supply for the table be desired. But if none were sown in October, they should be sown in the beginning of the month.

The early hot-spur is the most proper for sowing at this season; and it must be done in the manner directed last month, under a south wall, or other fence.

ɞ Sow Carrot-Seed. ɞ

Let a little carrot-seed be sown, in a warm border, at the beginning of this month; for there is reason to hope it will succeed, and produce young carrots for the table early in the spring, when they will be very agreeable.

ɞ Take up Carrots and Parsnips. ɞ

Long red
coreless carrot
Daucus carota

Your carrots, parsnips, and other kitchen-roots, should be taken out of the ground in the beginning of this month, and laid in sand for winter use.

For if these roots are suffered to continue in the ground, they will canker and rot: besides, if the frost should set in severely, the ground would be so hard, that it would be difficult to take up the roots when wanted.

Let, therefore, the advantage of a dry mild day be taken for digging up the roots, the tops of which must then be cut off close, the whole roots well cleaned from earth, and then carried into some convenient dry place to be preserved for use, in the following manner:

Lay on the floor a bed of dry sand, about two or three inches thick; place the roots upon the sand close together, observing to lay the crowns of the roots outwards.

Cover the roots with sand two inches thick, then lay more roots upon that, and then more sand; proceeding in this manner with a layer of sand, and another of roots, till all are deposited, covering the upper layer of roots with sand, and laying some dry straw over the whole.

℘ Potatoes. ℀

If any of your potatoes still remain in the ground, let them be taken up as soon as possible, before the severe frosts begin; for these roots are very soon affected by the frost, which renders them watery, and unfit for the table.

As soon as your potatoes are taken up, let them be laid in a dry room, and covered with dry straw a foot thick, as soon as the frost begins.

It will also be necessary to look them over from time to time, taking away all such as have any tendency to rottenness, for otherwise they will soon infect the whole heap.

Potatoes
*Solanum
tuberosum*

℘ Spinach. ℀

Remember to keep your beds of spinach perfectly clean from weeds; and wherever you perceive the plants stand too thick, let the smallest be taken up for use, so that every plant may stand singly. By this means the sun and air will have free access to the surface of the ground, to warm and dry it, which will cause the plants to thrive greatly.

You should also remember, in gathering spinach, to cut only the large outside leaves; by which means the inner ones will grow large, and be fit to gather in their turn.

℘ Artichokes. ℀

About the middle or latter end of the month, the leaves of your artichokes must be cut down close to the ground, and the plants earthed up, to protect them from the severe frosts of the winter. There are two methods of earthing, or as the gardeners call it, landing up artichokes. The first method is this:

Let trenches, about twenty inches wide, be marked out between all the rows, and the ground dug out a good spade deep, laying the earth, as it is dug up, over the rows of the plants, and observing to cover the crowns of them six or eight inches deep at least.

The second method practised by many gardeners is as follows:

The line is to be extended exactly along the middle of the spaces, between the rows of the plants, and a mark cut with the spade under the line. With these lines a kind of beds, four or five feet, are formed, having a row of

plants standing along the middle of each bed. The ground is then to be dug regularly bed by bed, digging close about and between all the plants; at the same time working, or rearing the earth gradually from the above lines or marks on each side the row of plants, into a ridge sloping equally on each side with the row of plants in the middle of the said ridge.

Red artichoke
*Cynara fativa
rubra*

By either of these methods the artichokes will be protect-ed from the frost, unless it be remarkable severe, when it will be necessary to lay over every ridge a covering of straw, or other long litter, which, with the earth thrown up, will be a sure protection to the plants.

Some gardeners, indeed, content themselves with covering the plants with long dung; but the plants are not so effectually protected by this method, as by either of the former.

You should remember, in dressing artichokes, that if any of the strong plants should now shew fruit, and you are desirous of having it, not to cut the leaves, but to tie them up close with a hay-band, and then to lay the earth over the roots as above directed, closing it well about the outsides of the leaves. By this method the plant will be preserved in a growing state, and consequently bring the fruit to perfection.

℘ Asparagus. ca

If your asparagus beds were not dressed last month, it must be done now, and the sooner in the month the better.

In order to which, let the stems or haulms of the asparagus be cut close to the surface of the beds, and carried away directly.

When this is done, let every weed on the beds be cut up with a sharp hoe, and drawn off into the alleys.

The beds being thus cleaned, stretch your line along the side of each bed, and with your spade mark out the alleys about eighteen or twenty inches wide; and let the alleys be dug out one spade deep, and the earth laid neatly over the beds. Remember, as you go on, to bury the weeds drawn off the beds a proper depth in the alleys, and to make the edge of every bed straight and full.

℘ Sow Radishes. ℆

If a little radish seed be sown at the beginning of the month, in a warm border near a wall, or other fence, there will be great hopes of success, provided the weather be not too severe. Those that survive the frost will come early in the spring, and are therefore valuable. Remember to sow the seed pretty thick, to do it in a dry day, and to rake it in lightly with an even hand.

℘ Sow Small Salleting. ℆

If a constant supply of small sallad herbs, such as mustard, cresses, radish, rape, and lettuce, be required for the table, they should be sown every ten or twelve days.

But the bed should now be made in a warm situation, where the earth is rich and light. The bed should be properly adapted to the length of a three-light frame, observing to raise it a foot or more higher in the back than in the fore part, and to make the surface very smooth.

When this is done, put on the frame, sinking the back part of it in the ground, so that the surface of the bed may be everywhere within six or eight inches of the glasses.

Double curled parsley
Selinum dulce

The seeds must be sown in shallow drills, and just covered, not more than a quarter of an inch at most, with earth.

This being done, put on the glasses, and as soon as the plants appear, let them have air, by raising the lights, or taking them entirely away, as you see necessary; remembering to cover them close every night.

By this method you may raise small salleting, during the whole winter, without the assistance of artificial heat, except when the frost is very severe.

℘ Lettuce. ℆

Remember to give your lettuce plants in frames fresh air every day, when the weather is mild and dry, by taking the glasses entirely off in the morning: but if the weather be very cold, or likely to be wet, let them be put on again in the evening, otherwise the plants may remain uncovered during the night; for the closer these plants are kept, the weaker they will be when drawn up.

The glasses must, however, be kept on when the weather is wet; but even then they must be raised a considerable height at the back of the frame; for the plants must have a quantity of fresh air.

But in severe frost weather the glasses must be kept close, and, if necessary, other coverings must also be used.

The same instructions must be observed with regard to those lettuce plants under hand or bell-glasses.

Celery
Apium graveolens dulce

℘ Celery. ℘

Remember to keep your celery now blanching well earthed up, for this will preserve it from the frost. The earth, after being well broken, should be laid up to the plants within six inches of the tops of their leaves.

But be sure to take care not to lay the earth to the plants too hastily; because the earth would by that means be forced into their hearts, and cause them to rot.

℘ Endive. ℘

Let more of your endive plants be now tied up to whiten; but be sure to chuse a dry day for this purpose.

When the leaves of the full grown plants are perfectly dry, let them be gathered up regularly in the hand, and tied together with a string of bass.

But if the weather be inclinable to be frosty, or even wet, the following method may be practised.

Draw up some of the best and largest plants, in a dry mild day, and hang them up by their roots across some lines stretched in a dry place, for a day or two, in order to drain off the wet from between the leaves.

When the plants are thus dried, let some barrows full of dry and light earth be laid in a frame, observing to raise the earth to the top of the back part of the frame, and let it come sloping to the front.

As soon as this is done, gather up the leaves of the endive evenly in your hand, and let the plants be buried in the above earth, almost to the tops of their leaves; and when the weather is very wet or frosty, let the glasses be close shut, and other coverings used when thought necessary.

If you have not a frame at liberty, earth may be laid in any dry open shed; remembering to raise the earth in a high ridge. In this earth, let the plants be placed as above directed, observing to cover the plants with long litter, when the frost is severe.

By either of the above methods, endive may be blanched in any of the winter months, and, consequently, a proper supply be procured for the table, provided care be taken to have a sufficient quantity of plants against the dreary season.

If you have neither the convenience of shed or frame, you may practise the following method.

Dig a small spot of ground in a border, under a south wall, or other fence, remembering, as you dig it, to throw up the earth in a high sharp ridge length-ways the border, making the south side as steep as possible; and let the endive plants be prepared as above directed.

When the bed is thus prepared, gather up the leaves of every plant close and regular, and put them into the earth on the south side of the ridge almost to the tops of their leaves. But remember that the plants are not to be set in an upright manner, but placed as it were on their sides, in a sloping manner, like the surface of the bed: one or two rows may be put in length-ways the ridge.

The plants, by this contrivance, will blanch freely; nor will there be any danger of their rotting, for too much wet cannot lodge on the surface of the bed. But you must remember to cover the plants in severe frosts, with peashaulm, fern, or some other dry long litter.

The endive plants in the bed must also be covered in hard frost; for these plants cannot endure severe cold.

𝕤𝕠 Cardoons. ℭ𝕽

As your cardoons advance in height, let them be earthed up: but remember to gather their leaves up very close and even, and to tie them together with a hayband; and to break the earth well before it be laid up to the plants.

A dry mild day should also be chosen for this work; for if the leaves of the plants are not perfectly dry when the operation is performed, they will rot.

𝕤𝕠 Onions. ℭ𝕽

Remember to pick out all the weeds carefully from the beds of your spring onions; for they will otherwise soon overtop and destroy the plants.

Spanish onions
Allium cepa

𝕤𝕠 Manure and Trench your Garden Ground. ℭ𝕽

Let the rotten dung from your old hot-beds be now laid on the surface of such parts of your kitchen-garden as want manure.

At the same time, let all such pieces of ground as are now vacant, be dug, trenched, and ridged up; that every advantage may be reaped from the influence of the sun, rains, and frost.

Let the ridges be dug about two or three spades broad, laid up rough, and as high and sharp as they will stand. These ridges will be easily levelled down in the spring, when the ground is wanted for the reception of seeds or plants.

Yew
Taxus baccata

THE NURSERY

⊷ Management of Seedling Plants. ⊶

You must remember to shelter your seedling exotic plants in beds, from the sharp frosty weather. This may be done by laying fern, peas-haulm, or other light substance, about the stems, and over the tops of the plants; observing to take it away when the frost breaks.

Or by placing some hoops across the bed, and throwing thick mats over the hoops, when the frost is very severe.

With regard to your plants in pots, it will be proper to plunge the pots to their brims in a dry, warm spot of ground; and, if the frost be very severe, to place hoops over the pots, and cover them with mats.

⊷ Management of New-Planted Trees and Shrubs. ⊶

The greatest care should be taken to protect the roots of new-planted trees and shrubs from frost; particularly those of the more tender kinds.

In order to this, let mulch or long litter be laid a considerable thickness over the surface of the earth between the plants, for this will prevent the frost from penetrating to their roots.

At the same time, let all your new-planted trees which are tall, be staked, and the stems tied fast to these stakes, that violent winds may not blow them to one side.

❧ Finish Transplanting. ☙

All the trees and shrubs you intend to transplant this year, must be removed before the middle of the month. Indeed it will not be prudent to defer it so long; for if the hard frosts should set in before the trees have taken root, they will in all probability miscarry.

❧ Dig and Trench Ground for New Plantations. ☙

Where new plantations are to be made in February or March, the ground should now be well dug and trenched; by which means it will be in fine order to receive the plants in the spring.

❧ Manure the Ground. ☙

Let dung be laid on the surface of such parts of the nursery that want manuring; but remember to chuse dry or frost weather for this work.

It will also be of great benefit to your young trees, if a little dung be now spread over the surface of the ground where they stand; for the rains will wash the salts of the dung, in which its virtues consist, into the ground among the roots.

Care and manipulation of tree stocks.

THE FRUIT-GARDEN

ᨠ Prune Peach, Apricot, and Nectarine Trees. ᨢ

Any time this month is a proper season for pruning peach, apricot, and nectarine trees; observing the same method as mentioned in the preceding month.

The last summer's shoots are to be preserved in every part, at proper dis-

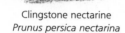

tances; for on these shoots principally all the above
trees produce their fruit.

At the same time, let the old naked branches,
which have no shoots upon them, be either entirely cut off, or shortened to some convenient branch
that supports such shoots; always remembering to

Clingstone nectarine
Prunus persica nectarina

cut them off close, and to make the cut very smooth.

In a word, let some of the old wood, in every part of the tree, be cut away
every year in the winter pruning, in order to make room for the last summer's shoots, a sufficient supply of which should be left in every part, at
convenient distances, for bearing fruit next summer; cutting away all that
are not wanted for that purpose.

At the same time, the young shoots that are left must be shortened, more
or less, in proportion to the vigour of the tree, and the strength of the different shoots. For by this means the shoots will produce a sufficient supply
of new shoots next year, for bearing fruit the year ensuing.

It may not be amiss to repeat the cautions given last month with
regard to these trees, namely, as soon as you have pruned one tree, to nail
up the branches before you begin another; and to nail the branches and
shoots straight, and close to the wall, at about six inches distant from
one another.

Prune Apple, Plum, and Pear Trees
ᨠ Planted Against Walls or Espaliers. ᨢ

The above trees may be pruned any time this month; but remember to
examine them attentively, and to cut out of every part of the tree all the old
and useless wood.

At the same time, wherever a supply of young bearing wood is wanting,
let a sufficient number of the best situated shoots of the last summer's
growth be left. But these shoots must not be shortened: each must be laid
in at its full length; for each of these shoots will, the second or third year,

begin to produce thick, short shoots or spurs, about an inch long; and upon these shoots, or natural spurs, only, the fruit of these trees is produced. Consequently, if the shoots laid in for bearing were to be topped, or shortened, they would produce no such shoots or spurs, and therefore no fruit: but instead of these spurs, or blossom-buds, they would send out strong, and entirely useless, shoots; by which means the tree would be crowded with needless wood, and, at the same time, not produce one tenth part of the fruit it would have done, had the branches been laid in at full length.

Hence it plainly appears, that neither the old nor young branches of any of these trees are to be shortened at this or any future pruning, either in summer or winter.

At the same time, all the branches should be carefully examined; and where there are any old naked branches, or such as support very little bearing wood, let them be taken away, to make room for training more promising branches, and form, in a regular manner, a constant supply of young wood.

Plum
Prunus

As soon as all the old and useless wood is cut away, let all the remaining useful branches be well examined; and wherever you perceive these stand too close, let some of them also be taken away, remembering to clear out those which grow in the most irregular manner, and such as can best be spared; but be sure not to let any two branches grow across one another, nor any remain at less than six inches from the next.

Remember also, when you take away any branch, to cut it off quite close; for no spurs, but those naturally produced, must be left.

Let all the branches, as soon as the pruning is finished, be laid in horizontally, trained straight and close, at regular distances, and immediately nailed to the wall, or tied to the espalier.

Your cherry trees, whether standards, or dwarfs planted against walls, should not be pruned.

With regard to the wall cherries, the same method before laid down for pruning plums, &c. must be observed. All such old branches as support but little or no bearing wood, must be taken away, in order to make room to train the full-bearing branches, together with the last summer's supply of young wood, in a regular manner.

At the same time, wherever a supply of new wood is wanting, remember to leave, in proper places, a sufficient number of the last year's shoots; but all those which are not wanted for the above purposes, must be now cut off close.

You must also remember not to shorten any of these shoots or branches: they must be lain in at full length; for cherry trees, like those of the apple, pear, and plum, produce their fruit principally upon spurs; and the branches, if not shortened, will begin to produce these spurs in the second year.

Be particularly careful in pruning morella cherry trees, always to leave a sufficient supply in every part of the tree of the last summer's shoots, about five or six inches apart; for this species of cherry tree produces the greater part of its fruit upon the last year's shoots.

❧ Prune Vines. ❧

Any time this month will be a proper season for pruning your vines, whether planted in vineyards or against walls.

In pruning vines, remember to cut out all the old useless wood, in order to make room for the bearing shoots or branches; and to leave, in every part, a proper supply of the last summer's shoots to bear fruit the next season.

For these shoots will, in the spring, produce from every eye, or bud, a young shoot; and on these young shoots the grapes are produced the same summer, the bearing shoots of vines being in general produced from branches one year old.

Raisins of the sun grapes
Vitis insolatae

It is therefore necessary to leave, at this pruning, a sufficient supply of the last summer's shoots in every part of the vine.

But in doing this, let the strongest and best situated shoots, and such as have the strongest joints, be chosen; and let each be shortened in proportion to its strength: that is, the strongest should be cut off at the fourth or fifth eye, and those that are weaker about the third.

For if the shoots are left longer, they will fill the vine, during the ensuing summer, with more shoots than you can find room to lay in. At the same time, the fruit on such shoots will be small, ill grown, and ill ripened. But if the shoots be shortened to the lengths above mentioned, they will each, next summer, produce three or four good shoots, and every one of these plants two or three bunches of fruit, which will grow very large, and ripen kindly.

You must remember, in shortening the shoots, to cut them off about an inch above an eye, and to make the cut sloping; at the same time not to leave any branches nearer to each other than ten or twelve inches.

Let care be taken to prune your vines in such a manner, that there may always be a succession of young branches near the bottom; because these will supply the place of old naked wood, which must every year be cut out as it becomes useless.

Nor should you ever suffer any of the old naked branches to remain, unless there be no younger branches or shoots properly situated to supply their place.

As soon as the pruning is finished, let the branches be laid in straight and regularly, about ten or twelve inches from one another, and nailed up neatly.

∞ Prune Gooseberry and Currant Trees. ∞

This is a proper season for pruning gooseberry and currant trees; a work which gardeners too often neglect, though the fineness of the fruit greatly depends upon it.

Let all the old wood be cut out as it becomes useless, and young branches left to supply its place; at the same time the branches should be kept free and clear from one another.

Nor must you suffer any suckers from the roots to stand for bearing branches; these must be entirely cleared away every year.

∞ Prune Raspberries. ∞

It is not yet too late to prune raspberries, which must be done in the manner directed last month. After which, the cuttings are to be cleared away, and the ground dug between the plants.

∞ Prune Standard Fruit Trees. ∞

This is the proper season for examining your standard apple or pear trees, either in the orchard or garden; and wherever you perceive any dead, or very old branches, let them be cut away, together with any large branches that grow in a rambling manner across the rest.

At the same time, where you observe the branches to stand too close, so as to interfere with one another, let the most irregular growers be taken away.

By dressing your orchard in this manner, you will have handsome and lasting trees, which will produce large and well-tasted fruit.

As soon as you have finished pruning, let all the moss, if any be found on the stems or branches, be cleared away.

∞ Transplant Peach, Nectarine, and Apricot Trees. ∞

You may still transplant peach, nectarine, and apricot trees, provided it be done when the weather is open.

If you intend to make an entire new plantation of these trees, let the method laid down in the Introduction to the Kalendar be followed.

But if only a few trees are wanted in different places, it will be sufficient to trench the border in the parts the trees are to stand, adding a little dung, and a proper quantity of good loam, where it can be procured; if not, fresh earth must supply its place.

Remember to let the trees stand fifteen or sixteen feet from one another, and the stem of each tree to stand four inches at least from the wall.

ᏳᏒ Transplant Apple, Pear, Plum, and Cherry Trees. ᏒᏳ

Any time this month, when the weather is open, will be a proper season to transplant apple, pear, plum, and cherry trees, where they are wanting.

Cherry
Cerasus

Remember, if these trees are to be planted against walls, to allow them sufficient room, a caution that has been too frequently forgot in plantations; for how often do we see them blended together, before the trees are half grown to their proper size; by which means the bearing wood is obliged to be cut away, and the trees are starved for want of nourishment; for their roots, as well as their branches, will interfere with one another.

Let your trees therefore be set fifteen feet from one another, at least; if sixteen the better. Apples and pears will require eighteen or twenty.

At the same time let the border be trenched up two spades deep, and some very rotten dung laid in: unless the earth of the border be naturally bad, when a quantity of fresh loam, should if possible be procured, and worked up well with a little rotten dung, and some of the earth of the border. In this compost the trees will thrive well: for fresh loam is of the utmost consequence.

ᏳᏒ Transplant Standard Fruit Trees. ᏒᏳ

Chinese date plum
Prunus

This is also a proper season for transplanting standard fruit trees. It may be done any time in the month, provided the weather be mild and open.

Remember not to set these trees nearer to one another than thirty feet, whether they be planted in the garden or orchard. The method necessary to be followed in making these plantations has been already laid down in the Introduction to this Kalendar.

℘ Transplant Mulberry, Medlar, and Quince Trees. ℜ

Mulberry, medlar, and quince trees, may now be safely transplanted, for they will succeed. The very same method is to be followed in planting these, as in planting other fruit trees.

℘ Plant Raspberries. ℜ

You may still make new plantations of raspberries; but the sooner it is done the better.

The plants must be set in an open spot, in rows four feet asunder, allowing three feet between plant and plant in the rows.

℘ Plant Filbert Trees, &c. ℜ

This is a proper season for planting filbert and hazel nut trees, where they are wanted.

They will both thrive in almost any situation, provided the ground be not too wet in winter; they are generally raised by suckers from the roots.

Filbert
Corylus maxima

These should be planted in rows ten or twelve feet asunder, and the plants six feet apart in the rows.

℘ General Directions for Planting. ℜ

The following instructions should be constantly observed in planting all kinds of fruit trees.

1. Let a hole be opened for each tree, wide enough to let the roots spread freely and equally every way; and let the ground at the bottom of the hole be well loosened with a spade.

2. Let the roots of the trees be pruned; that is, all the broken and bruised parts be cut off, the stragglers shortened, and the ends in general trimmed. For this will make them produce new fibres more freely.

3. Let no tree be ever planted too deep; that is, never let the upper part of the root be more than three inches below the common surface of the ground.

4. Let the tree be placed perfectly upright in the hole, and let the earth be well broken, and thrown in equally about all the roots, the tree being at the same time shook gently, that the earth may fall in equally between all the small roots and fibres.

5. Let the surface of the ground, when the hole is filled up, be trodden gently round the tree.

Hardenbergia
Hardenbergia

THE PLEASURE OR FLOWER-GARDEN.

❧ Plant Tulips, Ranunculuses, and Anemonies. ❧

You may still plant the roots of tulips, ranunculuses and anemonies, provided it be done in mild open weather and before the middle of the month.

With regard to the tulips planted in beds, let them be set in rows nine

Ranunculus
Ranunculus Creticus latifolius

inches asunder, the same distance being allowed between the roots in each row. The beds should be of rich light earth, situated in a dry part of the garden, for too much wet would rot the roots.

The ranunculuses and anemonies should also be planted in beds of light earth, laid up rounding, that the water in hasty rains may not continue long enough on the bed to rot the roots.

The beds where these roots are planted should indeed be covered, as they should be protected in winter from severe cold, and in the spring, when they are in bloom, from the rains and sun. The same distance in planting these roots, must be observed as mentioned last month.

But if they are planted in borders, it will be proper to plant them in small clumps or patches, each containing four or five roots, and to allow an interval of nine or ten feet between the patches.

The roots must not be planted more than two or three inches deep; the tulips should be four or five.

℘ Plant Crocuses. ℀

Crocuses, and other small bulbous roots, may also now be planted. But let them be planted in patches, as mentioned last month.

Remember not to put the roots above two or three inches under the surface of the ground.

℘ Plant Narcissuses, Jonquils, &c. ℀

This is also a proper season for planting narcissuses, jonquils, and indeed, all other bulbous roots that are still above the ground. But remember to do it in mild open weather, and to follow the directions given for that purpose last month.

℘ Set Perennial Plants. ℀

You may still plant double scarlet lychnis, double rose campion, double rocket, catch-fly, campanulas, bachelors-buttons, sweet-williams, wall-flowers, stock july-flowers, columbines, Canterbury-bells, tree primrose, Greek valerian, perennial sunflower, golden rod, perennial asters, holly-hocks, French honey-suckles, monkshood, peonies, London pride, gentianella, double daisies, polyanthuses, primroses, and many other sorts.

Dwarf Haage lychnis
Lychnis

Campanula
Campanula cetidifolia

But remember, in planting the different sorts, to let all the large or tall growing plants be placed backwards in the border or clump, and to set them at a good distance from one another.

Remember also to intermix the different sorts in such a manner that every part may have both an agreeable variety and a continual succession of flowers.

℘ Plant Box. ℀

It is not yet too late to plant box edgings to beds or borders, where wanting. At the same time all gaps or uneven places may be repaired.

℘ Transplant Hardy Flowering Shrubs. ℀

You may still, when the weather is mild and open, transplant roses, honey-suckles, syringas, lilacs, laburnums, bladder and scorpion sena, althæa frutex, double flowering cherry, jasmines, gelder rose, and many other hardy shrubs, for they will yet succeed.

Remember to take away the suckers, and to plant them in an open spot, where they will make pretty plants in two years time, and may then be removed into the clumps or borders.

Cherry laurel
Laurocerasus

☙ Transplant Forest Trees. ☞

Forest trees of all kinds may yet be transplanted, when the weather is mild and open. Remember to stake them properly, in order to secure them from the power of the wind, as soon as they are planted.

☙ Prune Flowering Shrubs. ☞

Let all the long rambling shoots of the last summer's growth be cut away from your flowering shrubs, together with all the dead wood; and the irregular branches shortened.

Where the branches of any shrub stand too close, let some of the worst of them be taken away, and the rest left at regular distances.

At the same time remember not to let the branches of any two shrubs interfere with one another; for every plant appears more agreeable to the eye when it is kept single, than when intermixed with another.

Flowering dogwood
Cornus florida

As soon as the pruning is finished let the ground between and round about the plants be dug one spade deep, and all the suckers sent up from the roots of the shrubs, taken away.

☙ Management of New Planted Trees. ☞

You must be very careful, when the frost sets in, to protect the roots of your new planted trees, particularly those of the more choice and tender kind, by covering the surface of the ground with mulch.

At the same time let stakes be firmly fixed in the ground near the taller trees and shrubs, and their stems fastened securely to the stakes. This should indeed be done now, and the sooner the better; for as long as the wind has power to rock them at their roots, they can put out no new fibres; or if any are shot out during a calm of two or three days, they will be broken, or at least disturbed, by the first high wind. You therefore cannot be too careful in this particular. Let the stake be strong enough to support the plant, and let the stem of it be tied to the stake in a neat and secure manner.

ᔕ Management of Auriculas, and Carnation Layers in Pots. ᔑ

Remember to defend your auricula plants and carnation layers planted in small pots, from the frost and heavy rains.

In order to this, let the pots be plunged up to their rims and close together in a bed covered with a garden frame; and when the weather is unfavourable, let the glasses be put on to defend the plants.

Carnation
Dianthus
caryophyllus

If you have not the convenience of a frame, let the pots be plunged in a bed of dry earth, having hoops placed across it; and when the weather is either very cold or wet, let the hoops be covered with mats or canvas.

But remember to take off the coverings, whether glasses, mats, &c. in dry open weather, when they should not be covered even at nights.

ᔕ Management of Seedling Flowers. ᔑ

If your pots or boxes of seedling flowers were not removed into a warm situation last month, let them be removed at the beginning of this.

The most certain method to secure the plants from hard frosts, is to plunge the pots and boxes into the earth of a dry warm border; and when the weather proves very severe, to cover them with mats or long litter.

Convolvulus
Convolvulus
tricolor

ᔕ Management of Hyacinths, Tulips, &c. ᔑ

Be very careful to shelter the beds where your choicest hyacinths, tulips, ranunculuses and anemonie roots are planted, in heavy rains, sharp frosts or snow, by drawing the mats or canvas over the hoops placed across the beds. For if either too much rain or snow be suffered to remain upon the beds, the wet will penetrate to the roots, by which means many of them must be destroyed, and all of them considerably injured.

ᔕ Management of Grass Walks and Lawns. ᔑ

As the worms at this season throw their casts up very fast and thick, the grass will become dirty, unless you take care to pole and roll it often.

Let therefore the long pliable pole be frequently used, in order to break and scatter the wormcasts; and the grass afterwards well rolled with a wooden roller. By this method the grass walks will be firm, smooth, and entirely clean; for all the worm casts will stick to the roller.

Remember to chuse the driest days for this work, and let it be constantly done once a week during the winter season.

This is also the season for clearing your walks from the leaves of trees, which being all fallen, should be cleared away from every part of the garden.

⊱ Management of Gravel Walks. ⊰

Many throw up their gravel-walks in ridges at this season, in order, as they pretend, to kill the weeds: but experience has sufficiently shewn that it will not answer the intention. It is therefore a much better method to let them continue as they are: for the ridging renders them entirely useless, and gives a very disagreeable appearance to the whole garden.

Let them therefore remain in their present situation, keeping them entirely free from weeds and moss, which will now spread apace, and rolling them once a week, when the weather is dry.

⊱ Prepare Compost for Flowers. ⊰

Your heaps of compost should be now turned, if omitted last month, remembering to break the clods very well, and to mix all the parts thoroughly together.

⊱ Clear the Borders. ⊰

Let all your dead annual plants, such as French and African marigolds,

African marigold
Tagetes erecta

lavateras, China asters, and other plants of that kind, be pulled up by the roots; and all the stems or decayed flower stalks of perennial plants, be cut down; and the borders cleared from the leaves of trees and all other litter.

When this is done, let the surface of the borders be gone over with a Dutch hoe in a dry day, and the surface raked smooth.

This being done, look round your borders, and wherever you perceive any perennial plants wanting, thrust a stick into the earth as a mark where it should be planted.

DECEMBER

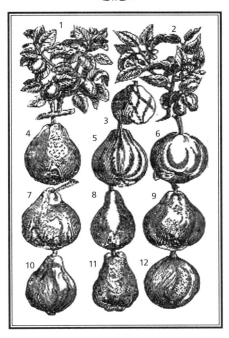

1. Quince Tree. *Malus cotonea.*
2. Portingall Quince. *Cydonium lusitanicum.*
3. Pear. *Pyrus.*
4. Winter Bon Chretien Pear. *Pyrus.*
5. Striped Pear of Jerusalem. *Pyrus.*
6. Burgamot Pear. *Pyrus palatinale.*
7. Summer Bon Chretien Pear. *Pyrus.*
8. Best Warden Pear. *Pyrus volemam.*
9. Pound Pear. *Pyrus librale.*
10. Windsor Pear. *Pyrus windsorianum.*
11. Gratiola Pear. *Pyrus cucumerinum.*
12. Gilloflower Pear. *Pyrus caryophyllatum.*

Tools of the gardener's trade. Equipment includes instruments for property survey.

The Works of this Month in the
KITCHEN GARDEN

℘ Plant Asparagus. ℞

If early asparagus be desired, a hot-bed should now be made for raising them.

In order to this, let the dung intended for the bed, be thrown up in a heap ten or twelve days before you use it; for in that space of time it will be in proper order.

Remember to make the bed two inches wider on every side than the frame; and three feet and a half high.

When the bed has been made two or three days, level the top, and cover it equally six or seven inches thick with earth, making the surface perfectly even; but do not yet put on the frame.

This being done, the asparagus plants are to be immediately placed on the surface, close to each other, in the following manner.

Let a small ridge of earth, about four inches high, be raised upon the surface, at one end of the bed. This being done, place a row of roots close together against the above ridge, and then another row of roots against the former; proceeding in this manner till the whole bed is filled with roots, except two or three inches on each side of the bed, which must be left to support some moist earth, which it is necessary to bank up against the outside roots, on each side of the bed.

This being done, let good light earth be thrown equally over the bed, till the crowns of the roots are covered above two inches thick; and two or three pots of water poured on the surface to wash the earth in among the roots; adding, after the watering, a little more earth, that the crowns of the roots may continue covered two inches thick.

In this manner the bed is to remain till the asparagus begins to appear through the covering of earth; when another parcel of earth, to the depth of three or four inches, is to be laid upon the bed; so that the crowns of the roots may now be covered five or six inches deep.

The bed being thus prepared, thick bands or ropes of straw must be fixed round the bed for the frame to rest upon. This is done in the following manner:

Asparagus
Asparagus officinalis

Let some bands of straw, about three or four inches thick, be made, and fastened down round the upper part of the bed, with stakes about two feet long, sharpened at one end in such a manner, that the upper part of the straw may be exactly level with the surface of the earth; remembering to thrust the stakes down into the dung of the bed. This being done, let the frame and glasses be immediately placed on the band of straw.

If any heavy rains or great snows should happen to fall during the time the bed continues without a frame, it must be defended with a good thick covering of straw or mats.

By this method the buds will rise very thick in about a month or five weeks time, and grow surprisingly fast.

When you perceive the heat begins to decline, which will happen in about eighteen or twenty days after the bed is made, it must be renewed by applying a lining of fresh dung to the sides. Nor should you forget, when the buds begin to appear, to cover the glasses every night with mats or long litter.

Remember to place the crowns of the roots upright when you set the plants in the bed, and to gather the roots of each plant close together, so that a bed adapted to a three-light frame, may contain at least three or four hundred roots.

The plants for this purpose should not be less than three, nor more than five years old.

❧ Set Beans. ❧

If you did not plant any beans last month, a few should be planted at the beginning of this; but if they are to succeed the former plantation, the middle of the month will be soon enough.

In order to this, let a piece of ground be prepared in a sheltered situation, and mazagan beans, for these will come the earliest, planted in rows two feet and a half asunder, and the beans four inches apart. They should be planted about two inches deep in the ground.

About the last week in this month a few Sandwich beans may be planted; they will come at a right time to succeed the crop of small early beans, planted at the beginning, or in the middle of the month.

They should be planted about three inches deep, in rows three feet asunder, and the beans five or six inches apart in the rows.

Broad bean
Phaseolus

At the same time, care should be taken to guard those beans which are up from the frost, by drawing the earth up to their stems as they advance in height; but remember to do it in a mild dry day, and when the surface of the earth also is tolerably dry.

❧ Sow Peas. ❧

Let a spot of ground be got ready, when the weather is open, for sowing another crop of peas, to succeed that sown in the foregoing month.

The ground being prepared, draw small drills about three feet asunder, and scatter the peas, which should be the earliest hotspur, pretty thick in the drills, covering them with earth about an inch and a half deep.

These peas may be sown any time this month, when the weather is open; but if they are to succeed those sown in November, the middle of the month will be the most proper season.

Peas
Pisum

Remember, if you have any peas above the ground, to draw some earth up to their stems, to protect them from wet and frost; but this must be done in a dry mild day, and the earth broken very fine before it is drawn up to the plants.

慨 Sow Carrots. 愂

If young carrots be desired early in the spring, a little seed may be sown any time this month, when the weather is mild and dry. And if the season proves any thing favourable after Christmas, a few young carrots may be expected pretty early.

In order to this, let a spot of ground, in a warm border, be prepared, the seed sown pretty thick on the surface, and immediately raked in equally with an even hand.

慨 Sow Lettuce Seed. 愂

Any time this month, when the weather is mild, a little lettuce seed may be sown on a warm south border; and, if the season should prove favourable, it will succeed tolerably well, and produce plants, which will be very useful in the spring.

慨 Sow Small Salleting. 愂

The seeds of mustard, cresses, radish, rape, and lettuce, should be sown once in ten or fourteen days, if a proper supply be wanted.

Upland cress
Lepidium

These seeds must be sown in a bed of light earth, covered with a frame; the seeds also must be covered near a quarter of an inch with earth.

The glasses must likewise, in general, be kept on the frames; but the plants must have fresh air every day, when the weather is mild, by raising the glasses on props. When the weather is very fine, which sometimes happens this month, the glasses may be entirely taken away; but be sure to keep the bed covered close with the glasses every night.

慨 Sow Radish Seed. 愂

A little radish seed may be sown any time this month, when the weather is dry and open. The plants, if they succeed, will come early in the spring.

In order to this, let a small spot of ground, warmly situated under a south wall, be prepared, the seed sown on the surface, and raked in with an even hand. The best sort for sowing, at this season, is the short-topped radish.

If the frost should be severe, you must cover the bed with peas-haulm, fern, or other long litter.

❧ Management of Cauliflower Plants. ❧

The cauliflower plants under frames must now be looked over, and all the decayed leaves, which are very injurious to the plants picked off, whenever they appear.

Be sure to take off the lights every mild day, that the plants may enjoy the benefit of the free air; but remember to put the glasses on every night.

When the weather is very wet, the glasses must not be removed, but propped up a considerable height at the back of the frame; for these plants require a large quantity of fresh air.

In severe frosty weather, however, it will be necessary not only to keep the plants constantly covered with the glasses, but also to lay a covering of straw, fern, or long litter, over the glasses, and round the outsides of the frame.

With regard to the cauliflower plants under hand or bell-glasses, the same management will be necessary for them as for those under frames.

❧ Management of Lettuce Plants. ❧

You must remember, every mild and dry day, to uncover your lettuce plants under frames; for a free circulation of fresh air is necessary to their growth: nor should you put on the glasses at night in very mild weather.

When the weather is very wet; the glasses must not be removed, but raised up a considerable height at the back of the frame, by which means a quantity of fresh air will be admitted to the plants.

In frosty weather, the plants must be covered close with the glasses; and if the frost be very severe, it will be necessary to add a covering of mats, straw, fern, or long litter.

Remember to take away all decayed leaves whenever any appear upon the plants, and to keep them entirely free from weeds.

❧ Earth Up Celery. ❧

The first mild dry day, when the plants are perfectly dry, let your celery be earthed up; but remember to break the earth very small, and to lay it up carefully against the plants, so as neither to break their leaves, not bury their hearts.

The plants should, if possible, be earthed up within four or five inches of their tops; for this will at once defend them from the frost, and blanch them a considerable length.

White plume celery
*Apium graveolens
dulce*

It will be proper, when the weather is very severe, to cover with peas-haulm, fern, or the like, some of your best celery plants; for by this means the plants will be protected from the frost, and the ground from being frozen, so that you may take up the plants whenever any of them are wanted for the table.

℘ Earth Up Cardoons. ∝

Your cardoons should, when the weather is mild and dry, be earthed up, in order to blanch them, and, at the same time, to defend them from the frost.

In order to this, let the leaves be gathered up regularly, and tied together with hay-bands. When this is done, let the earth be well broken, and laid up round each plant, as near the top as possible. In very severe weather, some dry litter should be laid up round your best plants, in order to preserve them from the frost.

℘ Earth Up Artichokes. ∝

If your artichokes were not earthed up last month, let it be done, if possible, at the beginning of this; at least some dry litter laid over them.

The leaves should all be cut down and cleared away; and then the earth laid over the rows of plants, in the manner mentioned last month.

But if the ground be frozen so hard, that you can not dig between the plants, or time will not permit your doing it be sure to lay some dry long litter over and round the plants, to protect them from the effects of the frost.

℘ Blanch Endive. ∝

More of your large endive plants may now be tied up, in order to be blanched, provided the weather be mild and dry.

In order to which, the leaves should be gathered up evenly in the hand, and tied together a little above the middle of the plant: but remember to let the plants be quite dry before you tie them up, for otherwise they will rot.

In very wet or frosty weather, endive cannot be blanched by this method. Some of the finest plants must therefore be drawn out of the ground the first dry mild day, and hung up two or three days by their roots in some shed, that the moisture may drain away from between their leaves. When this is done, they are to be blanched in the manner directed last month.

ஐ Mushrooms. ௸

The greatest care must now be taken to keep the frost and wet from your mushroom-beds. The best method of doing this is by covering them a foot thick, at least, with clean straw.

Remember always to examine the covering after heavy rains or snows, and wherever you find it wet to the bottom next the bed, let the wet straw be taken away as soon as possible, and its place supplied with dry.

Common mushroom *Agaricus campestris*

ஐ Trenching and Digging. ௸

Remember to employ every minute that can be spared in digging and trenching the vacant spots of ground, that they may be ready to receive the intended crops in the spring.

Let the ground be dug one or two spades deep, according to the nature of the crop you intend; observing to lay it up in ridges till the time you want to plant or sow it; by which means the ground will be greatly mellowed and enriched.

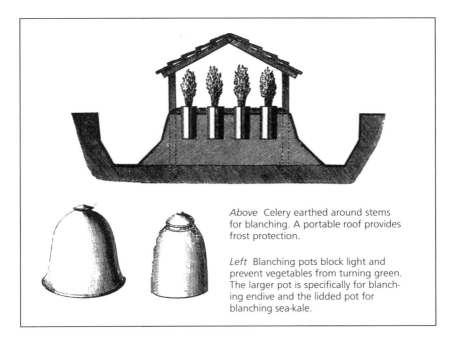

Above Celery earthed around stems for blanching. A portable roof provides frost protection.

Left Blanching pots block light and prevent vegetables from turning green. The larger pot is specifically for blanching endive and the lidded pot for blanching sea-kale.

THE NURSERY

❧ Management of New Planted Trees. ❧

Your new planted trees, especially those of the more tender kind, will still require attention. If therefore you omitted to cover the surface of the ground about their roots with mulch in November, let it be done now; and the sooner it is done the better.

Remember also to support the stems of all new planted tall trees with stakes, if you omitted it last month; for while any tree is rocked to and fro by the wind, there is not hope of its taking root.

❧ Management of Seedling Exotic Trees. ❧

All seedling exotic trees will, while they are young, require some shelter in severe weather. Remember, therefore, to protect them in the manner mentioned last month; but never let the covering remain a day longer than there is an absolute necessity.

At the same time, remember to cover the beds where your seeds, berries, acorns, &c. were sown in October, or the beginning of November, with peas-haulm, fern, or other dry long litter. And be sure to do this before the frost has penetrated far into the ground. This caution will be particularly necessary with regard to your beds of acorns, which will soon shoot after being committed to the ground, and consequently will be soon greatly affected by the frost.

Cockspur hawthorn
Crataegus crus-galli

❧ Dig the Ground Between the Rows of Trees and Shrubs. ❧

Every opportunity, when the weather is open, should be taken to dig the ground between the rows of trees and shrubs; taking care to bury the weeds properly, and not to injure the roots of the plants.

❧ Digging and Trenching. ❧

Let the digging and trenching such pieces of ground as are intended to be planted with shrubs in the spring, be now forwarded as much as possible. The ground should be laid up in ridges; because the frost will have much greater power to mellow it, when laid up in that form, than when dug in the common manner: at the same time, the rain will not lie upon it so long as on ground laid perfectly flat.

THE FRUIT-GARDEN

℘ Prune Apricot, Peach, and Nectarine Trees. ℂ

It is not yet too late to prune apricot, peach, and nectarine trees: nor will they be much injured even if the weather should prove frosty. If therefore the weather be not very severe, these trees may be pruned any time this month. Remember to follow the directions laid down in the two preceding months; and to nail up every tree, as soon as it is pruned, in a neat and regular manner.

℘ Prune Apple and Pear Trees. ℂ

Any time this month will not be too late to finish the pruning of your apple or pear trees against walls or espaliers: for as these trees are very hardy, there is not the least danger of their receiving any injury from pruning.

The same method must be used in pruning as was laid down in November.

℘ Prune Vines. ℂ

Your vines also, whether planted against walls or in vineyards, may now be pruned, observing the directions given last month.

↶ Prune Standard Fruit Trees. ↷

Remember to examine your standard fruit trees, whether planted in the garden or orchard, at this season; and wherever you perceive any dead or ill-growing branches, let them be taken away.

At the same time, where the branches stand too close, let them be thinned, observing to cut out such as grow the most irregular, and also those which grow across, or interfere with any of the others.

If you perceive any of the smaller branches near the upper part of the tree crowded too close together, let some of them be taken away. For these trees should be moderately thin of branches, and those kept at regular distances. By this means the trees will produce a great quantity of large and handsome fruit.

↶ Prune Gooseberry and Currant Trees. ↷

Your gooseberry and currant trees may still be pruned; observing the method laid down the preceding month; namely, to keep the branches thin, and at regular distances; to suffer no branches to remain that grow across each other, and to take away or shorten all such as grow in an irregular manner; to keep the hearts of the trees open, to cut out all dead wood, and the very old branches, and to clear away all the suckers from the roots.

↶ Prune Raspberries. ↷

If any of your raspberry beds still remain unpruned, let it be done now, observing the directions given for that purpose in October and November.

↶ Plant Raspberries. ↷

It is yet not too late to plant raspberries, provided the weather be open. The manner of preparing the plants, and of setting them, has been already described in the two foregoing months.

Herstine raspberry
Rubus idaeus

↶ Plant Gooseberry and Currant Trees. ↷

You may still plant gooseberries and currants for raising a supply of young trees. The best manner of doing this has been already mentioned in October and November.

❧ Transplant Gooseberry and Currant Trees. ❧

Gooseberry and currant trees may be transplanted any time this month into places where they are wanted, provided the weather be open.

Let these shrubs, if planted round the quarters of the garden, be set seven or eight feet distant from one another.

❧ Transplant Fruit Trees. ❧

You may still transplant most kinds of fruit trees, provided the weather be open; for it must not on any account be done when the frost is severe.

❧ Management of New Planted Fruit Trees. ❧

Remember to secure the roots of your new planted fruit trees from frost, by placing mulch, or some kind of long litter upon the surface of the ground about the trees, laying it as far every way as you think the roots extend.

At the same time, let all your new planted standard fruit trees be supported with stakes, if not already done; observing to put a piece of hay-band round that part of the tree where it is to be fastened to the stake; for this

'Duchess of Angouleme' pear
Pyrus

will prevent the bark of the tree from being rubbed off, when rocked by the winds against the stake.

❧ Management of Fruit Tree Borders. ❧

This is a very proper season for manuring, or adding fresh earth to fruit tree borders, where either or both are wanting.

Let therefore a quantity of fresh loamy earth be procured, and mixed thoroughly with some of the best rotten dung. Let this compost be laid upon the ground, dug in, and well worked up with the earth of the border. This will encourage the growth of the trees surprisingly, particular-ly such as are in a declining state, so that they will

Grey rennet apple
Malus

produce large, fair, and well-tasted fruit. But the sooner in the month the borders have this dressing, the better.

If you intend to make new borders for fruit trees, let the ground be dug when the weather is open; observing the directions given in the Introduction to this Kalendar.

Scilla
Scilla clusii

THE PLEASURE OR FLOWER-GARDEN

❧ Carnation Layers. ❧

Your carnation layers that are in pots, should be covered in hard rains, snow, and frosts; but remember, when the weather is open, and not very wet, to let the plants have constantly the benefit of the free air.

❧ Auricula Plants. ❧

Primrose
Primula denticulata cashmeriana

Be very careful to protect your auricula plants from wet, great snows, and hard frosts. If they are placed in frames, let the glasses be kept constantly over them in bad weather; if in a bed under hoops, let mats or canvas be drawn over them.

But whenever the weather is mild and dry, let the plants be constantly uncovered; for a free circulation of air is absolutely necessary.

Protect Your Beds of Hyacinths, Tulips, ❧ Anemonies, and Ranunculuses. ❧

Remember to protect your beds containing your choice hyacinths, tulips, anemonies, and ranunculuses; especially those of the two former, when the weather is very severe.

In order to this, some peas-haulm, fern, or other dry long litter should be provided; and when the frost is likely to set in hard, let a warm covering of it be laid over the surface of the beds; but remember to let it be removed when the frost is not severe.

As soon as the plants appear above ground, the beds should be arched over with hoops, and a quantity of large thick mats provided, in order to be in readiness to be thrown over them in hard weather.

Anemonie
Anemone hortensis tenuifolia

∾ Management of Seedling Plants. ∾

Your seedling flower-plants will also require some attention, in order to protect them from injuries during this inclement season.

With regard to those sown in pots or boxes, let them be plunged to their rims or tops in a warm border; and long litter laid on the surface, when the frost is severe.

∾ Management of New Planted Shrubs. ∾

You must remember to protect the roots of your new planted trees and shrubs, particularly those of the more tender kind, when the frosts are severe.

In order to this, a coat of mulch or long litter of a considerable thickness, must be laid on the surface of the ground about each plant.

The ground also should be dug between all kinds of flowering shrubs, when the weather is open.

∾ Management of Hardy Flowering Shrubs in Pots. ∾

Your hardy flowering shrubs in pots, such as sweet-williams, double scarlet lychnis, double rose campion, and other perennial fibrous-rooted plants, will now require attention, to protect them from the severity of the weather.

In order to this, let the pots be plunged to their rims in the earth of a dry warm border, at the beginning of this month. This will prevent the frost from penetrating to the roots through the sides of the pot; and with regard to their tops, they must covered in very severe weather with dry long litter; but let this covering be taken away as soon as ever the weather is any thing mild.

Rose campion
Silene coeli-rosa

If you have any frames to spare, the pots containing any of the above fibrous-rooted plants may be plunged into the earth in the frames, and covered occasionally with the glasses.

ଋ Prune Flowering Shrubs. ଓଌ

Examine your flowering shrubs, and prune all such as want that operation; but let it be done with a knife, not with the garden shears.

Remember, in doing this, to let all the long vigorous shoots produced last summer be taken off quite close, together with all straggling branches; and when the branches are crowded, let some of them be cut out in a regular manner.

Let every shrub be trained and pruned in such a manner, that it may stand entirely clear of all the rest: the branches of different shrubs should never be suffered to interfere with one another; for their beauty will be considerably impaired by being blended together.

Cherry laurel
Laurocerasus

As soon as the shrubs are all pruned, let the ground be dug between them; remembering to take away all the suckers, and to shorten all the straggling roots as you proceed.

ଋ Prune Forest Trees. ଓଌ

This is a very proper season for pruning all sorts of forest trees; for it may be performed in frosty weather, when very little other business can be done.

ଋ Plant Quicksets, and Other Fences. ଓଌ

Quicksets, and other species of thorn, may now be planted for rearing fences. And where the hedges are thin or naked at the bottom, they should now be layed down in such a manner as to render them thick in that part.

ଋ Propagate Shrubs by Suckers from the Roots. ଓଌ

You may now propagate roses, lilacs, and several other shrubs of that kind by suckers.

In order to which, let the suckers by taken up with care from the old plants in open weather, and planted out immediately in rows fifteen inches asunder; some of them will make good plants in two years time.

Sweet brier rose
Rosa rubiginosa

℘ Transplant Forest Trees, and Hardy Flowering Shrubs. ℜ

When the weather is open, you may still transplant forest trees, and the more hardy flowering shrubs.

But remember to cover the ground about them with mulch, as soon as ever any of them are planted, to keep out the frost, if any should happen.

℘ Prepare Compost. ℜ

Let all your heaps of compost be now broken up, and the several parts mixed very well together.

℘ Prepare Ground for Planting. ℜ

When the weather will permit, let the ground, either in the borders or any other part of the garden, where trees or shrubs are intended to be planted, be now well dug.

℘ Roll Grass and Gravel Walks. ℜ

Remember to let your grass walks and lawns be poled and rolled once a week at least, in mild weather.

Your gravel walks also must be kept very clean, and rolled now and then when the weather is mild and dry.